Carmen Meinert (ed.)
Traces of Humanism in China

Being Human: Caught in the Web of Cultures
Humanism in the Age of Globalization

Volume 6

Editorial

Globalization demands for setting up new cultural orientations. Different traditions and forms of life struggle for recognition throughout the world and have to meet the necessity of values and norms with universal validity. Similarities and differences in understanding the world have to be analyzed and recognized which requires a new reflection on what it means to be a human being concerning its anthropological universality, but also its diverseness and changeability.

The books of the series **Being Human: Caught in the Web of Cultures – Humanism in the Age of Globalization** are committed to a new Humanism, which not only highlights humaneness in its cultural and historical varieties but also presents it as a transculturally valid principle of human interaction in all cultural life-forms.

The series is edited by
Jörn Rüsen (Essen), Chun-chieh Huang (Taipei), Oliver Kozlarek (Mexico City) and Jürgen Straub (Bochum), Assistant Editor: Henner Laass (Essen).

Advisory board:
Peter Burke (Cambridge), Chen Qineng (Beijing), Georg Essen (Nijmegen), Ming-huei Lee (Taipei), Surendra Munshi (Calcutta), Erhard Reckwitz (Essen), Masayuki Sato (Yamanashi), Helwig Schmidt-Glintzer (Wolfenbüttel), Zhang Longxi (Hong Kong)

CARMEN MEINERT (ED.)
Traces of Humanism in China
Tradition and Modernity

[transcript]

In Cooperation with the Institute for Advanced Study in the Humanities, Essen, the Institute for Advanced Studies in Humanities and Social Sciences, National Taiwan University, the Faculty of Humanities of the University Duisburg/Essen

Humanism in the Era of Globalization –
An Intercultural Dialogue on Humanity, Culture, and Value
sponsored by Stiftung Mercator

Bibliographic information published by
the Deutsche Nationalbibliothek
The Deutsche Nationalbibliothek lists this publication in the Deutsche Nationalbibliografie; detailed bibliographic data are available in the Internet at http://dnb.d-nb.de

© 2010 transcript Verlag, Bielefeld
All rights reserved. No part of this book may be reprinted or reproduced or utilized in any form or by any electronic, mechanical, or other means, now known or hereafter invented, including photocopying and recording, or in any information storage or retrieval system, without permission in writing from the publisher.

Cover layout: Kordula Röckenhaus, Bielefeld
Typeset by: Martin Hanke (CHINA Buchservice, Gossenberg)
Printed by Majuskel Medienproduktion GmbH, Wetzlar
ISBN 978-3-8376-1351-3

Global distribution outside Germany, Austria and Switzerland:

Transaction Publishers
New Brunswick (U.S.A.) and London (U.K.)

Transaction Publishers	Tel.: (732) 445-2280
Rutgers University	Fax: (732) 445-3138
35 Berrue Circle	for orders (U.S. only):
Piscataway, NJ 08854	toll free 888-999-6778

Contents

Foreword	7
Introduction: In Search of Humaneness in China	9
CARMEN MEINERT	
Confucian Statecraft in Early Imperial China	19
WEIZHENG ZHU	
Footprints in the Water.	
Assessment in the *Zhuangzi*	49
PAUL D'AMBROSIO	
Reconsidering *Ren* as a Basic Concept	
of Chinese Humanism	69
ACHIM MITTAG	
Negotiations of Humaneness and Body Politics	
in Historical Contexts	83
ANGELIKA C. MESSNER	
Human Equality in Modern Chinese Political Thought	103
DENNIS SCHILLING	
Inventing Humanism in Modern China	131
KE ZHANG	
Bibliography	151
Table of Chinese Dynasties	171
List of Chinese Characters	173
Indices (of Names and Subjects)	181
Authors	205

Foreword

Our book series on "Being Human: Caught in the Web of Cultures — Humanism in the Age of Globalization" aims to inspire "an intercultural dialogue on humanity, culture, and values," so we consider it a matter of self-understanding to also present here the Chinese tradition of dealing with humanity. The editor, Carmen Meinert, has emphasized that this book does not pretend to cover the whole field of Chinese intellectual and conceptual history, and therefore deals with the encompassing idea of the essence and features of this tradition. This selectivity is all the more necessary when intercultural dimensions are addressed. In this wider perspective, the terms "civilizations" and their cultural "traditions" very often claim for a more or less closed set of phenomena clearly separated and distinguished from other "civilizations" or "cultures" and their "traditions". Nobody can deny cultural differences, but nobody can deny similarities, intersections, and changes either, which rule out an uncritical use of the concept of cultures as closed systems with a unique cultural code of human life.

Therefore one has to be very careful when entering — or even stimulating — an intercultural discourse on such an essential issue as humanity in the special perspective of humanism. I am very grateful to the editor and to the contributors that they are rather reluctant to tie themselves to general assumptions regarding humanism in general and Chinese humanism in particular. Their cautious approaches to these issues present a convincing way of coming to terms with the great challenge for the humanities in the context of globalization, namely, to think about culture in such a way that universal dimensions and specific differences in space and time are realized simultaneously. The intercultural discourse on basic cultural orientations today cannot start from presupposed principles or definitions of what humanism is about; rather, it has to work out these principles or definitions by bringing different traditions of thinking about the cultural nature of man into a productive interrelationship. In order to bring about such a productive interrelationship, two conditions have to be fulfilled: an attitude in which cultural differences are recognized and, at the same time, an attitude of critique, which addresses the failures and shortcomings of the other as well as one's own tradition. Both — recognition and critique — require a solid knowledge of the idea of humankind, humanity, and humanism in the rich variety of human life-forms in space and time. This book is a contribution to such knowledge. It presents aspects of Chinese thinking which have to be systematically taken into account if the present-day discourse on man wants to profit from the experience of a great culture. This book can be read as an impulse for the beginning of an intercultural humanism, as an attempt to open chances for humanizing human life in all its conflicting aspects, within and beyond one's own cultural forms. It shows that humanism is not a privilege of one tradition but a promise and a desire in all forms of cultural life, within which man has to realize his or her humanity.

Bochum, January 2010   Jörn Rüsen

Introduction: In Search of Humaneness in China

CARMEN MEINERT

The topic of this volume, *Traces of Humanism in China*, is anything but the remnant of a Western hope to find common ground for an intercultural discourse in a time of ever-increasing global interconnectedness and interdependency. In fact, in China too it very much mirrors the spirit of the time, as can be seen in the title of a recently published volume of photography shown in an exhibition in Canton and Shanghai during the years 2003 and 2004: *Humanism in China (Zhongguo renben)*.[1] That volume is an unvarnished collection of snapshot portraits taken in contemporary China, showing China's diverse ways of life in all their shades in a rapidly changing society — here with the *human being* at its center. It is remarkable that those photographs often depict individual lives, persons, whereas in traditional Chinese thought a human was seen more as a part of society, with certain obligations and clearly defined relationships. Yet, as a matter of fact, to find such a title circulating in China at the beginning of the 21st century is not surprising at all; rather, it pays tribute to a long indigenous tradition of humanism. Although the medium of expression, the photography of individuals, is a rather modern approach to the subject, the topic itself is an old friend and a reoccurring theme in the history of Chinese culture over the past two millennia. As Heiner Roetz has shown, the topic of humaneness *(ren)* kept reappearing as a reshaping force in transformatory processes of Chinese society throughout history.[2] Therefore, the attempt to redefine the place of the human being is not at all astonishing at a time when Chinese society, in the wake of an economic boom, has now attained one of

---

1 Wang/Hu 2003.
2 Roetz 1992. For a discussion of the crucial power of "change", that is, change in ethical systems concurrent with shifting political systems, see the article by Angelika Messer, particular pp. 86-88 in this volume.

the highest income disparities in the world,[3] with clearly delimited social strata at both ends of the scale.

Simultaneously, various other attempts to meet the needs of the times are noticeable as well, mostly in the form of a revival of real or quasi-traditional Confucian thought, and thereby of ideas of humaneness itself. Intellectual discourses in mainland China and in Chinese overseas communities since the 1990s have turned to Confucianism as an immediate reaction to the fear of losing sight of human values in the rise of a market economy.[4] Recent efforts of the Chinese government have been directed towards establishing humane policy (*rendao*) and harmony (*hexie*) based on the theoretical foundation of indigenous Chinese concepts in defense of cultural relativism and against Western concepts of human rights and individuality.[5] There is also the sudden yet comprehensive proliferation of Confucian Institutes appearing worldwide to parallel Germany's Goethe Institutes[6] — an outspoken sign of rediscovering (once again) Confucius (ca. 551–479 BC) as the ambassador of China.

There is no question about the fact that within the process of the great societal transformation that China is experiencing at present, the individual as well as society as a whole is searching to redefine their self-perception. Here, the official reinforcement of "traditional Chinese values" by an authoritarian

---

3   The distribution of family income is measured according to the Gini coefficient. Its application shows how China, since 1978, rose from a rather egalitarian society to become one of the countries with the most unequal distribution of income world-wide. Cf. Schucher 2007, Chang 2002, and OECD 2004.
4   These discussions in mainland China were published in the then most influential periodical *Dushu* (Review). See eg. Wang Hui 1995 and the article by Ke Zhang in this volume.
5   At the 17th National Congress of the Communist Party of China in 2007 the establishment of a "harmonious society" as the party's mainstream guiding ideology was proclaimed. For a summary of the Congress see Schucher 2007, and Zheng/Tok 2007. Heiner Roetz (2009) has pointed out some difficulties in bringing the current allegedly Confucian policy of harmony and humaneness in accord with traditional Confucian thinking. Moreover, the present political discourse might as well remind us of policies in Han dynasty China, the second century BC: Weizheng Zhu analyses in this book (p. 43) the use of Confucian Classical Learning, or Confucian statecraft, at the time simply as a means to make policies more appealing.
6   The first Confucian Institute was founded in Tashkent, Uzbekistan, in 2004. At the end of 2009 there were 282 Confucian Institutes in 88 countries. The Office of Chinese Language Council (short Hanban) envisions expanding further to have 1000 Confucian Institutes worldwide in 2020. It has been observed that the Chinese government uses the Confucian Institutes as organs of political propaganda and, as such, as attempts to influence academic research on China abroad.

government might help the national cause — just as it seemed to have helped in so many transformation processes throughout the ages. However, whether such principles will remain equally applicable outside the Sinic cultural sphere as ethical guidelines in a global context is more than questionable — particularly with regard to the intensely inward-looking aspect of Chinese culture, associated with a certain kind of Sino-centrism, and the resulting degree of resistance on the Chinese side to truly engage in an intercultural discourse with the other. In this regard, it remains to be seen whether the present Chinese search for "humaneness" is simply another extension of highly traditional discourses formed over the past 2000 years, or whether the current changes in Chinese society within a global context might lead to a certain "breaking with culture"[7] and as such to the development of innovative ideas and real alternatives for both individual well-being and social welfare that would allow for thinking outside the (well-known) box.

There is no doubt that Chinese culture has a rich humanistic tradition in its own right, even though of a kind quite different to humanistic concepts developed in the West. The Chinese-language terms which correspond to the Western term "humanism" are a phenomenon of the 20th century;[8] however, the focus of Chinese philosophy throughout the ages has been on man and society to such an extent that discussions on ethical and political concerns have often been at the expense of the development of metaphysics. As such, Chinese philosophy may be best described as a human-centered one, and may in this respect be called a particular kind of "Chinese humanism". However, it should be added that unlike Western humanism, this kind of Chinese humanism cannot be thought of as separate from a supreme power or nature. Since antiquity, traditional Chinese philosophies were embodied in the proposition of the "integration of heaven and man" on the one side, and of the "integration of knowledge and practice" on the other.[9] Humanism, or the way of man (*rendao*), had to mirror the way of heaven (*tiandao*).[10] Therefore, this particular Chinese humanism was not at all as secular as Western humanism and was by no means a counterpart of religion. Yet those great virtuous men whose writings ascended to canonical status were esteemed as sages (*shengren*) or immortals (*xianren*). Their lives and sayings as a man of

---

7 See Alfred Hirsch (2010) for his argument that a certain breaking with traditional culture is a necessary precondition for e.g. the establishing of the human rights idea in a society.
8 See the discussion of the different Chinese translations of the term "humanism" in the article by Ke Zhang in this volume, particularly pp. 133-137.
9 Cf. Tang Yi-jie 1991, p. 161.
10 For a discussion of the the relationship of nature and society see the article by Dennis Schilling in this volume, particularly pp. 106-108.

this world reflected the way of heaven — a divine principle, so to speak. It is this very fact that makes their writings not merely a source for ethical conduct, but also a source for spiritual orientation, to nurture the mind-heart (*xin*) for very inner-worldly purposes. The unity of heaven and man has characterized the entire history of Chinese philosophy. Thus, the core concern was not so much the search for truth. Rather, Chinese humanism emphasizes social relationships: how should the ruler govern, how should man behave, how should he take over responsibilities, and how should he fulfill his duties to society and to others.

This volume intends to simply give a glimpse of some of the humanist traces found in this *Chinese humanism*. However, it neither attempts to exhaust the topic to its full extent from a historical perspective, nor to cover all areas of knowledge and all schools of thought in China that were concerned with the *conditio humana*. From a historical point of view, the articles in this volume cover antiquity, when the foundations of the Confucian state ideology of imperial China were laid, and developments from early pre-modern China, that is, from the Song dynasty in the 12th century up to the debates of the 20th century. Except for the article by Paul D'Ambrosio, which deals with an early Daoist critique of the Confucian search for humaneness, the contributions here rather focus on aspects of humanism in the Confucian context; Buddhism, which despite its high degree of Sinification continued to be perceived as foreign, is therefore not treated in a separate article in this volume. Nevertheless, the articles in this book precisely demonstrate how Chinese intelligentsia over centuries and millennia dwelled on similar issues, once the socio-political order of Confucianism, with its very clear-cut social stratification, had been established. In order to open up the realm of Chinese humanism for the non-Sinologist reader as well, let me first establish here the following reference point with which to fathom the *traces of humanism* in China found in this book.

The time before the unification of the first Chinese empire, the Qin dynasty (221–206 BC),[11] under Qin Shihuang (259–210 BC), is known as the golden age of Chinese philosophy and is as such marked by a great intellectual and cultural expansion. It is the flourishing time of the Hundred Schools of Thought (*zhuzi baijia*) (770–221 BC), freely developing ideas that should have had a profound and lasting impact on all aspects of life, intellectual and spiritual outlook, social identity, rulership and diplomacy in China up to the very present. Among those competing schools of thought were the followers of Confucius and Mencius (372–289 BC), the Legalists following Han Feizi (ca. 281–233 BC), Daoists in the footsteps of Laozi and Zhuangzi (d. 286

---

11 A table of all Chinese dynasties is given on p. 171.

BC), Mohism developed by followers of Mozi (ca. 490–381 BC) and others. All these schools of thought affirmed that their canonical texts and their statecraft had universal value and would entreat the monarch to put their theories into practice in order to attain internal peace and stability for the empire. Their thoughts aimed at a political applicability in order to develop a society free from disorder (*luan*),[12] or in other words to bring about "no dissent under heaven" (*tianxia wu yi yi*).[13] As such, any ethical concerns were right from the start intimately connected with political affairs as well.

From the beginnings of the Qin empire in 221 BC to the demise of the last dynasty, the Manchurian Qing, in 1911, the approved way of rulership — despite numerous dynastic changes, foreign rulers, divisions, reunifications and major societal changes — remained the same: autocratic monarchy. And the remedy, to ensure stability, generally remained the same as well once it was established during the Han dynasty (206 BC–220 AD). Confucian statecraft was legitimized through the Chinese canonical texts, mostly referred to as the *Four Books and the Five Classics* (*Sishu wujing*), or the *Six Classics*, or from the Ming dynasty (1368–1644) onward as the *Thirteen Classics* (*Shisan jing*).[14] Once such a corpus of classical texts was established, it remained the sole and primary reference point for scholars throughout Chinese intellectual history. All later philosophical concepts are developed, strictly speaking, as comments on these classical texts. Even if philosophical discourse as a whole never emancipated itself from the limitations of the canonical scriptures, scholars from the circles of the New Confucianists more recently argue positively, in that this culture of exege-

---

12   See the article by Paul D'Ambrosio in this volume, which discusses the Daoist critique of the Confucian approach to the problem.
13   Cf. Weizheng Zhu's article in this volume, where the term "no dissent under heaven" is used.
14   Since all contributions in this book refer to some of these canonical texts, they shall be listed here: The *Four Books* (*sishu*) include (1) the *Great Learning* (*Daxue*), (2) the *Doctrine of the Mean* (*Zhongyong*), (3) the *Analects of Confucius* (*Lunyu*), and (4) the *Book of Mencius* (*Mengzi*). The *Five Classics* (*wujing*) are (1) the *Book of Changes* (*Yijing*, or *Zhou Yi*), (2) the *Book of Odes* (*Shijing*), (3) the *Book of Rites* (*Liji*), (4) the *Book of Documents* (*Shujing* or *Shangshu*), and (5) the *Spring and Autumn Annals* (*Chunqiu*); sometimes as the sixth classics (6) the *Book of Music* (*Yuejing*) was added. Alternatively, the *Thirteen Classics* of Confucianism are made up of (1) the *Book of Odes*, (2) the *Book of Documents*, (3) the *Rites of Zhou* (*Zhouli*), (4) the *Ceremonies and Rites* (*Yili*), (5) the *Book of Rites*, (6) the *Book of Changes*, (7) the *Commentary of Zuo* (*Zuozhuan*), (8) the *Commentary of Gongyang* (*Gongyang zhuan*), (9) the *Commentary of Guliang* (*Guliang zhuan*), (10) the *Analects*, (11) *Luxuriant and Refined Words* (*Erya*), (12) the *Classic of Filial Piety* (*Xiaojing*), and (13) the *Book of Mencius*.

sis itself meant the very continuity of Chinese intellectual history.[15] Yet because of this continuous self-reference to scriptures of Chinese antiquity until the very present, it is difficult to imagine — at least outside a Sinocultured point of view — that the Confucian version of humaneness could become a genuinely alternative system of ethics on a global scale.

When in 135 BC Confucian statecraft was adopted as *the* policy for establishing socio-political order, it marked the beginning of a process of appropriation of a certain set of ideas that proved functional enough to become developed and refined and to endure for about the next 2000 years — and to remain the yardstick of governing even under the three and a half centuries of foreign rule of the Mongolians (Yuan dynasty 1271–1368) and Manchurians (Qing dynasty 1644–1911). Not once throughout imperial history did the ruling class in China try an alternative philosophy of governance. However, the circumstances that led to the adoption of the Confucian and not the Daoist or Legalist teachings as Chinese imperial state ideology were almost random, and were the results of a number of historical coincidences rather than a preeminent teaching walking over inferior competitors.

This brings us right into the first story told in this book. Weizheng Zhu, one of the leading contemporary Chinese historians, detects a number of such historical coincidences and decisions that led in the earliest stages to the rise of the Confucian teachings as imperial state ideology. During the first half of Han dynastic rule (particularly during the 2nd century BC), a superstructure was shaped that was based on a very specific type of learning; Confucian Classical Learning was used for pragmatic reasons, only to make policy more appealing. And the first official paragon of Confucianism was constructed in the figure of the scholar Dong Zhongshu (ca. 179–104? BC), although, as Weizheng Zhu judges, Dong never really grasped the real meaning of Confucius. It is in this way, Weizheng Zhu argues, that "Confucian learning was transformed into a state-sponsored theology". A very specific mode of national self-perception was thereby also constructed. Moreover, it was also in the 2nd century BC that the knowledge of the *Six Confucian Classics* became the yardstick by which officials were chosen for government service — and it is here that the Confucian version of humanism became a matter of education: only the morally educated one, versed in Confucian classics, was regarded as *humane* and as such as a functional part of society. This decision laid the cornerstone for the later imperial examination system (*keju*) that lasted for 1300 years (605–1905) after its institutionaliza-

---

15 The argument in favor of this culture of exegesis is that those interpretations of one and the same text could differ radically that it is hard to believe that they were comments on the same canonical text. See Schmidt 2009, pp. 14-15 and Huang 2009, p. 33.

tion, and became probably the most important institution of the Confucian state; it would allow control over political ideology as well as providing a recruitment system for the central bureaucracy.

In a way, moral standards, the essence of human culture (*renwen*), were thus used for highly pragmatic reasons in political practice. It is precisely this fact which is the target of the Daoist critique of the Confucian version of humaneness (*ren*), as is discussed by Paul D'Ambrosio. Referring to one of the Daoist classics, the book *Zhuangzi* by Zhuang Zhou or Zhuangzi (d. 286 BC), and to the great commentator Guo Xiang (252–312 AD), Paul D'Ambrosio shows how a lack of concern is actually regarded as an alternative to get out of the disorder (*luan*) of society. Whereas the Confucianists try to establish and control order by means of clear-cut regulations for the human being as a part of society, and mount an educational campaign in order to reach the state of "no dissent under heaven", the Daoists advocate non-interference (*wuwei*) and rather remain in a natural state. From an official Confucian viewpoint, such a person was not regarded as a functional part of society and in this respect did not have the same value as a human being, because human value had to be gained through moral education. Yet for Zhuangzi it is more harmful than beneficial to cultivate particular virtues such as *ren* (humaneness), as they neglect the undivided whole. Although the official elite in imperial China was officially bound to Confucian values, nonetheless, in private a literatus would often find the naturalism of Daoism or the spiritual outlook of Buddhism more attractive. Yet the fact that both groups — Daoists and Buddhist — were not esteemed to the same degree as functional human beings who were part of society, can be seen, for example, from the official petition that a Buddhist monk should be spared from bowing to the emperor — an idea unthinkable from a Confucian point of view.[16]

With the first two articles, the reader may be able to grasp a rather fundamental tension inherent in society in imperial China: the Confucian state ideology that trained and controlled the Chinese elite for two millennia on the one hand, and its counterpoints, such as Daoism, that were present in the background throughout the centuries. The following articles in this volume show different facets of the Confucian ideal of humaneness (*ren*) and how the topic reappeared and became involved in various other discourses during times of great societal changes between the 16th and 20th centuries.

---

16 For the text "Treatise On Why The Monk Need Not Bow To The Ruler (*Shamen bujingwangzhe lun*)", composed in 404 by the aristocratic, learned monk Huiyuan (334–416) see Shi Zhiru 2010, p. 128.

Achim Mittag brings the reader right into the heart of Confucian humanism, namely, into a discussion of various meanings of the core virtue of *ren* (humaneness) — particularly with regard to Song dynasty (960–1279) Neo-Confucian sources. He demonstrates how misleading and narrowing it would be to settle for simply one single English translation of the term, such as humaneness or benevolence; instead he explores four different meanings of *ren,* ranging from a "keen sense of responsibility in one's action" to "benevolent government".[17] He thereby shows how moralistic and pragmatic concerns became more and more intertwined in discourses on *ren.* The sources quoted by Achim Mittag rest on the notion of a superior man leading the rest of society or humanity, which may be alien to a Western tradition of humanism.

With the contribution of Angelika Messner, another trace of humanism is discussed: the embodiment of moral values and the extension of humaneness to the medical field in times of societal change in the 16th and 17th centuries. Under the influence of Daoist and Buddhist currents of the time, moral self-cultivation (*xiu shen*) was embodied and practiced to nourish life (*yangsheng*), inspired by the strong voice of the Neo-Confucianist Wang Yangming (1472–1529). Here the notion of *ren* acquired yet another new meaning, namely "to feel or to sense". The Confucian way of attaining sagehood was no longer restricted to the field of learning of the canonical classics; in fact, a popularization of knowledge can be observed which made medicine as a practice of humaneness part of the higher culture as well. Just as *ren* (humaneness) was applied in the political sphere as statecraft (*shu*), as shown by Weizheng Zhu, it here found a new application in the skills or craft of medicine (*yishu*).

With yet another major societal shift in the late 19th century in the light of the imminent downfall of the imperial system in China, discussion of aspects of humanism was voiced through the social and political theories of progressive thinkers, here using the concept of human equality (*pingdeng*), as is discussed by Dennis Schilling. Although the arguments brought forward by scholars such as Kang Youwei (1858–1927) or Tan Sitong (1865–1898) recognize distinct humanistic traditions in Chinese thought influenced by Confucianism, Daoism and Buddhism alike, they nonetheless viewed traditional Confucian state ideology as the main source of inequality, namely, that human nature necessarily determined the stratification of human soci-

---

17 The scope of meaning covered by the term *ren* is well documented in the index on pp. 196-197, where under the entry of "*ren*" are listed various English translations of the term used in the different articles in this book. They exemplify the many shades, shifts in meaning, and areas of application of the semantics of *ren* throughout the ages.

ety.[18] Tan Sitong understood the notion of *ren* as a selfless act that meant a kind of existential transformation. By interpreting *ren* with a soteriological connotation, for Tan Sitong it came to have the specific meaning "to commit suicide" — an astonishing turn towards radicalization in the semantics of *ren* which can only be understood against the background of the socio-political situation of his time.

The article by Ke Zhang outlines modern Chinese responses to the encounter with the Western concept of humanism in the 20th century when, following the demise of the imperial system and thus the downfall of Confucian state ideology, a vacuum emerged for new discussion. In the ensuing attempt to formulate a modern Chinese humanism, traditional culture and particularly the political and ethical doctrines of Neo-Confucianism were — if only for a moment — totally refuted in the iconoclastic May Fourth Movement of 1919. What followed, however, was a gradual yet continuous reaffirmation of Confucian values in the Republic of China, the People's Republic of China and in Chinese overseas communities. Ke Zhang aptly describes, using the words of the contemporary overseas Chinese historian Yu Yingshi (born 1930), the predicament of modern Confucianism as a "drifting soul" that has lost its institutional foundation following the abolition of the imperial examination system in 1905.

It appears that presently Chinese society has halfway broken with traditional culture, yet is still somehow stuck in between — neither willing or able to fully let go of the familiar past, nor able to embrace the unknown future. One of the reasons might be the failure of Maoism, which in its original sense could — at least partly — be understood as a search for humanism on modern terms. Yet the attempts of Mao Zedong to establish a *new* human being and in this sense to completely break with traditional culture ended in the well-known disasters and in misery for the Chinese people. In this regard the present attempts to revive Confucianism are yet another expression of moving back and fro between tradition and modernity. Following the *traces of humanism* sketched in this volume the reader might fathom China's arduous path into modernity, which, as indicated in the beginning of this introduction, is still not fully accomplished. However, that the topic of humaneness continues to be an essential feature of the discussion is a sign of hope at a time of ever-growing global interdependency.

---

18 One of the reasons for the Chinese government and for Chinese society to not so fully embrace the concept of equal chances for all human beings, for human rights, might be the fact that according to traditional Confucian views human value had to be gained through a moral education; it is not given naturally to all human beings by birth.

Last but not least I would like to thank Prof. Jörn Rüsen, the head of the project "Humanism in the Era of Globalization" at the Institute for Advanced Study in the Humanities (KWI) in Essen (Germany), for his unquenchable zest in looking beyond the confines of the occidental history of ideas for alternative role models, ideas and inspirations concerning humaneness and for other possibilities to overcome difficulties arising from cultural difference in a world of cultural diversity continuously moving closer together. In this regard I am very grateful for the opportunity provided by Jörn Rüsen to enable me to contribute my Sinological expertise to this series "Being Human: Caught in the Web of Cultures" by editing this volume of traces of humanism in China. My thanks also go to Martin Hanke, who prepared the typeset manuscript, to Sebastian Lorenz, who kindly offered his expertise in preparing the indices and the language list, to the authors who keenly wrote their contributions — partly under great time constraints, and to Trever McKay who willingly prepared the English translation of the article by Weizheng Zhu on very short notice when the Chinese original had proved to challenging to other translators. May I close my introduction with the hope that this volume as a joint effort of scholars from the West and the East forms one step towards a mutual understanding in search of humaneness and in search of an intercultural humanism.

Confucian Statecraft in Early Imperial China*

WEIZHENG ZHU

Introduction (by Achim Mittag)

The following article by Professor Zhu is part of the first chapter of his projected book entitled *The Chinese Tradition of Humanism* (*Zhongguo de renwen chuantong*). The prospects of the Chinese manuscript's finalization are good for this year. The initial idea to have Prof. Zhu write this book came from Prof. Jörn Rüsen, director of the Humanism Project. Realization of this idea was made possible by a generous grant of the Stiftung Mercator, the Alfred und Cläre Pott-Stiftung, both in Essen, and additional support from the International Office of the University of Tübingen. This allowed Prof. Zhu to receive a Visiting Scholarship at Tübingen for the summer months of 2007 and 2008.

The notion of *renwen* as used in the proposed title of Prof. Zhu's book consists of the two characters "human" (*ren*) and "ornament" (*wen*). It originates from the *Book of Changes* (*Zhou Yi*).[1] Therein, the "ornaments of society" are paralleled with the "ornaments of heaven" (*tianwen*), the latter term referring to the changing stellar constellations. *Renwen*, or *renwen zhuyi* ("the teaching of humans' refinement"), is only one of several terms commonly used to translate "humanism".[2]

---

* The translation of the Chinese article by Weizheng Zhu was prepared by Trever McKay (Taibei). CM
1 *Tuan Commentary* to Hexagram 22 (*Bi*); Sung 1935, pp. 99-100.
2 Other terms are *rendao zhuyi* ("teaching of the way of man") and *renben zhuyi* ("teaching of man as the central focus of the worldview"). For a discussion of these terms in the early 20th century see also the article by Ke Zhang in this volume, pp. 133-137.

We might speculate that Prof. Zhu chose the term *renwen* on the basis of the second character *wen*, which has a wide range of meanings, from "text" and "scripture," to "literary writing" and "literature," to "refinement" and "culture". Thus, one may say that *renwen* comes closest to what is generally associated with Renaissance Humanism, namely the emphasis on literary skills in connection with the greatly encouraged study of ancient texts.

Here it should be noted that modern Chinese intellectual culture, to a large extent, has been shaped by the May Fourth or New Culture Movement, which early on acquired the meaning of denoting a whole period extending from 1915 to 1923, or even later. It was Hu Shi (1891–1962), figurehead of the May Fourth "liberal" intellectuals, who established the view of the May Fourth Movement as a "Chinese Renaissance".[3] However, as Prof. Zhu has shown, even before Hu Shi, the European Renaissance had impinged upon the minds of Chinese intellectuals of the transitional era from the Hundred Days' Reform in 1898 up to the Revolution of 1911.[4] Ever since, the conception of "renaissance" as connoting the *rite de passage* from traditional culture to modernity has been a principal concern for Chinese intellectuals. Suffice it here to say that we thus shall be prepared to read Prof. Zhu's book-length essay on the Chinese *renwen* tradition as an inquiry into the genesis of present Chinese intellectual culture.

Speaking of *wen* in the broad sense of "culture," a famous utterance by Confucius, recorded in the *Analects* (*Lunyu*), immediately comes to mind, namely Confucius' claim that he had been entrusted with preserving "this tradition of *wen*" (*siwen*).[5]

One will perhaps be surprised to find that Prof. Zhu's article does not start out with a reference to this claim, nor even mention it. No word is spoken about the philosophical currents of the Hundred Schools (*baijia*) in Confucius' age. Rather, we are taken directly into the time of the imminent collapse of the first Chinese empire founded by Qin Shihuang (r. 246–210 BC) in 221 BC. Still, Confucius is not left out; on the contrary, the article aims at delineating the rise of Confucian teaching up to its becoming the nucleus of the Chinese imperial state ideology. The time span considered is from the founding of the Han dynasty in 206/202 BC to the death of the powerful General-in-chief Huo Guang in the year of 68 BC, with a focus on the long reign of Emperor Wu (r. 141–87). We are presented with various facets which are not found in conventional depictions of the so-called "victory of Confucianism," such as, for example, the role played by Confucius' disciple Zigong (520–456 BC), a wealthy merchant, whose riches made Confucius and his teachings known to the world.

---

3 Yü Ying-shih 2001, pp. 299-324.
4 Zhu Weizheng 1989, pp. 82-91.
5 *Lunyu* 5.5.

The thread that runs through the article's ten sections is the insight that the said formation of the imperial state ideology was essentially shaped by the dynamics rooted in the tension between "scholarship" (or "learning," *xue*) and "statecraft learning" (or "way of governing," *shu*). To elucidate this tension, the article focuses on the initial stage of Classical Learning (*jingxue*), the study of the *Six Classics* as the very essence of *wen* and its use in the political practice of the Chinese imperial state.

It should not go unmentioned that Prof. Zhu has enriched our knowledge of the history of Classical Learning (*jingxueshi*) with many prolific studies. The reason why these studies have met with a great response within the Chinese academic world probably lies in the fact that Prof. Zhu's writings always lend themselves to readings between the lines that reveal his critical reflections about the world here and now. A case in point is the related episode of Han Gaozu's urinating in the caps of scholars coming to court for an audience (p. 23 below) — a pointer to the humiliations suffered by the Chinese intellectuals in successive political campaigns in the Maoist era.

I would like to conclude by emphasizing "the subtlety and richly allusive quality of Professor Zhu's prose,"[6] which in fact poses the greatest challenge to any translator. Trever McKay has met this challenge in a truly admirable way.

When the Foretelling of the Imminent Demise of "Feudalism" Began**

Kings and nobles, generals and ministers — such men are made, not born![7]

When a young peasant named Chen Sheng (d. 208 BC) urged on his cohorts with these words of revolt against the Qin dynasty in 209 BC, he had no idea how prophetic his statement was about the nature of the new empire that would emerge five years later.

The empire that succeeded the Qin was called the Han. One of the major distinctions it bore from the Qin was that the Han's founding leaders — from the emperor Liu Bang (256 or 247–195 BC) down to his generals, ministers, and high officials — were almost all common people and minor officials, or as the Chinese say, from the "cloth gown" (*buyi*) class.

Another way in which the founding of the Han empire differed from that of the Qin was that it came about not by conquest of one feudal state over the

---

6   Ruth Hayhoe, "Translator's Note". In: Zhu Weizheng 1990, p. xii.
** Here is the starting point of Weizheng Zhu's contribution translated by Trever McKay.
7   *Shiji* 48/1952; see also Watson 1993, p. 3.

others, but instead by various revolts among the common people — uprisings from below that overthrew the government of the ruling class above. These uprisings then merged at various points to eventually re-establish a unified center of power referred to as "the great unity" (*da yitong*). Han scholars likened (though obviously in a farfetched way) this manner of power change to the change of the "mandate of heaven" (*tianming*) by Tang, the founder of the Shang dynasty, and Wu, the founder of the Zhou dynasty, as referred to in the *Book of Changes* (*Zhou Yi*).[8]

The problem was that as far as Liu Bang or his rival, Xiang Yu (232–202 BC), the Overlord of Western Chu, were concerned, the purpose of their revolt was simply to displace the Qin emperor, in order to seize the "mandate of heaven" for oneself and be named emperor. This being the case, the depiction of the Han dynasty actually adopting the Qin political system arose and, at the same time, was confronted with the same difficult problem that Qin Shihuang, the First Emperor of Qin (r. 221–210 BC), faced after his conquest of the other Six Kingdoms, namely: How can this type of unified empire achieve internal peace and stability?

Saying the Han adopted the Qin political system implies that the system of power established by Liu Bang and his group of low-born generals and ministers basically copied that of the Qin. In the beginning, however, the Han system was streamlined, designed to adjust to changing needs. One very noteworthy divergence from the Qin is that Liu Bang enfeoffed his paternal relatives. This is something that Qin Shihuang repeatedly refused to do. Liu Bang, who was later conferred the posthumous title of *Gaozu* (or "Most Senior Ancestor"), thought that by sending his sons and nephews out to key areas where they could rule as kings, they could form the "arms and legs" of the empire and could band together to aid the imperial court in times of distress. He did not realize that after becoming kings of vassal states, these young rogues would actually form separatist forces, and eventually even scheme to overthrow the empire and enthrone themselves as emperor. It goes to show that Qin Shihuang had spoken wisely when approving Li Si's (280–208 BC) remonstrance against enfeoffing imperial princes. Li Si cautioned, "All the world has suffered from incessant war and struggle. This is because we have enfeoffed kings and dukes." We can see that enfeoffing one's own sons was, in essence, "setting up [antagonistic] armies".[9]

---

8   *Zhou Yi*, Hexagram 49, *Tuan Commentary*.
9   *Shiji* 6/239.

Establishing the Rites for Low-born Generals and Ministers

The story of Qin Shihuang's "burning books and burying scholars" (*fenshu kengru*) is well known. However, textual research done by the famous scholar Zhang Binglin (also known as Zhang Taiyan, 1869–1936) at the end of the Qing dynasty, showed that the policy of anti-intellectualism was put into practice long before founding of the empire, as indicated by the banning and destruction of privately-held books and cartographic materials. He also showed that the 460 or so men who Qin Shihuang in his later years had buried alive in the capital of Xianyang were primarily *shushi* (i.e. magicians, soothsayers, fortunetellers, practitioners of geomancy, etc.). Because *shushi* were also archaically known as "scholars" (*ru*), the dictum of "burying scholars" came into being.[10] Actually, the court-appointed erudites (*boshi*), who functioned as advisors to the Qin emperor, included scholars from all schools of thought, including followers of the later Confucian School. One example is that of Shusun Tong (ca. 250–180 BC), who was appointed to the post of erudite after the Second Emperor of Qin's (r. 210–207 BC) accession to the throne.

Perhaps the low-born Liu Bang was influenced early on by Qin's anti-intellectualism, so that before the "change of the mandate" he harbored a strong resentment against scholars — a disposition which gave rise to a series of colorful anecdotes. One of the most well known of these is about him urinating in scholars' caps. Whenever a scholar came to have an audience, he would pluck off the scholar's cap and relieve himself in it.[11] Nonetheless, as Liu Bang gradually got the upper hand in the war between Han and Chu (207–202 BC), he let "the good birds select the tree upon which to perch," or in other words scholars of various persuasions were free to seek refuge in the Han camp. Because of this, the Qin erudite Shusun Tong, who was a great opportunist, finally surrendered to Liu Bang, the King of Han, after having switched his allegiance nearly ten times.

According to the *Records of the Grand Historian* (or *Shiji*), Shusun Tong brought over 100 disciples with him to the Han camp. On noticing that the sight of his attire disgusted Liu Bang on the occasion of his first audience, Shusun Tong switched to a simple gown like that worn by the commoners of Chu for his next audience, which won him favor with his new ruler. Moreover, he recommended men from his "old gang of outlaws" to Liu Bang, which made Liu Bang like him even more. Thereupon, Shusun Tong was officially

---

10 Translator's note: Some have erroneously interpreted *kengru* to mean "buried Confucian scholars," as those of the Confucian school were also identified by the term *ru*. However, this new usage did not come about until later.

11 *Shiji* 97/2692.

made an erudite, making him the first advisor in cultural matters in the Han founding period. His greatest accomplishment, however, was to "draw up the court rites" (*qi chaoyi*) for the Great Han empire.[12]

Before this, during the 5th year of his reign as King of Han (202 BC), Liu Bang's was a policy of "battling wits, not force" in his war against Xiang Yu. As such, he used Han Xin's (d. 196 BC) army to attack and kill Xiang Yu, after which he turned against Han Xin and, catching him off his guard, snatched control of his army. This made Liu Bang the final victor among the warlords vying for dominance in the wake of Qin's collapse. Eager to be enthroned, he proclaimed himself emperor of the Han dynasty while still among his troops.

And yet, it never occurred to this commoner from Pei County, known in history as Han Gaozu, that his salt-of-the-earth band of brothers, who had come up just as he had without the benefits of social status, would be so ignorant of order. "The officials congregated together, drank wine and argued over their achievements, and when drunk would sometimes yell at random, picking up swords and striking at pillars, all of which troubled Gaozu."[13] Most frightful to the new emperor was probably the way one of his closest ministers, Zhang Liang (d. 185 BC) evaluated the situation: "This will only lead to revolt."[14] In other words, since the emperor used to be a commoner, were he unfair in his rewards to those who helped him, they could certainly be expected to band together and plot another revolt. This terrified the emperor, and he responded quickly, publically enfeoffing one of his most detested fellow townsmen, and in so doing effectively repressing the voices of dissent.

However, the imperial court was as chaotic as it had ever been. Shusun Tong, who had long been accustomed to speculating on what the emperor thought, saw this as an opportunity not to be missed, and said to the emperor: "Scholars are of no help in forays and conquests, but [are of help] in preserving what has been accomplished. Allow me to recruit scholars from Lu to work together with my disciples to draw up the court rites." Knowing that the emperor detested Confucian scholars' propensity for intricate ritual, Shusun guaranteed that the ceremonies would be different, saying: "I will use some of the ancient ceremonies and combine them with rites from Qin." To which the emperor replied: "Regulations should be easy to understand. If you think I could follow them, then write them as such."[15]

---

12 *Shiji* 99/2721-2726.
13 Ibid. 99/2722.
14 Ibid. 55/2042-2043.
15 Ibid. 99/2722.

This was quite a challenge for Shusun Tong. It took him over a year, in which he traveled east to Lu to seek experts in rites and music. He was ridiculed by two scholars before returning west to the Han capital of Chang'an to practice the court rites with the recruited scholars and his disciples. When all the princes and officials gathered together to perform the new court rites for the first time, the result was magnificent. "When the wine was finally set out in the hall, no one yelled with joy or failed to observe propriety." The emperor was overjoyed and said, "Not until today have I truly understood the prestige of being emperor!" Shusun Tong's scholars and disciples were then given official appointments and monetary rewards. They extolled him, saying, "Shusun Tong is indeed a true sage, knowing what is needed to rule the world!"[16]

This was the first time that a Confucian scholar stepped into the limelight in the Han court. Nearly one hundred years later, the great Han historian Sima Qian (ca. 145/135–90/85 BC) would look back on the 7th year of Han Gaozu's reign (200 BC), the time when the rites were established and music composed, and exclaim:

Shusun Tong is a rare genius in knowing what needed to be done. His establishment of the rites and his sense of propriety show that he could change to suit the times. In the end, he became the paragon of Confucianism (*hanjia ruzong*). An old saying goes, "A truly upright person often looks to not be so. The Way is indeed a curvy line." Does this not describe him well?[17]

Han Gaozu and his prime minister, Xiao He (257–193 BC), both died in 193 BC. Xiao He's political enemy Cao Shen (d. 190 BC) was then appointed as the new prime minister. He professed to be a strict adherent to Laozi's philosophy of non-interference (*wuwei*), which proposed that "governing a state is like cooking small fish" (i.e. they should be handled minimally).[18] As the *Laozi* also says, "When the people are not afraid of death, wherefore frighten them with death?"[19] Thus, he believed the best way to govern the empire was to remove hunger and suffering, which led to unrest and a view that death was a welcome reprieve. In the successive dynasties in medieval China, one political motto to which everyone adhered was: "Let Xiao [He] set the path and let Cao [Shen] follow it." In other words, once the basic structure of the administrative, military, financial, and cultural system was set in place at the beginning of the dynasty, there is

---

16 *Shiji* 99/2723-2724.
17 Ibid. 99/2726.
18 Lau 2001, pp. 86-89.
19 Ibid, pp. 106-108.

no point in questioning its adequacy. Rather, later officials should adhere strictly to the system established, "observing it without fail".[20]

The Unlearned yet Artful "Paragon of Confucianism"

Having gained the good favor of Han Gaozu, Shusun Tong was first promoted to the post of Grand Master of Ceremonies (*taichang*). This put him in charge of all matters related to religious and cultural affairs throughout the empire. Subsequently, he was made Grand Mentor (*taifu*), who was responsible for educating the heir apparent. According to tradition, it was none other than Shusun Tong who, by threatening to commit suicide, initiated the protests against Han Gaozu's plan to displace his heir in the later years of his reign, thereby ensuring that the crown prince (who is posthumously known as Emperor Hui, r. 195–188 BC) could preserve his succession rights as heir apparent.

At its outset, the Han dynasty placed even more emphasis on the military than had the Qin, at the expense of the civil government. Thus, the practice of basing important government appointments on martial accomplishments had already become custom. But just as the quick-witted Lu Jia (ca. 228–140 BC) had argued when he criticized Liu Bang's anti-intellectualism by asking: "Your Majesty obtained the empire on horseback; does your Majesty plan to rule it on horseback too?"[21], the crux of the matter was that it required experts of all types to bring the empire under orderly rule. Thus, in the early Han dynasty, the Court of Imperial Sacrifices (*fengchang*, later renamed *taichang*), which had been set up during the Qin dynasty to supervise all matters relating to the rites and ceremonies of the ancestral temple, rose to become the ministry with the greatest concentration of experts in civil government matters. This included experts in anything from religious offerings, music and dance, banquets at court, astronomy and calendrics, astrology and divination, medicine and sanitation, civil engineering and architecture, mining and minting, to the management of markets and the dredging of canals. Naturally, it was essential that the head of this ministry be a highly erudite scholar, not a man from the military ranks.

We can take for granted that Shusun Tong, who had served as an erudite under two dynasties, upon his appointment to Grand Master of Ceremonies did what he could do to staff the positions of his ministry with erudites. He most likely died towards the end of Emperor Hui's reign (i.e., prior to 188

---

20 *Shiji* 54/2030.
21 Ibid. 97/2699.

BC). According to the *History of the Former Han Dynasty* (*Hanshu*), in early Han the number of erudites already amounted to several dozen.[22] We can infer that a good part of this was the doing of Shushu Tong, who under Emperor Hui was reappointed Grand Master of Ceremonies and with whom he enjoyed a close relationship. It goes without saying that he would not alter the function of these erudites as political advisors who possessed a thorough knowledge of the past and the present (*zhangtong gujin*); neither would he change the policy of recruiting erudites from all intellectual strata, i.e. from the Daoist, Mohist, Confucian, Legalist, Logician, or *Yin-Yang* schools of thought. Had he not done this, how could he have been said "to know what is needed to rule the world"?

How to Bring About "No Dissent under Heaven"?

Han Gaozu greatly admired what Shusun Tong had done in establishing the system of rites and ritual, which gave him a taste of the high prestige with which the emperor was vested. In the process, it became clear what sort of "magical mechanism" the superstructure of the empire needed to function: this superstructure had to be shaped in a way that safeguarded the authority of the "son of heaven" (*tianzi*) as supreme ruler and, concurrently, as spiritual leader. To this end, the Han needed to adopt Qin Shihuang's "method of the ruler facing south" (*junren nanmian zhi shu*),[23] i.e. an ideology in which the ruler adopts a detached approach towards the meticulous workings of the bureaucracy, as pointedly summarized by the dictum found in the *Spring and Autumn Annals of Lü Buwei* (*Lüshi chunqiu*), namely that the ideal ruler "does nothing, yet he sees that there is nothing left undone".[24]

Qin Shihuang espoused an eclectic ideology that contained traces of all the intellectual currents from the Qin-Han transitional period as depicted in Sima Tan's (165–110 BC) "Treatise on the Essential Teachings of the Six Schools" ("Lun liujia yaozhi").[25] This eclecticism left an imprint on his pronouncements and conduct. While his personality was always changing, one word of advice from his advisor Li Si became his lifelong maxim. This advice is recorded in Sima Qian's "The Annals of Qin Shihuang": "Ensuring

---

22 *Hanshu* 19A/726.
23 The phrase "the method of the ruler facing south" originates in the context of introducing the Daoist concept of government; see *Hanshu* 30/1732. It should be noted, however, that this concept's underlying idea of "bringing about order without exertion" (*wuwei er zhi*) is associated with the Sage Emperor Shun — an association which has been ascribed to Confucius himself; cf. *Lunyu* 15.4.
24 Cf. Knoblock and Riegel 2000, p. 49.
25 Included in Sima Qian's autobiographical account in *Shiji*'s last chapter: *Shiji* 130/3288-3292.

there is no dissent under heaven (*tianxia wu yi yi*) is the only way to achieve internal peace and stability."[26]

The word he used for "internal peace and stability", *anning*, was originally an alternate term used by the ancient Chinese for winter. It described the atmosphere of frozen tranquility exhibited by all living things during the dead of winter. This mode of expression is in line with Qin Shihuang's belief that his empire possessed the "virtue of water" (one of the "five elements") and his ambition to act as God on earth. Li Si's proposed way to realize the emperor's aspirations came from condensing the art of ruling as laid out by legalist thinkers Shen Buhai (420–337 BC) and Han Feizi into his concise statement of ensuring there is "no dissent under heaven". What this means, in essence, was that neither the ministers nor the people could have any will of their own; all thoughts and intents must be consistent with that of the emperor, similar to the atmosphere of harmony exhibited by nature in the dead of winter. Thus, the emperor used the law to burn books as a way to keep the people ignorant. He used retribution in the next life as a way to force people to be virtuous. Many other means were also used to prevent seeds of dissent from being sown. He ultimately failed, however, just as the fabricated prophecy among the people had predicted: "Emperor Shihuang will die and the land shall be divided."[27]

It seems logical to expect the low-born generals and ministers who revolted against the Qin dynasty to learn from history. However, when Han Gaozu ascended to the throne, he was deeply troubled that he did not receive the same type of demigod reception that Qin Shihuang enjoyed. He later disseminated a number of myths through Empress Lü (d. 180 BC) about such things as his being conceived when his mother copulated with a black dragon and having propitious clouds that covered him when he was once fleeing the law for crimes he had committed.

Shusun Tong understood that in order to create a divine ruler, one must first create a sage-emperor. Early on he arranged for the Emperor's adopting an august demeanor as the "son of heaven". Of course, this new aura could only be established by having Han Xin arrested and Xiao He incarcerated. This demonstration of might to the other low-born generals and ministers clearly communicated the message that whoever chose to contradict him would pay the price.

It is still not clear whether or not Liu Bang knew the real reason the Qin dynasty fell. That is, Qin Shihuang's youngest son fabricated an imperial edict with Zhao Gao (d. 207 BC) and Li Si ordering the execution of the

---

26 *Shiji* 6/239.
27 Ibid. 6/259.

crown prince and the head commander of the army, so they could usurp the throne. However, the fact that before dying, Liu Bang wanted to make another son the crown prince indicates he already knew the greatest obstacle to preserving the empire came from within his own family and from the empress' family.

Just as he had anticipated, shortly after his death, power fell into the hands of Empress Lü. However, when the empress followed his example in eliminating dissenters, those still loyal to Liu Bang revolted. The Chancellor Zhou Bo, along with Chen Ping and others, took advantage of Empress Lü's old age and eventual death to initiate a coup d'état, accomplishing what has later been referred to as "securing the house of Liu," or safeguarding the dynasty through a powerful minister.

Virtually the same story repeated itself over and over in China's medieval history. I once wrote:

From the founding of the Qin empire down to the demise of the Qing empire, there were many dynastic changes, divisions and reunifications; yet the common mode of governing always remained the same, namely an autocratic monarchy. Hence, the pivotal question in the field of ideology and political thought was how to ensure the stability of this monarchical autocracy and how to exert and extend "the method of the ruler facing south". The solution was first revealed by Ban Gu in the early Eastern Han: "Use the political astuteness inherent in the Classics to augment the bureaucratic government."[28]

Here I do not plan to restate all the results of my research on the history of Emperor Wu's "banishing the Hundred Schools and revering only Confucian statecraft" (*bachu baijia duzun rushu*). In order not to repeat myself at length, I'll just summarize a previous article of mine in five points.[29]

First, the scope of the so-called "banishing" of the Hundred Schools in the beginning was restricted to the official erudites who advised the emperor on cultural and literary matters.

Second, this change of advisors was primarily directed at the so-called Huang-Lao School, which constituted the mainstream of the ruling ideology in the early Han dynasty. As the Han adopted the Qin dynasty's po-

---

28 Zhu Weizheng 2002, p. 2-3. The statement "Using the political astuteness inherent in the Classics to augment the bureaucratic government" originates from *Hanshu* 89/3623-3624 (in reference to three Western Han scholars Dong Zhongshu, Gongsun Hong, and Ni Kuan). It is also referred to by Pi Xirui in *Jingxue lishi*, p. 103.

29 See "Rushu duzun de zhuanzhe guocheng (The Course of Events that Led to the Historical Turning Point of Endorsing Only Confucian Statecraft)". In: Zhu Weizheng 2002, pp. 65-95.

litical system, the Huang-Lao School actually was a camouflaged continuation of the Legalist School's advocacy of "punishments and names" (*xing ming*).

Third, when Sima Qian wrote "Those who have studied the *Laozi* (i.e. Daoism) over the generations disparage Confucian teachings, and those who have studied Confucian teachings have disparaged the *Laozi*,"[30] he revealed that in the transitional period between Emperor Jing (r. 157–141 BC) and Emperor Wu, during which Sima Qian and his father Sima Tan lived, the Huang-Lao and the Confucian schools were openly denouncing one another.

Fourth, when Emperor Wu ascended to the throne in 141 BC at 15 years of age, Tian Fen (d. 131 BC), younger stepbrother of the Empress Dowager née Wang (Emperor Jing's wife), was eager at the time to take control of the court. He was the first to propose the slogan of "elevating Confucian statecraft and censuring the parlance of the Huang-Lao School".[31] However, when he attacked the imperial relatives' faction headed by the Grand Empress Dowager née Dou (Emperor Wen's [r. 180–157 BC] wife), he was rebuffed and lost out to the Grand Empress Dowager. This shows that the proposal and rejection of elevating Confucian statecraft was nothing but the outcome of a power struggle between the relatives of the grand empress dowager and those of the empress dowager.

Lastly, when Grand Empress Dowager Dou died in 135 BC, Emperor Wu appointed Tian Fen as chancellor, in revenge for his grandmother's oppression. He then "ousted the Huang-Lao School, the Legalist School of 'punishment and names', and all other schools"; in their place, he widely recruited "literati and Confucian scholars". Now, since Dong Zhongshu's "Three Treatises on the Relationship between Heaven and Man" ("Tianren sance") were submitted to the Emperor in the 5th month of 136 BC, i.e. one year after Grand Empress Dowager Dou's death, we cannot but conclude that these treatises had been written in order to provide the obligatory rationale for the enacted policy of recruiting only those for official erudites who were "versed in the *Six Classics* and Confucian statecraft".[32] So, the way in which our history textbooks have the story, claiming that it was due to Dong Zhongshu's proposal that Emperor Wu banish the Hundred Schools and revere only Confucian statecraft, mistakes the effect for the cause. This is not how history actually unfolded.

---

30 *Shiji* 63/2143.
31 Ibid. 107/2843.
32 *Hanshu* 56/2523.

Dong Zhongshu "Uses the *Spring and Autumn Annals* to Adjudicate Penal Cases"

It is not clear where Dong Zhongshu's (ca. 179–104? BC) academic thought originated. Sima Qian, the author of *Records of the Grand Historian*, was a student of his, and yet only included a short biographical entry of him in the chapter entitled "Biographies of Confucian Scholars" ("Rulin liezhuan"). In it, he merely states that Dong Zhongshu was from Guangchuan (known today as the region east of Zaoqiang in Hebei Province), that he "was appointed as an erudite during the reign of Emperor Jing for his study of the *Spring and Autumn Annals*" (*Chunqiu*), and that "he belonged to the tradition of the *Gongyang* School of the *Spring and Autumn Annals*".[33]

The *History of the Former Han Dynasty*, written one hundred years later, gave him his own separate biography. Apart from including his famous "Response to the Question of Nominating Able and Virtuous Men" and other writings, there is hardly anything added regarding his life or his teachers. The only other information about him in the same book is found in Liu Xiang's biography, where it states that in the beginning of the reign of Emperor Yuan, some scholars viewed him as "the paragon of present-day Confucianism" (*shi ruzong*). One thousand years later, during the Northern Song dynasty (960–1126), the book entitled *Rich Dew of the Spring and Autumn Annals* (*Chunqiu fanlu*) was published with his name on it as its presumed author. However, already during the Song, some expressed their doubt regarding the book's authenticity.

There is one thing that we need not doubt, however, and that is that Dong Zhongshu was the first to adjudicate penal cases on the basis of the *Spring and Autumn Annals*. These cases were major cases, involving primarily insubordination to superiors (including the emperor) and inciting revolt. Shortly after the Han dynasty was founded, Xiao He established the Han penal laws based on the penal system of the Qin dynasty. With Emperor Wu having expelled the Huang-Lao School and the Legalist School of "punishments and names," regarding the adjudication of criminal cases it implied that the legalist theories of Shang Yang (395–338 BC) and Han Feizi could not be openly used or consulted any longer as a way to give moral credence and legal backing to these adjudications.

Dong Zhongshu was the first to use Confucian statecraft to resolve this dilemma. He stated that Confucius' statecraft was embodied in the *Spring and Autumn Annals*. He also claimed that even though this chronicle-style history composed by Confucius in his later years related to "three ages" (i.e.,

---

33 *Shiji* 121/3127-3128.

the age that Confucius lived in and knew as an eyewitness, the earlier age that he heard about, and the age before that which he only knew about from written accounts), it nevertheless contained countless "great principles" (*dayi*) which explicated the basic ideas of how to deal with the interrelations and correspondences between heaven, earth, and man. Confucius thought that such principles were best not expressed openly, so he only verbally taught them to his most trusted disciples. These secret teachings were called "subtle words" (*weiyan*). They were originally passed on by Gongyang Gao, a second-generation disciple of Confucius, to the subsequent generations of his family until Gongyang Shou in the reign of Emperor Jing (r. 157–141 BC). It was he, together with his disciple from Qi, Humu-sheng, who wrote them down. This is known as the *Gongyang Commentary on the Spring and Autumn Annals* (*Gongyang chunqiu*). As Dong Zhongshu claimed to belong to the Gongyang School, he presumably clearly understood the judicial doctrine spelled out by the "great principles" couched in the "subtle words" and how they could be applied in the present.

To give an example, let us turn to the 36 instances of regicide recorded in the *Spring and Autumn Annals*. Some of these cases did not actually happen. Specifically, the one recorded for the 19th year of Duke Zhao's reign states, "The crown prince of Xu committed regicide against his father Mai."[34] Later it goes on to say "A state burial was conducted for the Lord of Xu and he was mourned accordingly."[35] From the term "regicide" we know that the Lord of Xu was killed by one of his subjects. Yet from the expression "a state burial was conducted" it is clear that the he did not die by any means from the medicine his son brought to him (the medicine was the basis for the charge of regicide). All three commentaries on the *Spring and Autumn Annals* note the contradiction in Confucius' wording in this passage. Only Dong Zhongshu insisted that the reason for using the term "regicide" is Confucius' most important principle in the *Spring and Autumn Annals*, namely "meting out punishments on account of intent" (*zhu xin*). From this it can be inferred that an official or a son who is in disagreement with his ruler or father can be found guilty, even if he never openly spoke out but merely hemmed and hawed when listening to his ruler's or his father's instructions.

This was a revelation to Emperor Wu's important oppressive official Zhang Tang (d. 115 BC). He appointed scholars from Dong Zhongshu's following to high positions and added into the Han penal code dreadful regulations such as "mete out punishments based upon one's intentions" and prohibitions against "harboring feelings that run counter to one's lips" (*fan chun*).

---

34 *Gongyang zhuan zhushu*, p. 291.
35 Ibid., p. 292.

Subsequently, the oppressive official Du Zhou was even more audacious in claiming that the ruler's will was law.

That which was deemed right by former rulers shall be recorded as 'laws' (*lü*). That which is deemed right by later rulers shall be added as 'ordinances' (*ling*) to expound these 'laws'. If laws and ordinances are taken to spell out what is right in the present, what point is there in using laws of the past?[36]

This shows that Emperor Wu's "revering only Confucian statecraft," as it was proclaimed at that time, in actuality amounted to endorsement of the scholars in the circle around Dong Zhongshu, who all claimed to "thoroughly understand the *Spring and Autumn Annals*".[37] Wielding and corroborating on Confucius' great principles couched in subtle words, they pandered to the fact that the emperor wanted a unification of all ideologies. This cooperation with political power is also expressed by the phrase "studying thoroughly the canonical texts to employ them for political application" (*tongjing zhiyong*).

What Is Meant by "Studying Thoroughly the Canonical Texts for Political Application"

During the Warring States period, Daoists, Confucians, Mohists, and Legalists all made use of the technical term in textiles *jing* (warp), or the set of yarns placed lengthwise in the loom, to denote the books that contained their schools' essential teachings. They also used the word *shu* (thoroughfare), or the main roads within a city, as a metaphor expressing the way to guide political and educational practices according to the teachings contained in such canonical texts (termed "statecraft" in this article). All schools asserted that their canonical texts and their statecraft (or *jing shu*) had universal value. As long as they advocated what was suited to the occasion and persuaded the monarch who was looking for internal peace and stability to put their theories into practice, the result would be "no dissent under heaven". Thus, these scholars would achieve the aim of "studying thoroughly the canonical texts for political application" (*tongjing zhiyong*).

As such, during the Qin-Han period the dominant school changed hands three times, from Legalist, to Huang-Lao Daoist, and finally to Confucian statecraft. Their common focus was to validate the ideology of monarchical rule which adapted to the changes of time. The only difference was the nucleus of their arguments. The Legalists' nucleus was "exercising the law" (*ji fa*), which Qin Shihuang was fond of; in the early Han, when the

---

36 *Shiji* 122/3153.
37 Ibid. 121/3128.

Han adopted the political system of Qin, the Huang-Lao School was centered on "non-interference" (*wuwei*); and down to the time of Emperor Wu, the Confucians were focused on "allowing plenty of desires inwardly, yet outwardly exhibiting benevolence and righteousness (*nei duo yu er wai shi ren yi*)".[38] All of these ideas made sense in their own day. In other words, during the Qin-Han period, "studying thoroughly the canonical texts for political application" was a common theme among these three schools as a way to occupy center stage in political ideology.

While there is nothing suspicious about the development of these three schools, there is plenty to be suspicious about regarding Dong Zhongshu. Researchers in the history of Classical Learning have not yet determined whether or not Dong Zhongshu actually studied the *Gongyang Commentary on the Spring and Autumn Annals* with Humu-sheng. When the policy of "revering only Confucian statecraft" was declared in 135 BC, Dong Zhongshu was deemed the top respondent to a query by Emperor Wu. That this happened after Dong Zhongshu's responses to three queries of Emperor Wu on the relationship between heaven and man clouds the whole affair in a shroud of mystery (see above).

Similarly, was the textus receptus of the *Rich Dew of the Spring and Autumn Annals* actually written by Dong Zhongshu himself? The compilers of the *Complete Collection of Books in the Four Treasuries* (*Siku quanshu*; compiled from 1773–1782) were hesitant to confirm his authorship. Only Zhang Binglin (1869–1936) of the late Qing dynasty was bold enough to state that

> [...] Dong Zhongshu became the 'pope' [of Han Confucianism] by establishing regulations and ordinances on the basis of Yin-Yang thought and by handing them down as models for the erudites.[39]

Dong Zhongshu's advocacy of "guilt by intention" (*zhu xin*) has had a lasting effect on later generations. To this day Chinese law does not specifically allow for a presumption of innocence. Its application also allows for punishing one's attitude, which has lead to many miscarriages of justice and, at the same time, has saved many a corrupt official. No wonder Dong Zhongshu was posthumously given the epithet of "paragon of present-day Confucianism".[40]

Unfortunately, Dong Zhongshu never did grasp Confucius' real meaning. The *Analects* (*Lunyu*) record that Confucius did not discuss "man's nature

---

38 *Shiji* 123/3160.
39 Zhang Binglin: "Xue bian (Changes in Scholarship)." In: id. 1984, p. 144.
40 *Hanshu* 36/1930.

and the way of heaven" and that he "respected the supernatural but kept his distance".[41] Yet in his old age Confucius wrote the *Spring and Autumn Annals*, wherein various calamities, such as solar eclipses or locust plagues, are recorded. From this it seems as if Confucius believed in the interconnectedness between heaven and man. However, he never stated it openly. Rather, he was truly "the one among the sages who went with the times," knowing all the societal happenings of the time.[42]

Dong Zhongshu superstitiously believed that every word from Confucius the sage was truth. As a result, he constantly added meaning into the canonical text of the *Spring and Autumn Annals* that is not there. For example, the *Spring and Autumn Annals* record 36 instances of solar eclipses and the same number of instances of regicide. Could it be that this is just a coincidence? Not for Dong Zhongshu. He speculated that this was a concealed message from Confucius, to reveal heaven's interconnectedness with man. Specifically, whenever something goes wrong with the affairs of man, an abnormality will occur in the heavens. These natural disasters are meant as a warning. As Confucius never taught about such an interconnectedness, Xun Kuang (ca. 312–230 BC), who in the transitional period from Qin to Han was revered by Confucian and Legalist scholars alike, spoke even more explicitly on the separate realms of heaven and man. Dong Zhongshu had to strive to augment his viewpoint by using the *yin yang* and "five elements" doctrines advocated by Qin Shihuang. As a result, Confucian learning was transformed into a state-sponsored theology.

Cheng Shude's book *Jiuchao lü kao* (*A Study of the Laws of the Nine Dynasties*)[43] contains a collection of fragments from Dong Zhongshu's *Collection of Adjudications Based on the Spring and Autumn Annals* (*Chunqiu jueshi bi*), which is no longer extant. From these it is absolutely not by accident that Dong Zhongshu until today is honoured with the epithet of the "paragon of Confucianism".

Emperor Wu and Gongsun Hong

In imperial China, from the Qin and Han to the Ming and Qing dynasties, the emperor was both monarch and spiritual leader. While the emperor could be stripped of his power by an usurper, there were no effective checks and balances in place to control the emperor's use of power. Therefore, the way of

---

41 He Yan (annotator), cited in *Lunyu zhushu*, pp. 43, 54.
42 Zhao Qi (annotator), cited in *Mengzi zhushu*, p. 176.
43 Cheng Shude 1988.

governing was largely shaped by the individual ruler's character. This has been termed the "rule of man" (*renzhi*).

Emperor Wu is a striking example of this. He reigned for a total of 54 years (141–87 BC), the later 48 of which he ruled with complete sovereignty. The biggest challenge to his autocratic power came from his whimsical and wanton nature. It has been said that his keenness for Confucian scholarship was just the result of his confusing "scholarship" (*xue*) with "statecraft" (*shu*). With his approval of having the erudites' official chairs specifically assigned to each of the *Five Classics*, Confucian scholarship transformed into Classical Learning.

However, in the subsequent 40 some years of his reign there are only two instances of his showing interest in Classical Learning. The first is his inquiry about a text in the *Book of Documents* (*Shangshu*) to Ni Kuan (d. 103), a scholar of Classical Learning who was famous for "adjudicating difficult cases by using interpretations of law cases from the past".[44] The second is when he held a debate between the two schools of the *Gongyang* and the *Guliang Commentaries of the Spring and Autumn Annals* to determine which school commanded the finest interpretations of Confucius' *Spring and Autumn Annals* and the great meaning couched in subtle words therein. However, what Emperor Wu was really interested in was Confucian statecraft, that is to say statecraft derived from the Classics.

From the *Records of the Grand Historian* we learn that the *Gongyang Commentary* was Emperor Wu's most revered canonical work of Confucian statecraft and thus held the same authority as a constitution, as it were. The one who, on account of his scholarship of the *Gongyang Commentary*, was raised into the highest ranks of nobility, was none other than Gongsun Hong (ca. 200–ca. 121 BC).

Originally a poor swineherd from the Kingdom of Zichuan (located in present-day Changle, Shandong Province, and the region east of that city), it was not until Gongsun Hong was over 40 years old that he began studying a mélange of teachings about the *Spring and Autumn Annals* and yet earned the reputation for "twisting the Classics to curry favor with the powerful".[45] In 130 BC, on the occasion of the second imperial "recruitment of the virtuous, excellent, and learned," he responded to the emperor's query by imploring him to value the art of statecraft and was subsequently made an erudite. He was over 70 years of age at the time.

---

44 *Hanshu* 58/2629.
45 *Shiji* 121/3124.

Gongsun Hong lived a frugal life, but proclaimed "the monarch's greatest lack was that of breadth and magnanimity,"[46] giving the emperor a license to indulge in wanton extravagance. Add to that his habit in court discussions to propose alternative schemes and options for the emperor to choose from, and it's a small wonder that we read in his biographical account,

> [...] thereupon, the "son of heaven" observed that he was honest and sincere in his conduct, resourceful in debate, well-versed in the law and in government affairs, as well as apt in using Confucian statecraft to augment the bureaucratic government.[47]

Because of this, the emperor turned a deaf ear to the warnings of the high officials at court that Gongsun Hong was very deceptive and promoted him from Imperial Censor (*yushi daifu*) to Chancellor (*chengxiang*), and enfeoffed him Marquis of Pingjin.

Apart from being adept at guessing what was in the emperor's heart, Gongsun Hong was also good at taking advantage of the emperor's trust in him to seek power for those scholars below him. He recommended that "50 pupils be assigned to each erudite"[48] and devised a system whereby they could be selected, taught, tested, and given official posts based on their scores. It was approved by Emperor Wu and made into law. Before this, the posts of "Erudites of the *Five Classics*" were already the exclusive domain of Confucian scholars. However, their role was limited to waiting outside the gates of the imperial courts perchance the emperor would seek their advice on cultural matters. After Gongsun Hong revised the laws so that the erudites could take on pupils, these pupils became the group from which future civil officials were chosen. Their lessons, examinations, rankings, and even their expulsion were all controlled by the erudites. This meant that the erudites' scope of functions was enlarged by the task of educating the future civil officials.

> From this point on, the number of literati that held official posts greatly increased — from the rank of high ministers to that of petty clerks.[49]

Gongsun Hong was unlearned yet artful, plotting and scheming to create trouble for Dong Zhongshu, Zhufu Yan (d. 126 BC), Ji An and other important officials whose learning and talents far surpassed his own. Because of this, few words of praise were ever spoken of him, whether in life or in death. He however knew how to utilize Emperor Wu's ambition for great achievements. He enticed promising youth from all across the empire to devote

---

46 *Shiji* 112/2950.
47 Ibid.
48 Ibid. 121/3119.
49 Ibid. 121/3119-3120.

themselves to learning Confucian statecraft by arranging for this to lead to the "road to official emoluments and benefits".[50] He seized the opportunity to turn the erudites from advisors into educators. This brought about the institutionalization of the policy to "revere only Confucian statecraft". The far-reaching effects of this were that people began to believe that if one grasped the ways of statecraft within the Classics, then "obtaining a high-ranking post would be as easy as picking up dirt from the floor," as the ancient Chinese described it.[51]

Although he himself did not believe in Confucius' ways of statecraft as derived from the *Six Classics*, Emperor Wu proclaimed it the yardstick in political ideology. Subsequently, he got enmeshed in self-contradictions by such policies as his military expansionism, the performance of the mountain-top *feng* and *shan* sacrifices (*fengshan*), and his commissioning of alchemists to find the elixir of longevity. When he gave Gongsun Hong permission to have the erudites be in charge of educating and promoting future civil officials, it is likely he did not fully foresee the extent to which this reform would affect the whole system of civil officials. History shows, though, that its effects were not limited to the Western and Eastern Han dynasties, but rather that it was the very source of the civil service examinations up to their abolishment at the end of the Qing dynasty.

It just so happened that in the very year when the Manchus abolished the civil service examinations in 1905, that the historian of Classical Learning Pi Xirui (1850–1908) actually wrote in defense of Gongsun Hong. Earlier, Pi Xirui had run afoul of the government for his support of the Hundred Days' Reforms in 1898 and had thus been handed over to the custody of the local government. According to Pi Xirui, Gongsun Hong's reforms must be understood against the facts that during Emperor Wu's reign scholars did not only adhere to what their teachers taught and the Confucian School was held in low esteem. Hence,

[...] if the study of Classical Learning was to be encouraged, the only way to do so was to offer the enticement of official emoluments and benefits.[52]

Clearly, this follows the logic of an argumentation that the end justifies any means. For the last hundred years the ghost of Pi Xirui's argument has haunted Chinese intellectuals time and again. Perhaps it's time we truly examined its veracity.

---

50 *Hanshu* 88/3620.
51 Lu Bi, in *Sanguo zhi jijie*, p. 611.
52 Pi Xirui, p. 73.

On the Followers of Confucius and Han Imperial Merchants

The Western Han dynasty lasted for 240 years, reaching its peak during the reign of Emperor Wu. Yet just as with climbing a mountain, reaching the peak marks the beginning of the descent down.

As the 6th ruler of the Han dynasty, Emperor Wu inherited a rich empire. The imperial granary and treasury were filled with grain and money. The prefectures, counties, and princedoms throughout the empire were largely at peace. And the capital Chang'an was the most flourishing city in the world at the time.

It took Emperor Wu six years on the throne to fully step out from under the control of his grandmother. Driven by his youthful zest for action, he decided to attack the Huns to the north, the Kingdom of Min-Yue to the southeast, and the barbarians to the southwest all at the same time. Successive victories extended the boundaries of the empire to double the size of the Qin empire. Yet, it came at a heavy price. Not only did he exhaust the money in the treasury, he also enraged the lower classes. Two years prior to his death he was forced to issue an imperial edict acknowledging that such large-scale military aggression was wrong.

The emperor should be concerned with preventing oppression, halting excessive taxation, promoting agriculture, resting troops and revising laws, so as to replenish that which is lacking; wearing out the military is not the only thing involved in ruling the empire.[53]

This is a quote from his famous "Majestic Terrace Edict of Self-Accusation" ("Luntai zuiji zhao"). From Qin Shihuang to this point in history, imperial China had seen two dynasties and eight rulers, all in a period of 132 years. Yet, this was the first time that an emperor ever admitted in an imperial edict that one of his basic policies implemented for dozens of years had catastrophic consequences for the empire and the people.

The results of Emperor Wu's constant military conquests were not entirely negative, though, much as was the case with Caesar and the later successors of the Roman empire some years later. Some good did come from bringing different peoples settled in distant regions who were constantly fighting each other under the sway of a civilized and culturally-advanced central government. Similarly, the implementation of Gongsun Hong's suggestion to have future civil officials be trained and promoted by the "Erudites of the *Five Classics*" had the effect of raising the quality of the whole group

---

53 *Hanshu* 96/3914.

of civil officials in terms of ethical norms and cultural values, while at the same time transforming the bureaucracy into a mechanism for exercising control over political ideology. At the very least, there were no longer any illiterate officials in the prefectures and counties; rather, most were law-abiding and capable officials who sought to promote internal peace and stability as a result of their education.

However, there were three things that Emperor Wu's edict did not discuss, which are the guaranteed downfall of any government, then or now: (1) the emperor was the first to begin amassing wealth (by heavy taxation), (2) he violated the rule of law; and (3) he practiced favoritism in making appointments.

In addition to the exorbitant costs associated with long-term expeditions against the "four barbarians" (*si yi*) and helping displaced people find a place to settle, the new imperial palaces he had built, several tours around the empire, lavish worship ceremonies, and quests for potions of immortality were even more extravagant than under Qin Shihuang. The imperial treasury that his forebears had amassed over time was completely emptied within 20 years of his ascending to the throne. In 119 BC, natural disasters and other calamities resulted in over 700,000 refugees in the region east of the Hangu Pass (Guandong). The situation was so severe that cannibalism soon broke out and insurrections sprung up in various regions. All of these posed a serious threat to the stability of the empire. Emperor Wu's countermeasures were threefold: use a currency made of deer hides, mint bad money, and implement government monopolies.

As we read in the *Records of the Grand Historian*, "At this time, there were white deer in the Imperial Park, while the Privy Treasury was stacked with silver and tin."[54] The Imperial Park mentioned here refers to the Shanglin Park encompassing Emperor Wu's private hunting grounds just outside of the capital. The Privy Treasury managed the emperor's private property and controlled the taxes levied on all forests, mines, wastelands, and aquatic resources from oceans and lakes. After decreeing the imperial overseer to skin the deer and cut up the tanned hides into pieces, the emperor demanded the marquises to put up capital for a piece of hide in lieu of the rank-based annuity they had to pay in tribute to the emperor. A square foot of white deer hide cost 300,000 copper coins.

Copper coins were in use during the beginning of the Han dynasty as well, which at the time were really an alloy of approximately seven parts copper to three parts tin. One *jin* (approx. 245 grams)[55] of the alloy could be

---

54 *Shiji* 30/1425.
55 See Nienhauser 1994, p. *xxxiii*.

used to mint 6,000 *dangbai* coins. However, Emperor Wu's Privy Treasury added minute amounts of silver to the tin when making the coins. The result was that one of the new *banliang* coins was the equivalent of 3,000 *dangbai* coins. The *gui* coin, that was one-tenth the value, was worth 300 *dangbai* coins. With this level of inflation, the profits for the Privy Treasury far surpassed what was made from selling the deer hides. And all of it went into the emperor's private coffers. Large amounts of the money extracted from these two ploys went to fund the lavish and wanton lifestyles of the emperor, his wife and concubines, offspring, and relatives of the families of his wife and concubines.

It's not unusual that Emperor Wu would start to think of merchants when his coffers were running empty. As most of the powerful men in the beginning of the Han were lower-class vagabonds from country villages and small towns, they were jealous and spiteful of merchants who made their riches from opportunistic ventures. This sentiment can be seen from Han Gaozu's listing merchants last in his categorization of the four classes (i.e., scholars, farmers, craftsmen, and merchants), and from his "increasing their taxes and levies as a way to humiliate them".[56]

Yet after the unification of the empire, trading between different regions became more and more prolific and the capital Chang'an became the heart of all crafts and commerce. The guiding policy of the Han dynasty of "encouraging agriculture and disfavoring commerce" (*zhongnong yishang*) eventually turned into the emperor selecting merchants to work as imperial procurers. Also, the emperor took control over the monopoly of salt and iron, effectively monopolizing basic resources as a way to amass wealth. The emperor's greed soon trickled down through the strata of society and made it impossible for nobility and officials to not lead luxury-loving lives. All this is mirrored in the descriptions contained in Sima Qian's historical and realistic accounts in the "Treatise on the Balanced Standard" ("Pingzhun shu"), "Treatise on the *Feng* and *Shan* Sacrifices" ("Fengshan shu"), and "Biographies of the Money-makers" ("Huozhi liezhuan").

In addition to this, it is interesting to note that the *Records of the Grand Historian* raises another interesting point, namely, how do we account for the fact that Confucius encountered difficulties at every turn during his life, but after his death suddenly rose to become a person of great import? According to Sima Qian, the answer lies with one of his 77 disciples: Zigong, a merchant from the feudal state of Wei. As a matter of fact, Zigong did not only approve of Confucius' scholarship (*xue*), but agreed even more with his art of statecraft (*shu*). As I have pointed out earlier, the characteristic

---

56 *Shiji* 30/1418.

trait of Confucian history during medieval China was the tendency of "scholarship to follow changes in the ways of governing" (*xue sui shu bian*). It is in Zigong that we find the first example of using the way of governing to guide the direction of scholarship. That is, while professing to propagate his master's teachings, he changed with the times, seeking to gain fame, power, and riches for himself and his own school. Of course there were many like him in later generations.

According to the *Analects* and the *Records of the Grand Historian*, Zigong was the second best of Confucius' disciples in the language and diplomacy. Only Zaiyu (522–458 BC) was better than him. In the later years of Confucius' life, Confucius increasingly praised Zigong's knowledge and talents. Zigong not only ensured means to provide for his ailing parents, he was also at Confucius's side when his master passed away.

In Sima Qian's "Biographies of the Money-Makers," praise is first given to Fan Li, who once helped Goujian, the King of Yue, in seeking revenge and establishing himself as king. After achieving this aim, Fan Li left politics, changed his name to Lord Zhu of Tao, and became a merchant. In the ensuing 19 years, he earned a fortune three times over.

This Lord Zhu of Tao was a forerunner of Zigong. The difference between the two is that Fan Li engaged in politics first and then moved on to trade. Zigong, on the other hand, engaged in trade and scholarship at the same time. He always praised his teacher, and in so doing elevated his own status. After Confucius' death, Zigong traveled to the different kingdoms giving counsel to various feudal lords. "Whenever he arrived, the feudal lords invariably split the court and welcomed him as an equal."[57] No matter what he tried his hand at, be it politics, trade, or administration, he always attributed his success to Confucius' teachings. "The one who caused Confucius' name to spread everywhere was Zigong," wrote Sima Qian.[58] Zigong had power and influence because of his wealth, which he used to persistently propagate the message that Confucius followed in the footsteps of the Duke of Zhou, with the privilege of first entering the Confucian pantheon.

Consequently, Confucius' influence increased manifold. By the time Emperor Wu banished the Hundred Schools, Confucius had risen to become the "lone sage" (*dusheng*) in cultural and educational matters. Viewing the policy of revering only Confucian statecraft from this angle perhaps puts it in a more historically accurate perspective.

---

57 *Shiji* 129/3258.
58 Ibid.

The Negative Side to the Use of the *Six Classics*

Striving to bring about "no dissent under heaven" was a common goal shared by all monarchs of the successive dynasties and usurpers throughout medieval China. It has been said that Emperor Wu was wiser than Qin Shihuang in that he choose Confucian learning as state orthodoxy, and enticed people to study only Confucius and the Confucian School's canonical texts through official emoluments and benefits — eventually bringing about a unification of thought.

Unfortunately, history does not corroborate this viewpoint. As early as after Confucius' death, Confucianism branched out into different factions, so that for the Warring States period (476–221 BC) the question arises as to whether Mencius or Xunzi should be considered the true leader of Confucius' fellowship. In the Han dynasty Shusun Tong and Dong Zhongshu were both given the title of "the paragon of Confucianism" and both claimed to know what was needed to rule the world. Again the question arises: whose teachings can be classified as the "state orthodoxy"? Further, there has been much debate, both in the past and the present, about Emperor Wu's revering only Confucian statecraft. Be it as it may, what the emperor was really interested in was not Confucian Classical Learning, but rather Confucian statecraft or Classics-based statecraft, which he used as a tool to make his policies more appealing, just like adding a decorative border on the hem of a lapel would make a jacket more attractive. Is this not a historical fact that has already been discovered by scholars of the Han dynasty?

But this is not all. In speaking of Classical Learning during the Han dynasty, mention must be made of Pi Xirui and Zhou Yutong (1898–1981), who during the 20th century took the approach of studying the transmission of and commentarial work on the canonical texts. They must be given credit for systematically pointing out that at the core of Han Classical Learning lay a divide between the "New Text School" (*jinwen xue*) and the "Old Text School" (*guwen xue*). Moreover, within the same school there were versions and varying interpretations of the same text, which led individuals in these factions to strive for appointment as an erudite. This implied, of course, that among the various exegetical schools in the field of Classical Learning a scramble for gains and profits broke out, each vying for pole position on the road to official emoluments and benefits.

This scramble for gains and profits led to new alignments and developments. The "Erudites of the *Five Classics*" were mostly experts in but one classic and its exegesis as passed down from their own teachers. Constant changes in the political situation of the time demanded that in one aspect or another, the most be made of each classic. This resulted in a division of labor in the study of statecraft in the classics. As Pi Xirui has described:

> Using the two treatises contained in the *Book of Documents*, 'Tribute to the Great Yu' ('Yugong') and 'Great Plan' ('Hongfan'), to regulate the waterways and to investigate the changes in the natural and the human world, respectively; using the *Spring and Autumn Annals* to adjudicate penal cases; and using the *Book of Odes* to admonish the ruler — all of these show how one canonical text was studied to harvest the benefits that derived from that particular text.[59]

However, a presupposition of "studying thoroughly the canonical texts for political application" is that the text must be without controversy. After Qin Shihuang's proclamation of a law banning books, a period of 30 years elapsed before its eradication under the Han Emperor Hui. During this period book collections suffered severely. Except for the *Book of Changes*, the *Five Classics*, which people claimed to be edited by Confucius himself in his later years, only existed in bits and pieces. After the ban was lifted, the manuscripts in circulation were mostly written in the so-called "new script" (*jinwen*), which was instituted as the official writing style in the Qin dynasty. These manuscripts were used by scholars in different parts of the empire. It is thus not surprising that both the texts and their readings and interpretations would contain discrepancies. Furthermore, there were many discoveries among the people of texts written in different forms of the "old script" (*guwen*) used before the Qin dynasty's uniformization of the script.

The policy during Emperor Wu's reign was to appoint erudites of the classics and their commentaries written in the new script, regardless of minor inconsistencies between the text recensions or interpretations. Thus, three erudites were appointed for the *Book of Odes*, with their interpretations evidencing some drastic differences. Also, for the *Spring and Autumn Annals*, two erudites were appointed — one for the *Gongyang Commentary* and one for the *Guliang Commentary*, leaving it to the emperor to settle the controversies between them by proclaiming that the *Gongyang Commentary* was more congruous with Confucian statecraft. Because of this, during the reign of Emperor Wu, official Classical Learning began to establish the tradition of "scholarship follows changes in the ways of governing".

Two emperors later, during the reign of Emperor Xuan (91–49 BC), it became common that there were chairs for different interpretations of a single classic, amounting to twelve "Erudites for the *Five Classics*," together with other scholars who were not yet given the rank of erudite. To add to the confusion, there were two other books that were also required

---

59 Pi Xirui, p. 90.

learning for the imperial family and children of nobility: the *Analects* and the *Classic of Filial Piety* (*Xiaojing*).

The complex situation is highlighted in the chapter entitled "Interpretation of the Classics" ("Jingjie") contained in the *Book of Rites* (*Liji*), which was compiled around this time. While unable to refrain from eulogizing the magnificence of the *Six Classics*, the author of this text admits that any excess in commenting on and interpreting the classics will unavoidably lead to fallacy:

> Thus, an errant reading of the *Book of Odes* leads to stupidity; the *Book of Documents*, to slander; the *Book of Music*, to extravagance; the *Book of Changes*, to deceit; the *Book of Rites*, to excess trivialities; the *Spring and Autumn Annals*, to disorder.[60]

Rule by a Chosen Sovereign or a Monarch from the Royal House?

As noted in the preceding section, the tendency for scholarship to follow changes in the way of governing was prone to run in the counter-direction, i.e. changes in the way of governing were induced by changes in the reading and interpretation of the *Six Classics*. Apart from this phenomenon, we can even observe how strained interpretations of the classics that aimed to draw deductions for the present brought about arguments that had the potential of undermining the existing societal and political order — which inflicted harm upon those who had fathered them.

This is elucidated, for example, by Dong Zhongshu in his going against Confucius' admonition to not discuss man's nature and the way of heaven. In so doing, Dong secretly adopted the doctrine of the "five elements" propagated by the *Yin-Yang* School, where the elements succeed each other by vanquishing the one preceding it. He also came up with the doctrine of "heaven's interconnectedness with man," in order to predict the outcome of certain affairs on the grounds of natural or man-made calamities and strange phenomena. At one point, a fire broke out in the ancestral shrine of Han Gaozu, located in the region east of the Liao River. Dong Zhongshu advocated that it meant heaven was not pleased that Emperor Wu's policies and teachings had not yet reached the "great ideal of absolute impartiality and justness". It just so happened that one of Dong's disciples was commissioned to check on the reasonableness of this memorial without knowing who wrote

---

60 Zheng Xuan (annotator), in *Liji zhushu*, p. 845.

it. His assessment was that it was written by a "complete fool".⁶¹ As a result, his teacher almost lost his head.

One of Dong's second generation disciples, Sui Hong, who lived during the reign of Emperor Zhao (r. 87–74 BC), learned that in the year 78 BC a large rock on Tai Mountain rose spontaneously, that in Changyi a withered tree came back to life, and that in the Shanglin Park a willow tree that had fallen to the ground became erected again. So he memorialized the throne, asserting that according to Dong Zhongshu's theory derived from the *Spring and Autumn Annals*, all of these are signs of a change of the "mandate of heaven. He pled with the emperor to search for a virtuous and able person to whom he should "abdicate the throne" (*shanrang*). Eventually, the general-in-chief Huo Guang accused him of spreading unfounded rumors to deceive the people, and had him executed.⁶²

Later on, after having extricated himself out from under the control of Huo Guang, Emperor Xuan no longer pretended to walk the path of virtue and began appointing eunuchs and relatives of the empress' family to important posts. During this time, Ge Kuanrao (d. 60 BC), a scholar well versed in the classics who had been appointed colonel in charge of public order in the capital Chang'an, was incensed by the fact that the emperor's father-in-law was leading the rich and powerful to act like monkeys and fighting dogs. He then memorialized the emperor, making the accusation that

[…] the way of the sage-rulers has gradually been abandoned. Confucian statecraft is no longer practised. Eunuchs have taken over the positions which (under the exemplary Western Zhou dynasty) were held by the Dukes of Zhou and Shao, and laws and ordinances have replaced the *Book of Odes* and the *Book of Documents* [as the early Zhou kings' guidelines of good government].

He then went on, saying,

[…] the five sage emperors ruled as chosen sovereigns, while the kings of the three dynasties [i.e., Xia, Shang, and Zhou] ruled as monarchs of a royal house. Monarchs pass the throne on to their offspring, chosen sovereigns to virtuous and able persons. It is just as the succession of the four seasons: once a season has reached its full, it wanes. If one is not a virtuous and able person, he is not entitled to occupy the throne.⁶³

This clearly implied that the present emperor, by his personal character and conduct, had already forfeited the right to rule and thus the tradition of ruling

---

61 *Shiji* 121/3128.
62 *Hanshu* 27B/1412; 75/3153-3154.
63 Ibid. 77/3247.

"all-under-heaven" by a chosen sovereign as practised from the Yellow Emperor to Yao and Shun should be reinstated. Also, the throne should be abdicated to a virtuous and able man capable of putting into practice the "way of the sage-rulers". Needless to say, this is another instance of a plea to abdicate the throne, something that even Confucius thought of as taboo. Ge Kuanrao was thrown into prison where he committed suicide.

Footprints in the Water.
Assessment in the *Zhuangzi*

PAUL D'AMBROSIO

> When flowers bloom they do not disdain
>   the plots of the poor;
> The moon shines on mountains and rivers
>   so that all are bright.
> In this world the heart of man alone
>   remains vile;
> In all things demanding that Heaven
>   show him favor...
> However calculated, events are controlled
>   by fate rather than man.
>
> *Jin ping mei*

Introduction

The Daoist classic the *Book of Zhuangzi*, or *Zhuangzi*,[1] presents a fascinating, carefree world where nature is the harmonious home for all things. Stories in the *Zhuangzi* often show people or animals taking advice from unexpected areas: crippled people, animals, and even plants can be sources of

---

1 Daoism as a school of thought is most closely associated with the classical texts *Classic of Virtue and the Way* (*Daodejing*) and the *Zhuangzi*. Unique because it does not advocate any definite principles, nor does it have any clear guidelines for "followers". Both the *Daodejing* and the *Zhuangzi* are obtuse and mysterious texts that are difficult, if possible at all, to understand with any degree of certainty. The Daoist classic *Zhuangzi* comprises thirty-three chapters in all, the first seven of which are referred to as the "inner chapters" because they are thought to be the only ones written by Zhuangzi or Zhuang Zhou (d. 286 BC), himself. The remaining chapters vary in their explanation, but on the whole seem to be a continuation (or some version thereof) of the first seven chapters.

inspiration that reflect on our ideas. This reflection is often aimed at showing us that something we think is important is perhaps actually irrelevant, muddled, or both. It shows us that the judgments we value are often artificial and useless; they misguide us and cause disorder (*luan*)[2]. We are given the opportunity to view the world without virtues, ethics, or any code of conduct. The *Zhuangzi* prefers a return to nature, to a place where there is no assessment and no values. It is only in this way that the *Zhuangzi* can recognize a society or situation free from disorder (*luan*).

There is a story in the *Zhuangzi* where Zhuangzi finds a skull, wondering aloud he asks how the skull came to be in the state it is in. He asks the skull whether it died a natural death or not, considering all types of things that could have gone wrong and caused it to die. Tired, Zhuangzi grasps the skull and falls asleep; later that night the skull appears to him in a dream. It tells Zhuangzi that his wondering was silly because it only involved ideas about the lives of man and foolish assessments about life. After dying it is no longer necessary to deal with the toils of life, something difficult for the living to grasp.[3]

This story, and many others like it, discusses the possibility of living a life free of human judgments in order to more fully live a natural life. Nature is not the chaotic nature of Thomas Hobbes (1588–1679); nor does it involve an overcoming like in Friedrich Nietzsche (1844–1900). The *Zhuangzi*'s nature is pure and simple. It is before assessment, judgment, or analysis and for this reason it cannot be argued for, or against; nor does nature put forth an argument — it simply is. Thus, nature is only an option, the option of returning home.

In this paper I will consider the *Zhuangzi*'s[4] reaction to the philosophical arguments of its day. I will show that the *Zhuangzi* is not convinced by the arguments of "assessment" (*shi* or *fei*)[5] that arise when thinkers deal with philosophical issue, mainly *luan*. If the *Zhuangzi* advocates anything

---

2   The term *luan* means disorder, chaos, out-of-order. Harmony (*he*) is often contrasted with *luan*. This term also takes on different connotations depending on different contexts and schools of thought. For the Daoist this term may be similar to "unnatural" or straying from nature. The Confucians may see mis-managing, or an incorrect understanding of relationships as major causes of *luan*.
3   See Yang Liuqiao 2007, pp. 197-198 and the translation in Graham 2001, p. 125.
4   We will take the *Zhuangzi* as mainly being themes either in or directly connected to those of the "inner chapters".
5   I have used "assessment" as an umbrella term, covering all types of judging, analysis, evaluation, morality, and basically any type of distinguishing or differentiating that involves valuing.

at all, it is a lack of concern for ethics, knowledge and any affirmations (*shi*) or denials (*fei*). All these kinds of assessments are unnecessary, and only serve to hinder one's nature. As we will later see this lack of concern is actually the option out of disorder (*luan*) in a society or situation according to the *Zhuangzi*.

Assessment in this paper is any type of distinction or categorization that involves a value judgment or gradation. This can include but is not limited to expectations, pre-set ideas, judgment, analysis, and — perhaps the most important aspect of classical Chinese thought — morality. We will focus specifically on morality and virtues to emphasize the difference between Confucianism[6] and Confucian moral virtues as opposed to the *Zhuangzi*'s complete lack of regard for these things. To consider this problem in all of its complexities, I will first demonstrate how assessments, which are primarily moral, are made in early Confucianism. Examining what might be the most important Confucian virtue *ren*[7] (humaneness, benevolence) I aim to show how *ren* and all virtues are suspicious and perhaps even dangerous concepts for the *Zhuangzi*. I will then move on to the idea of assessment itself. An alternative to assessment will be explored by looking at several stories from *Zhuangzi* and show that any type of assessment, expectation, or pre-set idea is troublesome at best. I will show an alternate route for dealing with *luan* given in the *Zhuangzi*. In the final section I will discuss the fact that the *Zhuangzi* goes so far as to ignore the distinction between reality and illusion. Finally, the conclusion will be the natural synthesis of these parts, exploring the alternatives that are left after casting away all types of assessment.

Tracing the Sages: Standards of Action

The classical tradition of Chinese thought has been described by philosophers and sinologists, for example A.C. Graham (1919–1991) in *Disputers of the Tao*, as a discussion over the best way to deal with chaos, *luan*, in society. Confucius (ca. 551–479 BC) himself grew up in a time when wars were common in terms of both area and time. It has since been hypothe-

---

6   The school of thought that is associated with Confucius and his followers. Major early thinkers include Confucius, Mencius and Xunzi. The influence of this school is spread throughout everything from government to cooking, and is (in some sense) still alive in China today
7   *Ren* is the highest virtue in Confucianism. It is the expression of correct understanding and virtuous action with regard to relationships. It is the thread that all other virtues depend on, and the complete expression of all virtues is the complete fulfillment of *ren*. For various meanings of *ren* see also the article by Achim Mittag in this volume.

sized that his thought is prompted by the prevalence of war and the lack of order or *luan* that was experienced throughout the country. Almost every other ancient Chinese thinker addresses *luan* as a central issue or problem. It can even be said that finding order in China is similar to the Western philosophical search for truth. The different schools of thought in the Chinese tradition can then be likened to different philosophers in the West. Schools of thought in China deal with differing thought, ideas, values, etc. all according to how they approach the problem of *luan,* just as different Western philosophies develop out of different approaches to finding the truth. However, such parallels are not relevant for this paper; what is relevant is the way that Confucius, the *Zhuangzi* and other schools of thought may have dealt with *luan*, or their own version of a common goal. Confucius' own way to deal with this problem was to look at ancient cultures and by laying in moral overtones, make these cultures models for virtues and rituals that would help organize society.

Confucius, by his own account, never claimed to be a sage. He always insisted that he was following the sages of old, e.g., Yao and Shun,[8] as a transmitter of their thoughts.[9] However, by taking the thoughts and norms of his day and interweaving them with morality in order to design a model for action Confucius proved to be more of a thinker than a transmitter. For example, two levels of man, *junzi* and *xiaoren*, were "moralized" by Confucius. Originally the difference was acknowledged from a political standpoint, not from a moral one. A *junzi* was the son of an official; a *xiaoren*, by contrast, was a normal person.[10] In the Confucian classic, the *Analects of Kongzi (Lunyu)*[11], Confucius refers to a *junzi* as a highly moral person, whereas a *xiaoren* lacks morality.[12]

---

8 Yao and Shun were the founders of the Zhou dynasty (ca. 1100–256 BC) and were kings whose teachings Confucius is supposed to be "transmitting". For Confucius these men are the real founders of the Confucian moral virtue, and he often calls on them as figures of authority.

9 References to the *Analects* throughout this paper will always be numbered according to the translation by Ames and Rosemont 1998. See *Analects* 7.1.

10 Fung You-lan 1980, p. 130. Before Confucius the term *junzi* was used to describe the son of an official, or someone politically important. Confucius used this term to define those who he thought to be excellent exemplars of his thought. Although it is nearly impossible to become a *junzi*, or sage, Confucius believed that anyone who tried hard enough, studied well, and kept conscious awareness of themselves, their thoughts speech and actions, could become a *junzi*.

11 See Ames and Rosemont 1998.

12 The *Analects* do contain passages where the terms *junzi* and *xiaoren* are purely political, but the emphasis is on the moral use of these terms in the *Analects* themselves and in this paper.

The Confucian model is one that encourages people to compare themselves to each other, but more importantly to sages of old.[13] Morality is defined as looking back at the actions of past sages that were assessed as moral and modeling one's life after them. By imitating a sage, one could become a sage. However, one will undoubtedly encounter situations that sages had not. In these new situations, Confucius advised his followers to continue the ideal of imitation to the best of their ability. By comparing one's situation to the actions of a sage in a similar situation, until the appropriate action becomes clear to them.[14] The thought behind this Confucian teaching was that practicing appropriate action would change a person's thought process, enabling the individual to begin to spontaneously act as a sage does. Graham comments,

[…] the [Confucian] "way" is what you would want to do if you had the wisdom of the sage.[15]

Confucius' hope is that by imitating the sages one will slowly be able to think and act — spontaneously — like a sage.

An idea in the *Zhuangzi*, which is strongly emphasized by its great commentator Guo Xiang (252–312),[16] is that the Confucian standard for action relies on the footprints (recorded actions) of others. By following actions of past sages, comparing one's situations with theirs, one literally accepts these sages as models, or molds for what is right. Recognizing these molds, i.e., footprints, as correct one accepts and incorporates their direction as the proper way for one's current situation. As long as the model's circumstances are close enough to one's own, one can be sure that by following the footprints the sage has left, i.e., their decisions, one will be led down the correct path.

There are many difficulties with this standard: first, and most importantly, this standard never examines who and/or what made the footprints. The footprints are *traces* of what has been done, but they are not the doer himself.[17] The doer (so-called *sage*) is no longer alive, and the elements of his situation might no longer exist in their entirety.

---

13 See *Analects* 4.17 in Ames and Rosemont 1998.
14 Graham 1989, p. 27.
15 Ibid., p. 29.
16 Guo Xiang was a famous commentator of the *Zhuangzi*. He was part of the "dark learning" or *xuanxue* movement, which sought to find common ground between Daoist and Confucian thought.
17 I have borrowed the term "traces" from Brook Ziporyn (2003). The traces are basically the recorded actions or any writings left by major thinkers in ancient China. See here Ziporyn 2003, p. 31.

By following the sages' footprints, one ignores the fact that times and circumstances might call for different action. For example, Confucius famously answers different students differently when posed with the same question because he thinks no two people are the same. From the perspective of traces Confucius' mistake was not broadening his viewpoint in order to show that just as one cannot give different students the same answer to the question, "What is *ren* (humaneness, benevolence)?" one cannot follow the *ren* actions of Yao or Shun and expect them to be *ren* today. If the concept of *ren* is explained to various people differently, and applied to each situation uniquely, then even the *ren* of Yao and Shun cannot be imitated and remain, infallibly, *ren*.

Secondly, *ren* is a judgment placed on the outcome of an action and not the act itself; nor is it the motive driving the action. When Yao or Shun acted they did not do so in accordance with virtue, they acted with spontaneity according to the circumstances they encountered. Later, after their actions were over, theses two sages were praised and admired as virtuous because the outcome of their actions was deemed appropriate to the circumstances.

When Confucius speaks of virtues he does not, because he cannot, give principles or laws that apply to the wide variety of personalities encountering diverse circumstances in the world. Confucius can only give examples of what to do because there are no guiding principles other than *traces*. For this reason, the *Zhuangzi* criticizes Confucius for mistaking virtues as causes, Guo Xiang comments:

Benevolence [*ren*] is the trace of undiscriminating love; righteousness is the effect of bringing things to completion. The love is not (caused by) benevolence, but the trace "benevolence" moves in it; the completion is not (caused by) righteousness, but the effect "righteousness" appears in it.[18]

When acting, one does not need to be concerned with virtues because they are not the causes for actions, they are the result of judgments placed after the actions have finished. Virtues are not the motives of the sages; the sages' actions were later deemed virtuous by others. So Confucius attempts to imitate actions already judged virtuous in the hopes that his situation, actions, and outcome will be similar enough to be considered virtuous. The Confucian standard for action is a hope that by imitating actions already deemed virtuous one will become virtuous — a project that is, from the perspective of the *Zhuangzi*, a contradiction from the start.

---

18 I consulted the *Zhuangzi* edition by Guo Qingfan 1983, here p. 283. The translation follows Ziporyn 2003, p. 51.

Ren: a Moral Brand

The notion of *ren* is singled out not only because it is a perfect example of tracing the sages, but also because it represents a core concept in Confucianism that the *Zhuangzi* is purposely lacking. *Ren*, which is often translated as humanity or "human-heartedness,"[19] is a central concept in Confucianism. The term itself appears as the topic of many discussions in Confucius' *Analects*, but was seldom discussed in literature before this book. Like the terms *xiaoren* and *junzi*, *ren* was popularized by Confucius, and has since retained the connotations he put forth.

In Confucius' *Analects*, *ren* can be understood as both a virtue and a pinnacle/culmination of all virtues.[20] As a specific virtue *ren* speaks to the respect and duty required in people's relationships. It is also often explained as being a virtue of love, but it is a kind of love with more rigid obligations. There is a specific hierarchy to relationships (such as between a husband and wife, or parents and their children); *ren*, understood as love, is a virtue that respects and acts according to these hierarchies. By loving people in the right way, in accordance with what is required by their relationship, one expresses the virtue *ren*. It starts by having the correct relations with family members, and then branches out to friends, co-workers, and strangers et al. In this way *ren* would become the thread holding together responsible and moral social relations. These threads are woven through, and therefore depend on, family relations. Having good family relations becomes the model for healthy social relationships. As a broader concept *ren* is the expression of a person who is well-rounded morally.

The fully matured expression of *ren* incorporates the different virtues discussed by Confucius in the *Analects*.[21] *Ren* then becomes broader as it takes a position of precedence over other virtues as encompassing them as a pinnacle. This crosses over into other areas of Confucian thought, such as rituals. For Confucius rituals are extremely important and he spends a lot of time discussing the proper way to conduct them. But the foundation for these rituals, or the precondition, is that the person doing them is "morally able" or someone who is *ren*.[22] And so *ren* is broad in the area of virtues, but also in almost every area of Confucius' thought. It is a central thread that weaves thoughts together while at the same time being an integral part of their make up. In the *Zhuangzi*, however, *ren* is not something to be sought after or even learned about.

---

19 See Fung 1948, p. 42.
20 Ibid., pp. 42-43.
21 See *Analects* 17.6 in Ames and Rosemont 1998.
22 Ibid., 12.1.

When the word *ren* does appear in the *Zhuangzi* it is not expressly denied nor is it accepted or advocated for at all. In fact, in several places the *Zhuangzi* questions apparently obvious aspects of *ren*, and other Confucian virtues. The *Zhuangzi* is suspicious in accepting virtues as inherently beneficial. The details or qualities of these virtues are almost never discussed; the suspension arises over the entire system of ethics, or the idea of virtues themselves. By questioning the system itself the *Zhuangzi* does not engage in talks about virtues, but rather comments on these discussions themselves and not their particulars. Looking closely at the virtue *ren* we can understand a model for the *Zhuangzi*'s approach to all Confucian virtues.

For the *Zhuangzi* the concept *ren* (along with other virtues) is not necessarily a good thing. Approaching this Confucian virtue with caution the *Zhuangzi* is more inclined to associate *ren* and all other virtues with harm rather than benefit. It comments directly on virtues given from the sages of old, saying

[…] Yao has already branded your hide with Goodwill [*ren*] and Duty [*yi*], and snipped off your nose with his Affirmation [*shi*] and Denial [*fei*].[23]

Virtues are coupled with *shi* and *fei*, because they are products of the system of *shi* and *fei*. This system and virtues themselves are harmful to one's nature. Leaving lasting impressions and taking away from one's nature these concepts (virtues, *shi* and *fei*) are clearly something one can do without. Examining this comment, perhaps too literally, virtues will leave one branded with markings that can be seen by others and may never fade. It is also important to note that in ancient China criminals were branded on one or both cheeks when found guilty of a severe crime, allowing everyone else to know instantly that this person is a criminal. Using this brand is perhaps meant to provoke this image of a mark made on a criminal's face. We can then understand the *Zhuangzi*'s view of *ren* as something that is there for everyone to see, and something that allows others to know one is dangerous. Obviously not dangerous in the moral sense, because *ren* (and in this respect can be seen as akin to saying "good" in the West) is almost always supposed to be beneficial or at least positive morally. It is a remark that declines to comment on the details or particulars of *ren* itself, and seems to be speaking to all virtues.[24] The "danger" is a danger associated with all virtues, the system of ethics itself, and is therefore not something that will be a

---

23 Yang Liuqiao 2007, pp. 79-80; the translation follows Graham 2001, p. 91.
24 The comment does also include "duty" (*yi*), another core moral concept, so it is probably safe to assume that all virtues can be subject to the same understanding according to the *Zhuangzi*.

warning sign for any ethical person. Only those people without ethics, or perhaps those with different ethical beliefs, will see one's moral brand as dangerous. Furthering this explanation, and perhaps thereby verifying it to some extent, we can see another "danger" of virtues.

In another place in the *Zhuangzi ren* is again brought up in a negative sense. The *Zhuangzi* states,

> [...] then again, to be ample in Power and solid in sincerity but lack insight into others' temperaments, not enter into competition for reputation but lack insight into others' hearts, yet insist in the presence of the tyrant on preaching about Goodwill and Duty and the lines laid down for us, this amounts to taking advantage of someone's ugliness to make yourself look handsome. The name for it is "making a pest of oneself". Make a pest of oneself and others will certainly make pests of themselves in return. I rather fancy that someone is going to be a pest to you.[25]

This comment shows how virtues can be used as a way to praise one's self and condemn others. (It even goes so far as to say that one who pushes goodwill, *ren,* and other virtues on others are like tyrants.) Although this may seem to conflict with the above branding and criminal image, it in fact does not. The branding mentioned above is not supposed to be recognized by all as something negative, it is only a warning for those with different ethical views or (like the *Zhuangzi*) those lacking ethics altogether. Those who wear the mark are most likely proud of it (proud to be a moral person) and might ridicule others who do not bear the same brand, or those who bear no brand at all. In terms of virtues and ethics this means that those holding one ethical view or advocating one virtue over another will disagree with those who oppose or disagree with them, trying to make themselves look better and others worse. For the *Zhuangzi* this is a mere beauty pageant where one attractive person tries to point out another's blemishes in order to look more beautiful themselves. This is exactly like the arguments of Mohist and Confucians over virtues, morality or *shi* and *fei* in general. Because they disagree, they each try to point out weakness in the other to make themselves look better. This will be discussed in more detail below.

Ren can easily be coupled with affirmation (*shi*) and denial (*fei*) because it is one type of judgment made from using *shi* and *fei*. All virtues, which are advocated over others or vices, are products of assessment. But having these virtues brands our hide, and using *shi* and *fei* cuts off our nose. Staying literal while we examine the second comment, we can see that *shi* and *fei* is heavily influential to our senses. By cutting off our nose, and thereby inhibiting the sense of smell, we are left in a world without fra-

---

25 Yang Liuqiao 2007, p. 40; Graham 2001, p. 67.

grances, good or bad. Unable to smell, one would miss out on any pleasant scent, such as the scent of flowers. Their enjoyment of, for example flowers, would be greatly hindered. They would be able to enjoy flowers using only their other senses. The benefit to this is that without a nose one would also miss out on the bad smells as well as the good ones. However, bad smells are not always bad. Smelling food that is rotten can help one avoid eating something that may hurt or even kill them. Similarly, smelling a fire could allow someone to escape from a potentially dangerous situation. The connection between *shi* and *fei* and the loss of a sensory organ is then probably aimed at showing how the use of *shi* and *fei* hinders one's ability to experience the world in its fullness. Naturally, most people have noses, and can therefore experience smell, just as people are born without different categories or a *shi* and *fei* system. But *shi* and *fei*, just like losing one's nose, is the interruption of one's nature that results in a loss of an undifferentiated full experience of the world.[26]

Ren, as a single virtue, and all other virtues like it, are also subject to a more basic criticism from the *Zhuangzi*. On a fundamental level all virtues stem from accepting (*shi*) or denying (*fei*), or discriminating between alternatives. The *Zhuangzi* cannot be convinced of this not only because it sees the *shi* and *fei* system, and especially virtues, as potentially harmful, but also because it does not dare to advocate a single viewpoint or understanding on any issue. Commenting on this the *Zhuangzi* writes,

[…] in my judgment the principles of Goodwill [*ren*] and Duty, the paths of "That's it [*shi*], that's not [*fei*]," are inextricably confused; how could I know how to discriminate between them?[27]

Chopping: *shi* and *fei*

Mozi (ca. 490–381 BC), the founder of the Mohist school of thought, was as influential as Confucius in his time.[28] He was also the first major oppo-

---

26 Interestingly cutting off one's nose (foot or other body part) was also a punishment administered to criminals. It was not only debilitating but also a type of branding that let everyone know you had done something wrong. Cutting off a body part in ancient China was especially bad because it meant that one would be missing that body part in the next world. So it was important for many Chinese to die with their body intact, and losing a body part was seen as extremely unfortunate. This attitude is continued today in China where people missing body parts, deformed or even handicapped are often openly subject to prejudices.
27 Yang Liuqiao 2007, pp. 27-28; Graham 2001, p. 58.
28 Mohism, a school of thought beginning with Mozi, was just as popular and widely studied as Confucianism until it came to an abrupt end in the begin-

nent of the Confucian school, and the Mohist school of thought continued to disagree with the Confucian school for years.[29] The source of this disagreement can be understood as stemming from their differing approaches to the problem of disorder (*luan*). China may have been a bit more stable for Mozi than Confucius, but they both experienced a similar excess of wars and political turmoil. Mozi, however, was not from an aristocratic stratum of society, but was more likely to have been a kind of wandering military adviser who later had his own group of extremely loyal soldiers. The relevance of their different lifestyles in their different philosophies is quite apparent. Mozi criticizes Confucius for being too elaborate in his ethics. The different relationships and detailed explanation of virtues and rites would take years to study, time that a man of Mozi's status did not have. Mozi saw the study of music or mourning for the death of a parent for three years as a luxury that could not be afforded by most, not a necessity. Even the concepts of virtues themselves, such as *ren*, are extremely different for the two schools. In Confucian thought we saw this virtue being realized through the recognition of different levels and different relationships. Starting with the family and eventually spreading outward to all aspects of one's life, human relationships are central to the Confucian tradition. Mohist thought denies this and claims that *ren* is an all embracing love that does not discriminate, even between family and non-family members.[30] Mozi's explanation and reasoning for this has very much to do with his military attitude and having all soldiers on the same level. To put it simply, the Mohists and the Confucians disagree on the particulars of virtues and rites. The Mohists deny (*fei*) practices and ideas that are affirmed (*shi*) by the Confucians. The Confucians, in turn, *fei* what the Mohists *shi*. Each school responds to the other thinking they are correct and the other is wrong, thereby leading to an argument over what is right.

The *Zhuangzi* wants to remain outside of this argument, and comments on the argument as a whole, not on its particulars. According to the *Zhuangzi*, things can be sorted, but there is no reason to make assessments ("the sage sorts out but does not assess"[31]). This means that the *Zhuangzi* stays outside of the system of *shi* and *fei*.

Assessment is not limited to the "good" and "bad" of morality, but exists at a more fundamental level, that of *shi* and *fei*. The *Zhuangzi* openly at-

---

ning of the Han dynasty (3rd century BC). Because many of the tenets of the Mohist School and Confucian tradition are in opposition, these two schools were often involved in dialogue that included judging and criticism.

29 Fung 1948, p. 49.
30 Ibid.
31 Yang Liuqiao 2007, pp. 25-26; Graham 2001, p. 57.

tacks both the Mohist and the Confucians, but the attack does not simply deny the Mohists, Confucians, or both. The *Zhuangzi* comments on how silly and unnecessary it is to argue over virtues and *shi* and *fei*, remaining outside the argument itself. Criticizing the Mohist and Confucians the *Zhuangzi* does not advocate a different *shi* and *fei*. Nor are the ideas of *shi* and *fei* being thrown out, or *fei*ed. Without affirming or denying anything it is difficult to say that the *Zhuangzi* takes a position. Instead we can say that the *Zhuangzi* takes the position of no position — by disregarding and therefore not validating the discussion. The *Zhuangzi* does not want to be a position; it wants to be position-less. (Notably, it is futile to speak of a "non position," because to even acknowledge is often considered taking a position).

The non-position of the *Zhuangzi* is one that recognizes and wishes to stay in a muddled state before *shi* and *fei*. It is a position before any position, including any type of language — but then how can it be expressed? The *Zhuangzi* remarks:

[...] heaven and earth were born together with me, and the myriad of things and I are one. Now that we are one, can I still say something? One and the saying makes two, two and one makes three. Proceeding from here even an expert calculator cannot get to the end of it. [...].[32]

Here it is clear that things are not clear. Even in speaking, the *Zhuangzi* has done something that goes counter to what it wants to say. It would prefer not to speak at all, but now that there has already been so much that has been said, the *Zhuangzi* would like to add a few words to remind us of where we came from, and that we do not need right and wrong, or *shi* and *fei*. The act of speaking goes against what it says, but it cannot be expressed without speaking, so the *Zhuangzi* opts to speak despite itself. From this perspective *shi* and *fei* are added; they are not part of our original nature.

Right and wrong are discarded because they are not needed. They are artificial add-ons to our natural being, which is why (as the Confucians stress) they must be *learned*. Hence the earlier comment of being brands on our skin, i.e. added on to what we were already given by nature. The *Zhuangzi* has nothing to do with virtues or ethics at all. It sees these add-ons as harmful to (human) nature. There is no need to move past "the myriad of things and I are one".[33] Any time one moves past this they are dealing with artificial distinctions. There is a story in the *Zhuangzi* where a student approaches a Daoist sage in an attempt to learn something. The student mentions that he has learned about virtues and how to differentiate *shi* and *fei*

---

32 Yang Liuqiao 2007, p. 24; Graham 2001, p. 56.
33 Yang Liuqiao 2007, pp. 24; Graham 2001, p. 56.

from the ancient sage Yao. Upon hearing this, the Daoist sage is disappointed in the student. He dismisses the student saying "Then what do you think you're doing here? [...] Yao has already branded your hide with Goodwill and Duty, and snipped off your nose with his [*shi*] and [*fei*]."[34] When the student presses his questions, hoping to learn at least a little, the sage adds that the student is now without the ability to see the world in all its colors (as commented above).

This harsh dismissal shows us that for the *Zhuangzi shi* and *fei* of any kind, and most specifically virtues, are infringes on one's nature, distorting the way one views the world. Using *shi* and *fei* to divide up the world also means that things are divided out and the myriad variations within the world are destroyed as they are divided. Using *shi* and *fei* to consider alternatives means that the greatest alternative, the undivided whole, is neglected.[35] The *Zhuangzi* has no need to invoke *shi* and *fei*, it is pre-assessment — distinguishing, but not assessing.

Swimming, Crying and Spitting: an Alternative

When the *Zhuangzi* speaks it does so to show us how silly assessment is, reminding us of a more basic and natural way to live. Of course the *Zhuangzi* cannot throw out distinctions — the basic needs of all things require distinguishing — but there is no need to judge. In short it is a way of living that can be more effective, less stressful, and more fun than having to think about *shi* and *fei*, or morality. This point is illustrated in the *Zhuangzi* by the swimmer story. Confucius was walking by a treacherous waterfall where even turtles and fish would not swim. Suddenly Confucius saw a man swimming in these deadly waters. Believing that the man was attempting suicide, Confucius was surprised to see him suddenly stroll out onto the bank, singing. Assuming that the man must have some mysterious secret to be able to stay alive in such waters Confucius questioned him. (Perhaps he was worried that he would find no footprints in the water.) The swimmer replied that he had no special way of staying afloat, saying:

I began in what is native to me, grew up in what is natural to me, matured in what is destined for me; I enter with the inflow, and emerge with the outflow, follow the Way of the water and do not impose my selfishness upon it.[36]

---

34 Yang Liuqiao 2007, pp. 79-80; Graham 2001, p. 91.
35 Yang Liuqiao 2007, pp. 25-26; Graham 2001, p. 57.
36 Yang Liuqiao 2007, pp. 213-214; Graham 2001, p. 136.

Given the topic of this essay there are two major ways of reading this story. The first is to read this story as an allegory for human interaction in society and situations, especially those circumstances that are not neatly organized or are in disorder (*luan*). The second way to read this story analyzes it as it speaks to assessment and how the character Confucius assumes and applies virtues to almost all actions. Following the first reading we can understand the waterfall and the treacherous waters below it as being a society or a situation in a state of *luan*. The swimmer has no problem diving right on into the waters and is able to flow through the danger unharmed because he does not attempt to do anything about it. He remains uninfluenced by his surroundings. Of course he is required to move through the waters, or with them, but he does not try to do anything. There is no method that he uses or idea that he upholds when he swims. It is an allegory for moving through a situation or a society where things are in chaos, or at least not ideal (according to Confucius this means not the Zhou dynasty (ca. 1100–256 BC)). The *Zhuangzi* is telling us that we can move through a situation or society in chaos without trying to control or change it. We can engage in these situations successfully without manipulating them. And we have no need to concern ourselves with what is going on around us; we only need to dive in and go with the flow. In this way the approach given in the *Zhuangzi* differs drastically from that given in the Confucian model. We can gain an accurate understanding of this difference by looking at the Confucius character in the story, thereby reading according to the second way mentioned above.

Confucius is taken a bit off-guard twice in this story, and each time it only shows his lack of understanding because of his presumptions. The first time Confucius is surprised when he sees the swimmer emerge from the water in a light-hearted manner. The waters are so dangerous that Confucius assumes anyone swimming in them must be trying to kill himself. Standing on the bank, Confucius does not experience the water; he merely observes and makes a judgment based on his past experiences. He assumes that he has the situation figured out, but the swimmer shows him that he has not. Like Confucian virtues, it is a case of taking what one thinks things should be like and applying them to a different situation.

Secondly, Confucius is taken aback when he asks the swimmer how he is able to survive. Again, Confucius has made an assessment, and looked for footprints for guidance. He thinks that the swimmer can only survive because of some special technique, but this is not the case at all. In fact, the swimmer can stay alive in the water without any technique. The swimmer does not impede the water, but simply lets himself flow naturally with nature.

It is difficult for Confucius to fathom such a method of action. Confucius wants to act deliberately by following the traces of sages so as to achieve virtuous effects. He advocates planning, making decisions, and figuring things out, especially when faced with chaotic situations. The swimmer does none of these things. On the contrary the swimmer acts naturally and does not impose himself on the situation. Situations are like waters; they can be dangerous. However, if one just follows their inflow and allows oneself to emerge with the outflow, one is likely to move naturally, have a good time, and in this case — stay alive. Imposing oneself on a situation would assume that one knows how to positively (or morally) affect the situation. But how can one assume knowledge about something that has not yet happened? There are those who presume to know, but the *Zhuangzi* has a story for these people too.

In the second chapter of the *Zhuangzi*, with its many logical arguments, the comment is also made that, "the sage does not work for any goal, does not lean towards benefit or shun harm".[37] This passage goes on to explain that expecting is also a mistake. Even if there is good evidence that something might happen, it does not necessarily mean it will happen. Later the passage unfolds with a story of Lady Li, the daughter of a military man. One day, after Lady Li was taken by the kingdom of Jin, she cried and cried, longing to go home. After living for some time in her new home, she found it quite pleasing and regretted having cried.[38] Even though everything seemed completely horrible at first it actually turned out to be quite nice.

This story shows that when one tries to impose their own pre-set ideas about something onto to a situation it is often the cause of misery. If Lady Li had not had pre-set ideas she would not have been disappointed but free to explore and enjoy her new life. Later, when she became happy it was also because of her predetermined ideas: assumption of how horrible things would be turned out to be wrong and so she became happy. The changing back and forth of emotions was all due to pre-set ideas.

This story speaks directly to both Confucian philosophy and to the example provided by the swimmer. Confucius assumed that the waters were too dangerous for anyone who wanted to live, and he then assumed that the swimmer must have some special way to survive the waters. The first assumption expressed belief in a certain outcome, which then gives one the authority to act morally. The second assumption supposes the need to act in a special way beyond what is natural; it assumes that something extra must be learned (like morality). In both cases these assumptions are discarded. Without knowing the outcome one has no authority to act deliberately to invoke moral claims. On a more fundamental level, there is nothing special to be learned, morality does not need to be added to nature.

---

37 Yang Liuqiao 2007, p. 29; Graham 2001, p. 59.
38 Yang Liuqiao 2007, p. 29; Graham 2001, p. 59.

These stories clearly express that the *Zhuangzi* believes morality to be wrong. Wrong not because it is not right, but wrong because it is not needed and only adds harm. The swimmer needs no special way; Lady Li assumes she knows an outcome and later regrets this assumption. When acting one needs neither a special method nor does one need to preoccupy oneself with predicting the result. Special methods only carve out our natural ability, eliminating the fullness (of experience/life/nature etc.) and for this reason morality is said to cut off one's nose. Results cannot be known, and therefore any attempt to assume an outcome is futile. For this reason the *Zhuangzi* does not have any assessments, let alone an ethical system. In fact from the *Zhuangzi*'s perspective using assessments, ethics, or virtues is something one only does when the society or situation is already in, or in order to cause, a state of disorder (*luan*).

Using an allegory to express its point, to speak about effective and fluid human interaction, the *Zhuangzi* likens men to fish. As fish swim in a river men make their way through this world. Trying to set directions for one another, giving moral advice causes disorder (*luan*).

> The Way lost, only then Power: Power lost, only then Goodwill (*ren*): Goodwill lost, only then Duty: Duty lost, only then the Rites. The Rites are the Way's decorations and disorder's head.[39]

The most basic, the "way" (*dao*),[40] is the most natural; it exists before any type of moral judgment, virtue or assessment. When judgments are made the "way" becomes lost and only then does morality exist. If the "way" is lost men are like fish on a dried river bed. They praise sages and condemn criminals, but this is nothing more than the fish on a dried river bank spitting on one another to stay alive. The fish would rather ignore each other in a full river, just as people are better off without the (moral) directions of others, moving around in the "way".[41]

---

39 Yang Liuqiao 2007, p. 247; Graham 2001, p. 159.
40 The term *dao* is often translated literally as "the way" or "way". Similar to "good" in Western philosophy with regard to the fact that different schools, and different thinkers employed this term with the same basic role, however they defined it differently. For the Confucians this term *dao* has moral connotations, and it means the way one should act, the way one should study and strive to carry out. The Daoist use of this term has nothing to do with morality, studying or striving, but is exactly opposite. The Daoist "way" is before morality, suggesting that one does not concern oneself with neither studying nor striving.
41 Yang Liuqiao 2007, p. 78; Graham 2001, p. 90.

In Reality, Outside Morality: Where to Go

Graham comments the *Zhuangzi* is "outside moral philosophy altogether," he further says that "the only judgment assumed [...] is that aware reactions are better than unaware ones".[42] To this extent he is in-line with this essay, but he adds (and cautions) that awareness "is not more than preferring truth to falsehood, reality to illusion".[43] This comment, I believe, has dangerous overtones. It seems natural enough to move from aware actions to truth and falsehood, reality and illusion. But, as we saw in the introduction, Confucianism, and Chinese philosophy as a whole, are not interested in truth/false and/or reality/illusion dichotomies. Chinese philosophy is interested in the question "what should I do?" and not "what is true/real," which is the focus of the Western philosophical tradition.

Above we saw in the story of the swimmer that the sage is not in control of what is happening, and only tries his/her best to go with the situation. There cannot be any *shi* or *fei*, true or false, good or bad. These ideas only intervene and get in the way of acting naturally. Furthermore, the *Zhuangzi* often acts on the basis that dreams and illusions are just as real as any reality.[44] To say that the *Zhuangzi* wishes to assess the difference between reality and illusions would be to make the mistake Herbert A. Giles made when he translated the "butterfly dream". Giles translated this story of Zhuang Zhou dreaming he was a butterfly and then awaking, as a story about Zhuang Zhou remembering his true self and discerning the dream from reality. As Hans-Georg Moeller points out, the butterfly dream is not about self, remembering, or discerning dreams from waking.[45] In fact the story, and the *Zhuangzi* as a whole, are concerned with just the opposite. The *Zhuangzi* is more interested in living fully in each situation one encounters. Just as the diver must adapt to currents in the water, one must adapt to new circumstances without trying to *figure them out*. As Guo Xiang comments on the butterfly dream, "[b]eing a butterfly while dreaming is genuine".[46] Illusions and reality are difficult (if impossible) to discern; in any case the *Zhuangzi* thinks that one should approach all situations as being real. At the end of the Lady Li story, the author also comments on dreaming and its "realness".

While we dream we do not know that we are dreaming, and in the middle of a dream interpret a dream within it; not until we wake do we know that we were

---

42 Graham 2001, p. 144.
43 Ibid.
44 Yang Liuqiao 2007, pp. 79-80; Graham 2001, p. 91.
45 Moeller 2006, pp. 48-50.
46 Ibid., p. 51.

dreaming. Only at the ultimate awakening shall we know that this is the ultimate dream. Yet fools think they are awake. [....] You and Confucius are both dreams, and I who call you a dream am also a dream.[47]

Here it is clear that, according to the *Zhuangzi*, we cannot be sure whether or not we are dreaming, or if we will wake from one dream only to find ourselves in another. But this does not matter, because whether we are in a dream or not we must still live as the butterfly, or Zhuang Zhou — living fully in whatever circumstance we find ourselves in. Even when Zhuang Zhou wakes he does not question whether or not he was dreaming, he forgets his dream and goes on without trying to figure it out. He is not concerned with any type of assessment, including determining whether something is real or not. In life one needs only to be like the swimmer; flowing with the natural patterns of the situation.

Conclusion

According to the *Zhuangzi* there is no need for assessment. All types of assessing are add-ons to our original nature. Judging things, calling something *shi* or *fei*, does not enhance one's life, it dampens it. Assessments like *ren* (humaneness, benevolence) are especially bad because they make people think that they have the authority to make the "right" choice. These people may also believe that they have the authority to tell others what to do, because they know what *ren* is, they have studied and practiced it. However, it is precisely this that makes the *Zhuangzi* weary of an idea like *ren*. Because *ren* requires so much effort, and represents a personal change, it is obviously far from the natural. For the *Zhuangzi* the sages are those who keep their original nature, not people who learn artificial ideas and use them to guide their and other's lives. I venture to propose that if there were any "humaneness" in the *Zhuangzi* it would be humaneness without humaneness, or that *ren* in the *Zhuangzi* is precisely the absence of any Confucian conception of *ren*.

Acting according to what one thinks is *shi* and *fei*, or acting according to what one thinks one should do imposes goals and plans that influence decisions. They try to imitate what they think is best and because of this cannot react naturally to their situation. With preset goals and ideas one assesses and tries to manipulate situations, ignoring their natural direction, trying to twist things. They seek others (like the swimmer) who seem to have a special skill for the purpose of learning to better manipulate, but there is no special skill to be learned. They think they know what is best

---

47 Yang Liuqiao 2007, p. 29; Graham 2001, pp. 59-60.

(like lady Li) and are therefore pulled in a certain direction, victim to strong emotions whether things do or do not go their way.

If one lives like the swimmer, in accordance with natural patterns, one avoids many problems. One will not be controlled by strong emotions because one has no pre-set ideas that would influence oneself. There is no reason to judge the actions of others and attempt to follow their traces. Because one is not imitating anyone, there is no need to try and figure things out; one can react directly to the situation, without consulting others or their traces. Even the question of whether something is real or not is thrown out. The only thing left is the person and the situation (including others). There are no ideas to get in the way, and no traces to follow. There is no reason to dry up the river and spit praises at one another, or look for traces of other fish. When the river is full there are no praises to be spat, no footprints to follow, nothing to consider; swimming naturally, one can lead a happy carefree life.

Reconsidering *Ren* as a Basic Concept of Chinese Humanism*

ACHIM MITTAG

> When the horse stable had burnt down and the Master returned from court, he said: "Did this hurt anyone?" He did not ask about the horses.[1]

"Did this hurt anyone?" This is a simple question consisting of only three characters (*shang ren hu*), embedded in a dramatic, yet not really earth-shaking episode that features a fire in the horse stable of Confucius' residence[2] — yet there is hardly any saying by, or ascribed to, Confucius (551–479 BC) which can highlight in such a concise way what is commonly depicted as Chinese humanism. It is this human-centered orientation, the focus on man and the *conditio humana*, which is generally regarded as *the* prime characteristic of Confucian philosophy. Anything else is subordinated to human beings, be it deities or beings of the supernatural world, and be it beings of the animate and inanimate nature, i.e. animals and plants. As the eminent Song Confucian commentator Zhu Xi (1130–

---

* This small piece is dedicated to Jörn Rüsen, the *spiritus rector* of the Humanism Project, in deep gratitude for his unique friendship.
1 *Lunyu* 10.12. I follow Christoph Harbsmeier's translation published on the *Thesaurus Linguae Sericae* website (http://www.tls.uni-heidelberg.de) The *Four Books* (*Sishu*), comprising the *Analects* (*Lunyu*), the *Book of Mencius* (*Mengzi*), *The Great Learning* (*Daxue*), and *The Doctrine of the Mean* (*Zhongyong*), are cited by the *pian* or *zhang* divisions as used in Zhu Xi's *Sishu zhangju jizhu* (and followed in Legge's translations).
2 Chinese commentators thoroughly discussed the episode, coming to the conclusion that the horse stable referred to in the episode belonged to the residence of Confucius' family; it was most likely not one of the state's horse stables. See *Lunyu zhengyi* 13/422-423.

1200) in his later canonized commentary of Confucius' *Analects* (*Lunyu*) hastened to point out, it is not that Confucius did not care about (*ai*) horses, but "his fear that someone might have been hurt weighed heavier"[3].

At the heart of Confucian philosophy lies the notion of *ren*, commonly translated as "humaneness," "human-heartedness," "benevolence," "virtue," "love". It is the central notion of the *Analects*, where it occurs in almost sixty instances. As Heiner Roetz has convincingly shown, the principle of "reciprocity" (*shu*) is at the center of Confucius' concept of *ren*.[4] This principle of reciprocity is primarily conceived negatively and expressed by the Golden Rule: "What you do not wish done to you, you ought not do to others." The Golden Rule reoccurs, in variant wordings, in various instances of Confucius' sayings, such that it may well be considered the main doctrine of Confucian ethics. Yet it should be noted that occasionally the principle of reciprocity is also framed positively, as is the case in Confucius' answer to the question of what is to be understood by *ren*, "The man of *ren* is one who desiring to maintain himself sustains others, and desiring to develop oneself one develops others."[5]

Before Confucius, a web of norms and values had developed in Western Zhou (c. 1045–771 BC) aristocratic society, laid out in the ubiquitous system of rites (*li*) and based upon the principle of *do ut des* ("I give in order that you will give"). This conventional, class-bound ethics was transcended by Confucius' notion of *ren* centered around the principle of reciprocity. Its principally universalist conception introduced a radically new element of ethical thinking. This marks, following Heiner Roetz, the breakthrough of a "post-conventional" ethics as the main characteristic of the Chinese Axial Age.[6]

It is clear that any study of Chinese humanism must start out with the notion of *ren*. As a translation term, one may be tempted to settle with one of the conventionally used terms, preferably with "humaneness". It must be cautioned, however, that such a choice obscures some facets of what has been meant by *ren* in later periods of Chinese thought, in particular in Song (960–1279) Confucianism. In the following I want to discuss four such facets, drawing attention to *ren* as (1) being closely related to one's conduct and actions; (2) focusing on the notion of "caring for someone" (*ai*); (3) being in accordance with common sense, or "human sentiments"

---

3 *Lunyu jizhu* 5; cited from *Sishu zhangju jizhu*, p. 121.
4 Roetz 1992, esp. chap. 10, pp. 195-241; Roetz 1995, pp. 58-61 and pp. 69-79.
5 *Lunyu* 6.28. Cf. Fung Yu-lan 1952/53, vol. 1, pp. 70-71.
6 Roetz 1992.

(*renqing*), as the ultimate standard of conduct; and finally, (4) positing a crucial principle of government.[7]

In view of these four facets, it seems that *ren* could perhaps better be rendered as "a keen sense of responsibility in one's action," "conscientiousness," or "benevolent government". The following remarks intend to give some clues to this proposal; they are not meant as a systematic exploration into the notion of *ren* and its historical development.

Ren as Being Closely Related to One's Conduct and Actions

In an essay on the two cardinal virtues of *ren* and *zhi*, "wisdom," Wang Anshi (1021–1086), famous Song dynasty scholar and statesman who put important reforms into effect, reflects upon Confucius' saying that "The man of wisdom (*zhizhe*) is active (*dong*), the man of conscientiousness (*renzhe*) quiescent (*jing*)".[8] In essence, Wang Anshi argues that this distinction is not to be misunderstood as contrasting a *vita activa* with a *vita contemplativa*. Both the wise man and the conscientious man engage actively in the affairs of society: "There never has been a conscientious man who was not wise, nor a wise man who was not conscientious." The difference, Wang explains, lies in that the conscientious man possesses *ren* "by nature" (*wu suo you*), while the wise man must constantly strive for it: "He acts only after thought and speaks only with conscious deliberation." Yet in both their conduct of affairs, there is eventually "nothing that does not follow the sense of responsibility in action (*ren*)".[9]

To elaborate, Wang Anshi refers to the first part of Confucius' saying cited above, according to which "The wise man loves the rivers and streams, the conscientious man loves the mountains".[10] Wang comments that rivers and streams flow incessantly, whereas mountains are still and reposeful, "and yet in their usefulness [to men] they both are the same".

The catchword here is "usefulness" (*li wu*), or to be more precise, the usefulness of all things of the animate and inanimate nature for the benefit of man. The *Wenyan* commentary to the first Hexagram *Qian* of the *Book of Changes* (*Zhou Yi*), which is traditionally ascribed to Confucius, juxtaposes this notion of "putting the things of nature to use for the benefit of man" (*li*

---

[7] For the second and fourth facet, cf. Ding Shouhe 1996. Regrettably, I took notice of Ding's article only after completion of this essay.

[8] *Lunyu* 6.21; "Ren zhi" in *Wang Jinggong wenji* 37/1066-1067; translated by Williamson 1935–1937, vol. 2, pp. 350-352.

[9] Ibid.

[10] *Lunyu* 6.21.

wu) to the notion of "embodying *ren*" (*ti ren*);[11] this juxtaposition opens our eyes to grasping the meaning of *ren* as denoting the wise and responsible use of the bountiful resources of nature.

Hence, if we accept "humaneness" as a translation term of *ren*, it should be understood in analogy to the bounteous, constantly goods-producing, and thus "active," mountain of Wang Anshi's essay. In other words, *ren* denotes a state of mind, which might well be rendered as "humaneness" or "human-heartedness," yet in addition, must be essentially conceived as having a *Sitz im Leben*, i.e. the real challenge is to practice *ren* in everyday life. As Wang concludes his essay, only a sage (*sheng*) of Confucius' caliber is able to do so for a period of more than three months.[12]

This section is pointedly summed up by Zhu Xi, who in one of his "recorded sayings" (*yulu*) frankly tells us:

Ren resides in the matters [of everyday life]. If *ren* were not to become manifested in these matters, whereto should we gaze to see it?[13]

Ren as Focusing on the Notion of "Caring for Someone" (*ai*)

The everyday practice of *ren* is rooted in a "sensitive concern for others," to use Mark Elvin's propitious translation term for *ren*,[14] and is basically realized in form of "taking care for others" (*ai*).

As to the notion of "sensitive concern," suffice it here to refer to Mencius' notion of commiseration (*ceyin*) and his subsequent illustration of such a feeling by the alarming experience of seeing a child that is about to fall into a well.[15] Acting spontaneously out of a feeling of commiseration can qualify as *ren*, yet there is more to *ren* than such cases. As Zhu Xi remarks in another "recorded saying":

Ren constitutes the root, while [the feelings of] commiseration are compared to the sprouts. Love among siblings (*qin qin*), benevolent government of the people (*ren min*), and care for all things of the animate and inanimate nature (*ai wu*), then correspond to the branches and leaves.[16]

---

11 Cf. Sung 1935, pp. 5-6: Here "embodying *ren*" and "putting all things of the animate and inanimate nature to use for the benefit of man" are specified as two of the "four virtues" (*si de*) practiced by the gentleman (*junzi*).
12 Wang Anshi refers here to *Lunyu* 6.5, where Confucius' favourite pupil Yan Hui is said of having "nothing in his mind contrary to *ren* for three months".
13 *Zhuzi yulei* 6/116.
14 Elvin 1996, p. 271.
15 *Mengzi* 2A.6.
16 *Zhuzi yulei* 6/118.

The metaphor of the tree of "virtue" (*de*), to which Zhu Xi alludes,[17] would be complete with having identified its trunk. From other "recorded sayings" we may infer that Zhu Xi would approve of likening the trunk to the notion of *ai*, "[to] care for someone". In fact, Zhu Xi, in his analysis of the relationship between the two notions of *ai* and *ren*, consistently defines *ren* as constituting the inherent "principle" (*li* or *daoli*) of *ai*.[18]

The close and partially complimentary relationship between *ai* and *ren* had already early been established by no less authority than Confucius himself. In a much-cited saying in the *Analects*, Confucius answers a question about *ren* by enunciating, "It is to care for others" (*ai ren*).[19]

A similar note is struck in the *Discourses on Salt and Iron* (*Yantie lun*) from the first century AD, in particular in a passage, which includes the above-cited saying of Confucius on seeing that the horse stable had burnt down. In this passage, the deterioration of the moral and ritual order, paired with the rise of corruption and evil practices, is analyzed to the effect that the primary cause of such a decline is seen in the neglect of discussing *ren* and *yi*. Clarifying what is meant by these two notions, the text points out:

Ren is that by which care [or others] is put into effect. *Yi* is that by which matters (*shi*) are handled in an appropriate way (*yi*).

Elaborating on *ren*, the text goes on, saying,

[…] taking care of others (*ai ren*), the gentleman (*junzi*) reaches out to all things of the animate and inanimate nature. He puts in good order what is in close reach and reaches out to what is distant.[20]

One source of an imperfect understanding of *ren* in Western literature certainly stems from rendering *ai* as "love," a common translation firmly established since the Jesuits. However, throughout the literature of the Classicist Period (ca. 323 BC–317 AD), *ai* is predominantly used in the sense of *caritas*, expressing an affection which animates a person who is genuinely fond of someone in need as, e.g., a mother's love for her child. *Ai* mostly implies a hierarchical relationship, a movement from above to below; a case in point is the expression of a general's "taking good care" (*ai*) of his soldiers.[21] The complimentary term of the soldiers' "love" of their com-

---

17 Cf. *Zhuzi yulei* 6/111, where *ai* is said to be the "root and trunk" (*ben bing*) of *de*.
18 *Zhuzi yulei* 6/111; "Ren shuo" in *Zhu Xi ji* 67/3542-3544, here p. 3543.
19 *Lunyu* 12.22.
20 *Yantie lun* 15/567.
21 E.g. *Shi ji* 48/1950.

mander is *lian*, "to have tender affection for someone".²² Where ever *ai* occurs without implying a hierarchical relationship, it is mostly to be taken as meaning "holding in esteem" (*aixi*).²³ In addition, it is safe to assert that there are hardly any examples of *ai* as expressing the mutual affection and tenderness felt by lovers, that is, love between the sexes.²⁴

Here is not the place to elaborate on the semantics of *ai*; yet, in order to forestall criticism, it is necessary to draw attention to one much-cited passage in the *Book of Mencius* (*Mengzi*), at which *ai* is referred to in the context of Mencius' discussion of "intuitive knowledge of what is right and good" (*liangzhi*).²⁵ There we read a sentence which, in a common translation such as provided by James Legge, is rendered as follows: "Children carried in the arms all know to love their parents, and when they are grown a little, they all know to love their elder brothers."²⁶ A more faithful translation, however, should read: "Children who are at the age of upholding babies (*hai ti zhi tong*) all know what is meant by caring for one's siblings (*ai qi qin*)."

"Caring for one's siblings" fully describes the Mencian position in the extensive discussion about the extension of people's concern and care (*ai*). As is well known, at the one extreme of this debate, Mozi (ca. 479–438 BC) proposed the concept of "ubiquitous and indiscriminate care" (*jian'ai*), whereas, at the debate's other extreme, Yang Xiong (53 BC–18 AD) argued that "To care for oneself is the epitome of *ren* (*zi ai, ren zhi ye*)."²⁷ Here, as in many other instances, it becomes crystal clear that a translation

---

22 See e.g. fn. 21 above.
23 For a relevant example, see fn. 24 below.
24 According to Unger (2000, p. 1), *ai* encompasses the broad range of meanings of "love," from sexual love to humaneness. However, Unger fails to provide any examples of *ai* in the former meaning. — There are a few occurrences of *ai* in the *Book of Odes* (*Shijing*), where a modern reader *prima vista* takes *ai* to be meaning "love". However, such a reading is constantly thwarted by the traditional commentaries to the *Book of Odes*; a case in point is Ode no. 42, "Jing nü," first stanza, third line: *ai er bu jian*. Quite naturally, one will read this line to be meaning "I love her, yet I don't see her"; in fact, Zhu Xi lends authority to such a reading. However, traditional *Odes* exegesis takes *ai* in the sense of "holding in esteem" (*aixi*), understanding the line as expressing the poet's esteem of the "retiring girl" (Legge 1960, vol. 4: *The She King*, p. 68), who is "submissive and obedient" and therefore would be a good mate for the ruler; see *Mao Shi zhengyi* 2/310c; Legge 1960, vol. 4, p. 69, fn. According to the "Lu School," *ai* is a homophone for *ai**, "secluded," so that the line in question would read "[the retiring girl] lives in seclusion and cannot be seen"; cf. *Shi sanjia yi ji shu* 3A/205-206.
25 *Mengzi* 7A.15.
26 Legge 1960, vol. 2: *The Works of Mencius*, p. 456.
27 *Fa yan* 12 ("Junzi"), 18/515. Yang Xiong makes reference to a discussion begun by Xunzi; see *Xunzi* 29 ("Zi dao"), p. 396.

of this sentence as "To *love* oneself is the epitome of *ren*" goes astray and would obscure the said debate.

In short, *ren* must be understood in close connection with the notion of *ai*, the translation of which as "[to] love', instead of "[to] care for," has definitely contributed to a continued miscomprehension of *ren*, however.

Ren as Being in Accordance to Common Sense, or "Human Sentiments" (*renqing*)

The foremost example of Christian grace of charity is the popular story about St. Martin's cutting his own military cloak in half to share it with a scantily dressed beggar. Such a behavior could never be qualified as *ren*. One could imagine a Confucian version of this story; it would feature an army officer on horseback, who, on meeting a beggar, would turn his horse, ride straight up to the next *Yamen*, the seat of the magistrate, and submit a report revealing the intolerable living conditions, which then would pressure the magistrate into taking decisive action and launching relief measures.

The point here is that, under the framework of Confucian values, the cutting of the cloak in half would be considered as utterly going against common sense. Not only would the cloak be wrecked, but also the two men, the officer and the beggar, would not have left enough to shield themselves against the cold so that, in a worst case scenario, both men eventually might even freeze to death.

Important is that the notion of "common sense" adds another dimension to the complimentary notions of *ren* and *yi*; the latter term being commonly translated as "righteousness," "[sense of] justice," or "[sense of] moral obligation". This new dimension is governed by practical and pragmatic, and not, in a narrow sense, moral concerns. It is exactly this dimension which is referred to in the above-cited definition of *yi* in the *Discourses on Salt and Iron*, where *yi* is paraphrased as "handling matters in an appropriate way" (*yi**).[28] This paraphrase is not alien to Zhu Xi: "Let's see how it works to substitute *yi* by the character *yi**."[29] In other contexts, this ability of "handling matters in an appropriate way" is often termed *quanyi*, "to act according to expediency, to take measures of expediency".

This pragmatic dimension of expediency has at an early stage been added to the concept of *ren*, as a result of the criticism to which time and again the narrow, moralistic concept of *ren* allegedly held by Confucius

---

28 Tessenow 1991, pp. 320-321 (fn. 41). See the quotation above on p. 73.
29 *Zhuzi yulei* 6/120.

and other followers of the early Confucian School was subjected by their opponents. Such a criticism was notably voiced in the *Book of Zhuangzi* (*Zhuangzi*), from which originates the metaphor of "pushing a boat on land" (*tui chuan yu lu*),[30] which satirizes any attempts to install a rule of *ren* on the basis of early Zhou ethics and rituals. It appears that in the course of the development that the concept of *ren* underwent in the early imperial period, and in response to such criticism, the two threads of moralistic and pragmatic thought became more and more entangled.

This phenomenon is suggested by an interesting dialogue between the aforementioned Yang Xiong and an anonymous interlocutor.[31] Challenging the former, the interlocutor argues that "large utensils" (*da qi*) are not being employed for trifling matters because "a large houseboat or a war wagon are not being used to transport a jug of wine or to expedite a jar of mixed pickles".[32] What is being meant here is that men of the educated nucleus who dictate the current beliefs cannot be expected to deal with everyday issues.

Refuting this view, Yang Xiong responds that utensils certainly can be used properly only for specific purposes, but this does not apply to men because "The gentleman is not an utensil"[33], i.e. the gentleman is an "allrounder" and not bound to one single field of expertise or skills: "There is nothing which he will not deal with (*wu suo bu shi*)."[34] By analogy, *ren* as being the distinctive attribute of the gentleman cannot possibly be partitioned; it encompasses both the moral high ground and the lowlands of pragmatic action.

In Song Confucianism, the supreme criterion of pragmatic action was commonly expressed by the notion of "human sentiments" (*renqing*). Hence, what runs counter to human sentiments, i.e. human experience (*fei renqing*; *bu jin renqing*), can never be described as *ren*.

All what the sages did to practice the way,

says Wang Anshi,

was to hold to human sentiments and nothing else. When inquiring into matters and finding something that was not apt, or when investigating the meaning of texts

---

30 See *Zhuangzi* 14 ("Tian yun"), p. 373.
31 See above, p. 74.
32 *Fa yan*, 12 ("Junzi"), 18/497; translated by von Zach 1939, p. 63.
33 *Lunyu* 2.12.
34 Gloss by the comentator Wang Rongbao; see fn. 32 above.

and discovering something that was not comprehensible, then they judged it as not according to the Way.[35]

It is noteworthy that in Song writings we actually find the notion of "human sentiments" employed with regard to the two spheres addressed in Wang's dictum, the sphere of human action and the sphere of texts.[36]

The ubiquitous use of the notion of *renqing* in Song writings has evoked the suggestion to translate it by "common sense". Common sense describes well the kind of rationality that emerged in the Song dynasty due to the broadening of the horizon of knowledge as a result of a rising general literacy and the widespread use of printing technology.[37] In Song Confucianism, the concept of *ren* has inextricably been tied to this notion of common sense, which was commonplace among the ordinary educated Song people.

Ren as Positing a Crucial Principle of Government

In the previous section, *ren* appeared together with *yi* ("righteousness") in a pair that by itself must be considered one of the most important concepts in Chinese intellectual history. Yet this is not the only combination in which *ren* figures prominently. Of great importance are also the conceptual sets of the "four beginnings" (*si duan*) and the "five virtues" (*wu chang*), which include *ren*, "propriety" (*li*), "righteousness" (*yi*) (see above), "wisdom" (*zhi*), plus — for the "five virtues" — "trust" (*xin*); these five are often discussed in analogy to the "four seasons" (*sishi*) or the "five elements" (*wuxing*), respectively. These three conceptual sets dominate Zhu Xi's discussion of *ren* as the first and foremost virtue.[38] It goes without saying that Neo-Confucian philosophy in general was heavily influenced by this discussion, in particular after publication of an anthology entitled *The Essence of Human Nature and Principle* (*Xingli jingyi*) in 1713.[39]

---

35 "Cewen shiyi dao" in *Wang Jinggong wenji* 33/1147.
36 As to the sphere of texts, several examples from the *Book of Odes* exegesis can be adduced; see Mittag 1993, pp. 85-87 and 105-108.
37 Cf. Lee 2004b, p. xix: "Rationality is a complicated idea and the lack of an exact Chinese expression that coincides with its meanings casts doubt as to whether it was ever an articulated idea in China's long intellectual history. However, skepticism towards received wisdom and willingness to challenge it, since it runs counter to daily human experience, are fundamental to the rise of rationalism. Thus, common sense was very important to the rise in a rudimentary skepticism that, in turn, was fundamental to an overall change of intellectual outlook."
38 Tessenow 1991, pp. 103-104.
39 Chan 1975.

The Ming-Qing formation of a state orthodoxy in the fifteenth to nineteenth centuries centered upon Zhu Xi has greatly contributed to obscuring the lingering influence of yet another set of notions revolving around *ren*. This is the triad of "wisdom" or "knowledge" (*zhi*), *ren*, and "fortitude" (*yong*). Its *locus classicus* is found in *The Doctrine of the Mean* (*Zhongyong*), where it is introduced as denoting three complimentary aspects of one overriding principle guiding the efforts of putting into practice (*xing*) "the consummate way of all-under-heaven" (*tianxia zhi dadao*).[40] It is significant to note that the triad of *zhi*, *ren*, and *yong* lies at the core of the longest and most important section of *The Doctrine of the Mean*. In response to a question asked by Duke Ai of Lu (r. 495–468 BC) about government (*zheng*), this section expounds a political ethic presumably authored by Confucius himself. Consequently, the triad of *zhi*, *ren*, and *yong* can be rightly said to be central to Confucian political ethics.

That in Song Confucianism this centerpiece of Confucian political philosophy gained paramount significance is largely due to the labor of one single scholar and statesman, namely Sima Guang (1019–1086), the conservative antagonist of the above-quoted Wang Anshi and author of the great chronicle *Comprehensive Mirror for Aid in Government* (*Zizhi tongjian*). Throughout his political career, Sima Guang did not get tired of admonishing successive emperors, whom he served, on these three essential virtues of the ruler, which were juxtaposed by three essential tasks faced by each and every regent. As Sima Guang wrote in a memorial presented to the throne in 1061,

[…] I have heard that the way of achieving good order depends on but three things: first, assigning virtuous men to offices (*ren guan*); second, giving rewards in a way that generates trust (*xin shang*); and third, executing necessary punishments (*bi fa*).[41]

In this memorial Sima Guang elaborates on the three virtues in the following way:

Your minister humbly observes that there are but three great virtues for the ruler: benevolence (*ren*), acumen (*ming*), and rigor (*wu*).
Benevolence does not mean genial indulgence. Establish transformation through education (*xing jiaohua*). Improve administration (*xiu zhengzhi*). Nurture the folk (*yang baixing*). Bring all things of animate and inanimate nature to use for the benefit of man (*li wanwu*). This is the benevolence of the ruler.

---

40 *Zhongyong* 20.
41 Translation inspired by Bol 1993, p. 153.

Acumen does not mean petty spying. Understand the principles of the "way". Recognize security and danger. Distinguish the wise from the foolish. Discriminate between right and wrong. This is the acumen of the ruler.

Rigor does not mean violent ferocity. Choose that which agrees with the "way" and do not doubt. Slander cannot confuse him. Flattery cannot move him. This is the rigor of the ruler.

To be benevolent yet not have acumen is like having good fields without ploughing them. To have acumen yet not be rigorous is like finding the weeds around the shoots but not pulling them out. To be rigorous yet not benevolent is like knowing how to harvest but not to plant. If these are all complete together, the state will be ordered and strong. If one is lacking, it will decline. If two are lacking, it will be in danger. And if none of the three is present, it will perish. Ever since there were people this has never changed.[42]

More important than the four rather general principles of good government associated with *ren* in the section just cited above is the notion of "trust" introduced in the preceding citation concerning the ruler's three essential tasks. For Song Confucians in general, and Sima Guang in particular, trust was everything; all will likely erode if not collapse should there be an erosion of trust. In spite of all disputes, trust was generally regarded as encompassing two major components; the first is confidence that the government is competent and capable (*cai*); and the second, that it is being honest and straight (*de*).

Thus, *ren* as a principle of rulership may well be understood as the ruler's capability of generating trust in government by managing and balancing *cai*, "competence, expertise," and *de*, "moral virtue". As Sima Guang tells us time and again, this is primarily achieved through selecting the right officials for appointment.[43] It is in this respect that *ren* was considered the fundamental idea of rulership, as explicitly expressed in the *Wenyan* commentary already cited above (see Section 1): "The superior man, embodying *ren*, is fit to preside over men" (*junzi ti ren zuyi chang ren*).[44]

Sima Guang's *Comprehensive Mirror for Aid in Government* rests on this notion of *ren* as a fundamental principle of government,[45] and through the *Comprehensive Mirror for Aid in Government*, which from the South-

---

42 Translation, with slight changes, adopted from Bol 1993, p. 153. Note that Sima Guang speaks of "acumen" (*ming*), instead of "wisdom" or "knowledge" (*zhi*), and of "rigor" (*wu*), instead of "fortitude" (*yong*).
43 See Ji 2004, pp. 12-21.
44 Cf. Sung 1935, 5-6. For the *Wenyan* commentary of the *Book of Changes* see p. 71 above.
45 Ji 2004, *passim*.

ern Song (1127–1279) onwards became the primary textbook for the lectures in the Imperial Seminar (*jingyan*),[46] it continued to be pervasive in Late Imperial China.

It is true that there are few references to *ren* in this particular sense. Yet this very scarcity is a sign of extreme familiarity, so that a single reference will be vast in its implications. Take the explanation of what is to be understood by the epithet of *ren* traditionally attributed to a unicorn (*qilin*). Conventionally, the unicorn's characterization as an "animal of *ren*" (*ren wu*) had been explained in the way that a unicorn's horn, capped by a chondral substance, could not kill anybody and that a unicorn would not carelessly step on any creatures, or tear off plants.[47] However, as we can learn from one of Zhu Xi's "recorded sayings," there were contemporary scholars who, also in this particular context, obviously understood *ren* as the primary faculty of ruling and, hence, took the *qilin* for a lion as the king among animals.[48]

Concluding remarks

From the last section, we may conclude that the notion of *ren*, connotating a fundamental, yet rather unspecified principle of rulership, continued to play a significant role in Song and post-Song political ethics (i.e. from the 11th century onward). At the same time, however, it lost its principal place in the debate over moral ethics. The radical shift in this latter debate was signaled by none other than Wang Anshi, namely in his famous essay on Mencius' distinction between the "kingly way" (*wangdao*) and the "way of the overlord" (*badao*).

This essay opens with the bold thesis that in pursuing the "the consummate way" encompassing the "four beginnings" of *ren*, *yi* ("righteousness"), *li* ("propriety"), and *xin* ("trust"), there is no difference between the "true king" (*wang*) and the "overlord" (*ba*). As Wang Anshi maintains, both the true king and the overlord may exert themselves for the welfare of the people to the same degree. Yet the difference lies in the "heart," or "mindset" (*xin*), as the ultimate source of these efforts. Whereas the overlord's conduct and action are motivated by utilitarian, or political, considerations, the true king solely acts upon moral principles. Hence, the kingly way begins with the "art

---

46 See Hartwell 1971, p. 701.
47 *Shuowen jiezi* 10A/21a-b (p. 470b).
48 *Zhuzi yulei* 6/120. The reference is here to *Mengzi* 2A.2 (Legge 1960, vol. 2, p. 195), where a sage is compared to a unicorn among the quadrupeds.

of one's heart" (*xinshu*), i.e. one's habit of virtuous mind (*Gesinnung*), nurtured by the ruler and his officials alike.[49]

We have here the clearest exposition of what Max Weber later would term an "ethic of intention" (*Gesinnungsethik*). Due to Zhu Xi and the notorious instrumentation of the tangible notion of *xinshu* to castigate political foes, as happened posthumously to Wang Anshi in the first place,[50] Late Imperial Chinese moral philosophy developed much along the trajectory of that sort of "ethic of intention". Under the impact of this discourse, *ren* slowly receded into this and that citadel of moral philosophy.

---

49 "Wang ba" in *Wang Jinggong wenji jianzhu* 30/1060-1062.
50 Mittag 1996, p. 48.

Negotiations of Humaneness and Body Politics in Historical Contexts

ANGELIKA C. MESSNER

Social life in history changes constantly; and a closer look at the specific circumstances of change in Chinese history shows that the traditional claim for moral self-cultivation (*xiu shen*) with its highest goal, namely to become a great man (*da ren*) or a sage (*sheng ren*)[1] in terms of *ren* (humaneness, benevolence, compassion) always became virulent and explicit when people faced shifting socio-political realities. This has been convincingly shown by Heiner Roetz.[2]

The point of departure for this paper is the insight of Alasdair MacIntyre that "moral concepts change as social life changes".[3] By focusing on 16th and 17th century discursive formations of *ren* (humaneness, benevolence, compassion) we shall go further and ask what dimensions of meaning this ethical term embodied. By taking into account the semantics of *shen* (the self, the body), which since ancient times referred to the corporeal constitution of man and simultaneously to the individual personality, this paper traces notions of humaneness, which go beyond the issue of representation. In other words, this article discusses the ways a mere abstract cultural concept (humaneness, benevolence, compassion) was mapped onto and into the body, furthermore how this concept interleaved with concrete bodily manner of being. Finally, this paper examines how these shifting body-mappings were fostered by changing socio-political realities.

---

1 On the distinction between these two terms see Chow 1993, p. 212.
2 See Roetz 1992.
3 MacIntyre 1966, p. 1

Introduction

Among the unspoken presuppositions which have long influenced major metanarratives of Chinese history, those based on an imperialist epistemology — and which constantly presumed differences between Western and non-Western civilizations — suggested the moral and intellectual superiority of the Western hemisphere.[4] Historical writing in the Western hemisphere has been informed by the major dichotomy "East (stagnation) and West (dynamics and progress)" for a long time. The metanarrative of the classic (European) modernity solely relies on the notion of ever-growing technological and scientific progress with special reference to human rights beginning with Pico della Mirandola (1463–1494), and the literary and cultural movement in Western Europe in the 14th and 15th centuries, which emphasizes human value and dignity as opposed to religious belief. The East, in strong contrast, lacked any comparable tradition, and the Chinese terms which refer to humanism today, namely *rendao zhuyi*, *renben zhuyi*, *renwen zhuyi* had not been elaborated until the early 20th century by Chinese intellectuals, who were eager to conceptualize a Chinese modernity (and humanism) taking Europe as an example,[5] thus negating every trace of (genuine) humanism in Chinese history.

However, it is well known that the term *ren* has existed since ancient times and has always held the potential subversive power of questioning existing rules of society. To grasp a sense of *ren* in Chinese historical contexts, one must ask what the term might have implied in various scholarly communities. Based on several readings and analyses of the classics such as the *Analects* (*Lunyu*) of Confucius (551–479 BC), the *Book of Mencius* (*Mengzi*, Mencius 372–289 BC), the *Xunzi* (Xunzi 312–230 BC)[6], the *Great Learning* (*Daxue*) and the *Doctrine of the Mean* (*Zhongyong*) — both formerly part of the *Book of Rites* (*Liji*)[7] — as well as of excerpts of the Neo-Confucian writings of Zhu Xi (1130–1200) and of Wang Yangming (1472–1529), and finally of the writings of Tan Sitong (1865–1898)[8], historians have shown the significant role of *ren* in the Chinese context.[9] The following quotation offers a brief and comprehensive philological interpretation of "humanism" in Chinese history:

---

4 See Hung 2003, p. 254-280.
5 See the article by Ke Zhang in this volume.
6 His essays were collected into the book called *Xunzi*.
7 The *Liji* is one of the *Five Classics* of the Confucian canon.
8 For Tan Sitong see the article by Dennis Schilling in this volume.
9 See for instance de Bary 1970, pp. 145-245; Chan 1970, pp. 29-51.

Ren "humanity". *Ren* has been variously translated as benevolence, perfect virtue, goodness, human-heartedness, love, altruism, etc. None of these expresses all the meanings of the term. It means a particular virtue, benevolence, and also the general virtue, the basis of all goodness. In the *Book of Mencius* (6A.11), it is "man's mind". In Han times (206 B.C.–A.D. 220), Confucianists understood it to mean love or "men living together". To Han Yu (768–824) it was universal love. Neo-Confucianists interpreted it as impartiality, the character of production and reproduction, consciousness, seeds that generate, the will to grow, and who forms one body with Heaven and Earth, or "the character of love and the principle of mind". In modern times, it has even been equated with ether and electricity. Etymologically, *ren* means man in society, as the Chinese character for *ren* consists of both the word for man and the word for two (signifying a group). In both the *Book of Mencius* (7B.16) and the *Doctrine of the Mean* (ch. 20) *ren* is equated with man. [...] Furthermore, "love" is the correct translation for *ai*, and it would confuse *ren* and *ai* in Zhu Xi's dictum, "*ren* is the character of love," and Mencius' saying, "the man of *ren* loves others". [...] "Humanity" takes care of all the Neo-Confucian interpretations, for humanity certainly possesses the characteristics of life-giving and the like, and it is man who forms one body with Heaven and Earth.[10]

This elaborated summary, part of the Appendix within the *Source Book on Chinese Philosophy* (1963), obviously aims at contributing to scholarly exchange between East and West. Wing-tsit Chan (1901–1994), the renowned scholar and translator of Chinese philosophical texts into English, author of hundreds of books and articles on Chinese philosophy in both English and Chinese, hereby exemplifies scholarly argumentative strategies to meet given stereotypes and lack of knowledge in regard to the roots of the "idea of humanism" in Chinese thinking.

In 1933, some thirty years before Chan's text had been written, Hu Shi (1891–1962) explained that the humanist movement in early 20th century China resembled Italian Renaissance humanism in the 16th century.[11] He thereby expresses the general views held by many young Chinese intellectuals in early 20th century, namely that Chinese history was nothing one could rely on. These thinkers mostly saw themselves as the starting point of a new future, e.g. of the "journey of humanism" in modern China.

Whereas Wing-tsit Chan establishes sense and meaning in China through a backward-looking teleological philology, Hu Shi aims at establishing a new culture through future-oriented pragmatic perspectives on humanism. Scholars in the context of the People's Republic of China today,

---

10 Chan 1963, pp. 788-789. The transcription system has been changed from Wade Giles into Pinyin by A. Messner.
11 This was part of a lecture he delivered in July 1933 at Chicago University. See Hu Shi 2003.

again, variously stress the absence of humanistic traditions in Chinese history[12] by emphasizing the close connection of the concept of humanism with the Enlightenment, which according to them had never taken place within the Chinese context.

In opposition to the latter view and in response to the so called "revival of Confucianism" in contemporary East Asia, scholars in Asian contexts today are concerned with the question of how Confucian traditions can still function as cultural resources for national ideology, and how a modern system of ethics (including humanistic ideas) can be developed on the basis of Confucian classics.[13] These discussions exclusively rest upon indigenous textual transmissions of ethics, yet they nowadays time and again stress the bifurcations "East/West" from the other way round. This, however, is an additional oversimplification and reduction of historical realities.

Change: Shifting Political and Ethical Systems

This essay is neither meant to be an attack on the above-mentioned efforts to revive Confucianism nor on reactionary teleological philology. It is rather an attempt to move our attention away from the comparative framework of the given topic and instead to dwell on the crucial power in Chinese history, namely, on change.

Recent scholarship holds that the seventeenth century, by comparison, was the period of the most far-reaching and profound shifts in political, demographic and economic terms in Chinese history.[14] It is well known that the Manchu consisted of only about 2 million people when they occupied China, a country with as many as 200 million people in 1644. Their numerous aggressions towards the civil population from the 1620s into the 1670s were accompanied by local bandits, scattered armed forces and local rebels. The devastation eventually extended across the whole country, including the South, which, moreover, was afflicted by epidemics with more than 70 million victims.

It is also known that a growing literacy since 16th century and the ever-increasing numbers of candidates on the traditional examination routine fostered a surplus of licentiates (*shengyuan*), who, especially in the South, never got an official position. As early as 1400 the relatively stable structure of imperial power, local elites and village peasants began to disperse. The

---

12 See for example Wang Hui, http://www.pum.umontreal.ca/revues/surfaces/vol5/hui.html.
13 See for instance the discussions by Lee Ming-huei, Academica Sinica, Taipeh, or by Peng Guoxiang, Qinghua University, Beijing.
14 For an overview see Schmidt-Glintzer 2003, p. 128.

social categories "official-literati," "peasants" and "artisans" gradually became anachronistic. In about 1600 the heredity classifications no longer matched the actual local status classifications. Furthermore, the gradual increase of the population from about 60 million in 14th century to about 200 million in 1600[15] stimulated these processes of transformation. Both led to the imperial loss of control over the country and its "working resources".

The gradual loss of control on behalf of the central power was additionally fueled by monetarism ("silver era": from 1550 to 1650) during the period of the Ming economy.[16] The protestant Dutch and English invaded the trade territories of the catholic Spanish and Portuguese in order to extend their own power, with the outcome that there was a drastic decrease in Chinese silver imports. This again led to a hoarding of silver and to the decay of the copper-silver relation.[17]

At the same time, the Ming imperial power gradually lost its immediate influence on local municipal areas due to the evolving possibility of commuting the "working tax" into "money tax". A tight net of organized markets on the municipal level[18] gradually fostered a kind of commercial energy, which, moreover, was intensified by a drastic increase in population. Under these circumstances, to rent land becomes only one option among various other possible sources of income. Hence, the gentry and the commercial companies both increased their social power.

Traditional societal structures tended to dissolve in favor of the formerly disdained status of traders. This, however, did not lead to a lesser significance of the official examination in the minds of the people.[19] In opposition, the number of educated citizens had increased gradually since the 15th century, which again fostered a rising number of examined scholars. Many of them, however, waited in vain for an official post as the respective number of official posts was not increased. Moreover in the 17th century, an increasing number of officials and examination aspirants, so-called Ming loyalist scholars (*mingyi*), who were loyal to the former Ming dynasty (1268–1644), refused to serve under the Manchu (1644–1911). Thus, a surplus of educated people was in urgent need of alternative careers.[20] Writing and publishing of handbooks and encyclopedias for every day usage

---

15 See Skinner 1977, pp. 19-20.
16 See von Glahn 1996, pp. 113-166; Marks 1998, pp. 127-143.
17 See Atwell 1982, pp. 68-90 and Atwell 1986, pp. 223f.; Wakeman 1986, pp. 1-26.
18 See Kuhn 1990, p. 31.
19 See Elman 2000, p. 200.
20 For detailed information on the numbers of candidates who never got an official post see Elman 2000, p. 141.

(*riyong leishu*), and, as we shall see, practicing medicine became favored ways to make a life outside the conventional ways of career.

As Roetz has shown, whenever in Chinese history societal volatilities and renovations evolved — *ren* (humaneness, benevolence) always appeared or re-appeared as a reshaping force, i.e. significant marker of reformatory discourses. Whenever ritualized life-reality (*li*) failed in correlating with the social reality, *ren* was claimed in terms of goodness and sincerity as well as in the notion of a deeper layer of the human being. As a core element *ren* (humaneness) was enforced to help reshaping the lost values. Shifting social roles and, specifically, societal realities called for a renewal of values with regard to "*ren*". Thus, according to Roetz, Chinese intellectual history, on the one hand, can be traced in the ever-changing tension between etiquette (*li*), which retains people hierarchically and socially and, on the other hand, the call for "humanity" (*ren*).

Yet, those who, in varying times and circumstances, called for a re-evaluation of human virtues and held *ren* to be the virtue of paramount importance, can at the same time be regarded as implicit advocates for the disintegration of conventional hierarchies.

These insights give reason for historical investigations of the material logic of *ren*. By way of focusing on the relation between discourses and practices we shall explore "communities of practices," in which *ren* either implicitly or explicitly served as a concept for orientation. When self-cultivation practices (*xiu shen*) and techniques of respecting and nourishing life (*yang sheng*) in the 16th and 17th centuries amalgamated to certain extend, *ren* served as crucial link. Thus, when scholars in 17th century attempted to elevate the status of the medical field, they referred to *ren* as well.

Empathy: An Intrinsic Feature of Humaneness

Self-cultivation in Neo-Confucian terms, which from 1313 until the early 19th century was regarded as an orthodox practice in the imperial examination system, roughly consisted in studying and memorizing the canonical classics as well as to exercise the "virtues righteous" (*yi*), benevolence and humaneness (*ren*). To practice benevolence (*wei ren*) first and foremost meant that one had to overcome one's selfish desires (*ke ji*) and return to the observance of the rites (*li*). This way one could attain the perfect virtue of the original mind (*ben xin*), which then could be equated with the heavenly principle (*tian li*). These explanations on the matter by Zhu Xi (1130–1200) were regarded as orthodox in the imperial examinations.[21] They relied on a

---

21   See Elman 1993, p. 63.

conceptual bifurcation of *xin* (the heart/mind) divided into a moral mind (*dao xin*) and a human mind (*ren xin*). This bifurcation was fundamental to the vision of human nature, in which humaneness as the chief Confucian virtue could only be achieved by overcoming and controlling all selfish desires and motives.

This bifurcation of the mind into a human (*ren xin*) and a moral virtue (*dao xin*) was moreover reflected by the distinction of matter (*qi*)[22] and principle (*li*), which again mirrored two conceptual ways of being: the metaphysical sphere (*xing er shang*) and the physical/experiential sphere (*xing er xia*). The first included the cosmic force heaven (*tian*), nature (*xing*), principle (*li*) and tranquility (*jing*). The latter included the phenomena activity/movement (*dong*) and *qi*. As Martin W. Huang underlines, the antagonism between the metaphysical and the physical/experiential sphere was not necessarily understood as being dualistic by Zhu Xi and other Neo-Confucian thinkers; nevertheless it implied that illness could arise (only) from the physical/experiential realm.[23]

The bifurcation of the mind (*xin*) demanded that one should eliminate one's personal desire and aspiration, because they were generally considered as selfish. This again reflects the Song Neo-Confucian bifurcation between private and public with its ideal of the priority of "public" over "private".[24]

These bifurcations and antagonisms have gradually become blurred through the transgressing notions put forward by Wang Yangming (1472–1529), and, as we shall see, in the 16th and 17th centuries, Wang's views had been gradually developed and essentially supported on the basis of Daoist and Buddhist perspectives of the time. Moreover, both Buddhist and Daoist views play a major role in the late 16th and early 17th century's medical and "self-cultivation for nourishing life" (*yangsheng*) writings.

The 17th century in China is marked by an *epistemological revolution* which occurred among the elites who turned from Neo-Confucian anthropocentrism and rationalism to both a commitment to empirically based in-

---

22 There is no appropriate single translation for *qi* in Western languages. The terms "energy" and "life force" can be regarded as most approximate within medical contexts. In the case shown here, "matter" seems as most appropriate in its opposed position to principle (*li*). Yet, without clarification of the very semantics of these terms in the Western contexts, they also appear as vague and ambiguous. On the many different possibilities for translating *qi* into Western languages see Kubny 1995, pp. 67-79.
23 See Huang 2001, p. 27.
24 On the implications of these Song Neo-Confucian conceptions for the civil service examinations see Elman 1994, pp. 126-130.

quiry[25] and, at the same time, to a cosmological re-integration of men. By reversing the conventional Neo-Confucian tendency to reduce the human being as well as material things to an attribute of *li* (principle) or the *dao*,[26] many Chinese scholars now stress the primacy of *qi* (life force), which represents the notion of the visible, the concrete and the tactile. *Qi* (life force) appears already in earliest texts as an important feature of *ren*, which then explicitly means "to feel, to sense," but is not necessarily restricted to the sense of compassion. When parts of the body are numb (*bu ren*: are without sensation, have no feeling), the physician had to search for the possible causes and to determine the therapy strategies. Or, for instance, when someone is frightened time and again, it caused obstruction of the tendons. This numbness-disease was supposed to be cured by massage and tinctures.[27] Diagnostic and therapeutic strategies in these cases, since earliest times, have thoroughly relied upon the specific concern for *qi* as well as blood circulation in the vessels.

The strong parallelism between philosophical, literary and medical language and their underlying theories of *yin yang* as well as the "five phases" (*wu xing*) can hardly be ignored in contemporary Chinese everyday language.[28] This parallelism also especially helped to shape late imperial literary discourses.[29] These specific body-related semantics of *ren* (to sense, to feel) await a closer investigation into the medical explanations and definitions regarding the human body in relation to self-cultivation (*xiu shen*) for the attainment of sagehood.

It was this emphasis on *qi* which had been already established centuries before[30] and which had been further developed by the prominent philosopher and scholar-educationist Wang Yangming in terms of his "Learning of the mind-heart" (*xinxue*). His radical critique of the officially approved doctrines handed down from the Song founders of "Learning of the *dao*" (Neo-Confucianism) was partly formulated in a conventional rhetoric:

What do we mean by "person" (*shen*)? It is the physical operation of the heart. What do we mean by "heart"? It is the luminous and intelligent master of the person. What do we mean by "cultivating the self" (*xiu shen*)? It means to do good

---

25 This has especially been shown by Elman 1990 and Elman 1993, pp. 59-80, here particularly p. 60.
26 See for instance Ng 1993, p. 38.
27 Within the *Huangdi neijing suwen* (1978) we find several passages dealing with this phenomenon, such as for instance "Xueqi xingzhi 24," p. 381.
28 See Yu 2009, pp. 34-35.
29 See Berg 1993; Cullen 1993.
30 See *Zhengmeng* by the prominent Song Neo-Confucian scholar Zhang Zai (1020–1077).

and getting rid of what is bad. Can the self (*wu shen*) by itself do what is good and get rid of what is bad, or must the luminous and intelligent master of the person/self first want to do so and only then will one physically start to do what is good and get rid of what is bad? Therefore, those who want to cultivate themselves must first rectify their hearts (*zheng qi xin*).[31]

The claim to rectify one's heart was old and well known. Yet, Wang Yangming claimed that everyone could possibly achieve the highest goal, namely sagehood, independently from scholarly attempts as well as from constant learning and memorizing the canonical classics, by which means he suggested a kind of democratization of sagehood. Accordingly, sagehood was no longer reserved for the Confucian scholars. The possibility to choose a path according to its own circumstances highlighted a "philosophy that asserted the epistemological priority of personal action and experience".[32] This inspired late Ming (16th and 17th centuries) and early Qing (17th century) Neo-Confucian philosophers to insist on the possibility of choosing alternative paths to self-cultivation and enlightenment.

It is well known that Wang Yangming was at the same time an official and successful general, who, in his late years, was send to central Guangxi in the South of China to launch a surprise attack against the *Yao*[33] "bandits". Since according to him "all beings of blood and *qi*" (*you xue qi zhe*) shared the same innate, moral and intuitive knowing (*liangzhi*) and as such, everyone (including "non-Chinese" (*manmo*)),[34] could achieve accomplishment. On occasions he was in charge of formulating policies, and on his campaigns directed against aggressive non-Chinese people he put forward his proposals on how to transform or to "civilize" non-Chinese people.[35]

The sense of right and wrong is knowledge possessed by men without deliberation and ability possessed by them without their having acquired it by learning. It is what we call innate knowledge. This knowledge is inherent in the human mind,

---

31 See "Daxuewen" in Wang Yangming 1978, pp. 335-336.
32 See Furth 2007, p. 16.
33 The appellation of the ethnic group as *Yao* has been in use since the Song dynasty. In late Ming and early Qing dynasty they lived mostly in the western part of Hunan province and in Guangxi province. For a detailed description of the ethnographic representations of the Yao and other ethnic groups, which lived in various parts of late Imperial China, see Hostetler 2001.
34 See "Chuanxi lu 2" in Wang Yangming 1992, p. 250. Translation in Wang Yangming 1963, pp. 166-167.
35 This however did not prevent him from conducting military campaigns. On the just mentioned occasion he succeeded — with more than 13,000 soldiers in all — to prompt the decapitation of some 3000 "bandits". For details and excellent discussion of this highly ambivalent issue, see Shin 2006, p. 101.

whether that of the sage or of the stupid person, for it is the same for the whole world and for all ages.[36]

These instructional ideas challenged the traditional emphasis on looking only for one single orthodox line of transmission of the way towards accomplishment and opened the possible multiplicity and particularity of different sagely lives. This encouragingly new and different way of philosophizing invited everyone to choose the path according to his own circumstances.[37]

Wang Yangming used the ancient idea "forming one body with heaven, earth, and all things" (*yi tian di wanwu wei yi ti*) thoroughly as a sign of being a sage:

> The heart-mind of a sage regards Heaven, Earth, and all things as one body. [A sage] looks upon all people under heaven without regard to their being inside or outside [one's family] or their being far or near. [A sage] treats all who have blood and *Qi* as if they were one's brothers and children, [and a sage] wants to safeguard, educate, and nourish all without exception, so as to fulfill one's desire of forming one body with all things.[38]

This is an essential and fundamental step towards self-accomplishment: men who feel part of the whole universe cannot but do and be good. Wang even extends the ancient narrative employed in *Mengzi* (2A.6) in order to illustrate his idea that man's nature is essentially good: everybody would feel commiseration at seeing a child about to fall into a well. Wang goes beyond this notion by emphasizing that this commiseration is not simply due because the nature of man is basically good, but because "one's humaneness extends to form one body with the child" (*qi ren zhi yu ruzi er wei yi ti*).[39]

This notion of "forming one body with all things" can be seen as a strong argument for "empathy" as a connecting link of society. Empathy here appears to be defined by humaneness. But this foundation of all moral conduct and self-cultivation is by no means restricted only to human beings, animals and plants, but to all things in the universe: when one feels a sense of regret at seeing tiles and stones broken and destroyed, it is because

---

36 See "Chuanxi lu 2" in Wang Yangming 1992, p. 265. Translation in Wang Yangming 1963, p. 167.
37 See Furth 2007, pp. 16-17.
38 See "Chuanxi lu 2" in Wang Yangming 1992, p. 258. Translation in Wang Yangming 1963, p. 118.
39 "Daxuewen" in Wang Yangming 1978, p. 325.

"one's humaneness forms one body with tiles and stones" (*qi ren zhi yu washi er wei yi ti*).[40]

These clear statements are strong arguments in favor of empathy, i.e. humaneness as the all-encompassing bond of things and beings in the world.

Qing (Emotions, Passion and Love): Virtue and Foundation for Self-Cultivation

Only about a century later, similar arguments had been formulated by a scholar, whose plans for a traditional career of being an official were frustrated due to the reasons mentioned above: Feng Menglong (1574–1646). He is known as the compiler of the *History of Love/Emotions* (*Qingshi*)[41] and as the self-proclaimed founder of a cult/teaching of emotions (*qingjiao*). He was one of the so-called town-hermits (*shiyin*), like the writers Tang Xianzu (1550–1616) and Yuan Hongdao (1568–1610) — one among hidden people (*yinren*, *yiren*) or extraordinary people (*yiren*, *qiren*), who nurtured their aloofness and eccentricity as a trademark of their autonomy.[42] According to Feng Menglong, *qing* (emotion, love, passion), by comparison, is the essential condition of life, in the sense of being "the string which [binds] all scattered things [lit. coins] together [on the earth]".[43]

This definition entails a major implication, namely, to transform the conventional understanding of emotions and passion. Song Neo-Confucian perceptions of the emotions (*qing*) were heavily influenced by the antagonism of the aforementioned two ways of being, the physical/experiential sphere (*xing er xia*) and the metaphysical sphere (*xing er shang*). As introduced above, the latter included the cosmic force heaven (*tian*), nature (*xing*), principle (*li*) and tranquility (*jing*), whereas the phenomena activity/movement (*dong*) and *qi* belonged to the physical/experiential sphere. Although Zhu Xi and other Neo-Confucians did not necessarily emphasize a dualism, they implied that illness could only arise from the physical realm. In this view, emotions are morally suspect.[44] The bifurcation was partly generated by the controversies regarding the status of principle (*li*) in relation to *qi*, the all embracing and pervading "matter". Principle was to be investigated through inquiring into things (the experiential realm) by constant

---

40 "Daxuewen" in Wang Yangming 1978, pp. 327-328. For a commentary on this passage by Wing-Tsit Chan, see Wang Yangming 1963, p. XXXIX.
41 The title is also translated as "Anatomy of Love". See for instance Santangelo 1994, p. 168.
42 See Hsu 2000, pp. 40-77, here p. 42. See also Hsu 2006.
43 See Feng Menglong 1993, p. 1.
44 See Huang, 2001, p. 27; see also Metzger 1977, pp. 82-85.

learning (*gewu*) in order to eventually achieve accomplishment.[45] But *qi* could also be seen as subordinated to principle (*li*), and thereby, the dualistic view was highlighted. However, Zhu Xi had already stressed that everything within the metaphysical realm had to be investigated and fathomed by exploring things (within the experiential realm),[46] and such synthesizing Neo-Confucian approaches fueled the controversies about value and worthlessness of the desires to achieve refinement and accomplishment within the 16th century. Desires (*yu*) now appear as an enhancement of the emotions, since they were considered to belong to the concrete experiential realm, i.e. they were supposed to be explored through experimental ways in order to achieve, eventually, the unity with principle (*li*).

These epistemological concepts influenced Feng Menglong's views on emotions. Yet his promotion of the cultivation of *qing* (love and passion) also implied the idea of transgressing former perspectives on emotions and passions (*qing*).[47]

It has always been one of my ambitions to compile a history of *qing*, and ever since I was a young man, I have been known to be *qing*-crazy. Amongst my friends and equals I always pour out all my heart, sharing with them in both good times and bad. Whenever I hear about a person who is in unusual distress or is suffering a great wrong, even though I may not know him, I always render my help to him if he seeks it; should it be beyond my ability to help him, then I sigh for days, and at night I toss about, unable to get to sleep. And whenever I see a person rich in emotion, I always desire to prostrate myself before him. Should there be some obdurate person whose intentions and words are at odds with my own, I always try to guide him unobtrusively with *qing*; only after his absolute refusal do I refrain.[48]

A self, formerly defined through morality and ritual, and whose emotional life had to be controlled and rather eliminated, now becomes celebrated for its emotional features and the transforming potential of its passion, emotions and love (*qinghua*). By now emotions/passion/love have become designated as the new virtue[49] within the general course of late Ming (16th century) romanticism and individualism.

This paper aims at shedding a light on the relationship between practice and theory, i.e. at traces of the above shown shifts in socio-economics, socio-politics as well as in the epistemology of concrete social practices. Social practices cannot be traced without taking into consideration the

---

45 See Bauer 2001, p. 257.
46 See ibid., p. 271.
47 Cf. Wong 1969; Volpp 2003, pp. 152-154.
48 See Feng Menglong 1993, n.p.; see also Mowry 1983, p. 12.
49 Judith Zeitlin observes the herewith connected emerging cultural paradigm of obsession (*pi*) for things. See Zeitlin 1991.

realm of implicit knowledge, which again relies fundamentally upon the human body as well as upon historical research and which must consider the materiality of social practices.[50]

What follows is a brief portrayal of the medical field in the 17th century China, firstly because, as already noted above, this field has been chosen by many contemporary scholars as an alternative avenue through which to conduct their lives and this, again, was closely connected with the aforementioned flourishing book market. Secondly, the medical field had already been proposed in the 14th century as an integral part of the scholarly agenda. For example, the popularization processes of medical knowledge fostered the shaping of identity among medical professionals as a significant part of the higher elitist culture. Thirdly, because of the obvious reason that these newly developing identities required, rather urgently, the conceptual elevation of their former low status of being plain physicians, they thus referred to the virtue of humaneness/benevolence (*ren*) as the highest trait of a good physician.

Last but not least, I will look closely at a specific medical text from the early 17th century, whose controversial claim that the heart (*xin*) is not the ruler of the human body is supported by a new cartography of the human body and, moreover, by referring to the similarities of three teachings (*sanjiao he yi*) Confucianism, Buddhism, and Daoism, which in general had been strongly emphasized in late Ming times (16th century).

Cultivating and Respecting Life

Since ancient times the claim for personal transformation towards accomplishment has meant exhausting one's life potential by cultivating ethical aspects of one's personality: to rectify one's heart (*zheng xin*) and to follow the heavenly principle (*xu xin shun li*)[51] finally would lead to an empty mind-heart.

This claim remains unchanged in the 17th century as well. Yet the aforementioned, newly emphasized significance of the emotions becomes manifest in slight shifts in the perception of transforming processes. The claim for the authenticity of the emotions and passion fostered the exploration of new ways to accomplishment.

The rise of monistic philosophy on *qi* in the 17th century indicated a specific focus on what has been characterized by de Bary as "vitalistic,"[52] be-

---

50 See Reckwitz 2008, p. 189.
51 See *Zhuzi yulei* 1986, chp. 8, p. 25.
52 See de Bary 1975, pp. 194-195.

cause the mind-heart (*xin*) was to be seen as a spiritual faculty embodied in physical force and a manifestation of the dynamic life force (*qi*).

Both, the heart (*xin*) and *qi* were often similarly referred to such as "alive," "living," "life giving," or "life renewing" (*sheng*). Moreover, with the revival of syncretistic movements in the 16th century[53] the "cosmic grounding" of the human being attracted more and more scholars, and the unity of the three teachings Confucianism, Buddhism, and Daoism (*sanjiao he yi*)[54] is reflected in literary works, private writings and published handbooks — including the medical *congshu* (collectanea) and *leishu* (books arranged by categories) — which offered concrete, applicable knowledge for everyday purposes (*riyong leishu*) alike.

Thus, popularized fields of knowledge such as "self-cultivation for the nourishing of life" (*yangsheng*) and medicine concomitantly challenged anthropocentric Neo-Confucian epistemology. It is well known, for instance, that in the late 16th century, Buddhist, Daoist and ancient Chinese wisdom teachings such as the oracle book *Book of Changes* (*Yijing*)[55] became regarded more and more as an integral part of scholarly fields of knowledge.[56] Moreover, examination candidates at the highest levels were obviously well informed about epistemological concepts and notions on reincarnation, karma and retribution.[57]

The ongoing processes of re-reading and re-interpreting earlier (canonical) medical works[58] as well as the integration of the aforementioned syncre-

---

53 See Ch'ien 1986. The relations between the Ming empire and Buddhism changed many times. Towards the end of the 14th century the emperor in his attempt to control the Buddhist monasteries and monks also ordered the closure of most of the smaller monasteries. He allowed only a small number of larger monasteries to survive. In the 15th century the state lost its control over Buddhist activities. See Brook 1999, p. 174 and Rummel 1992, pp. 9-38. Towards the end of the Ming dynasty Buddhism was used by the gentry as place for generating new "official" authority as an alternative to the traditional hierarchical social roles. They employed monasteries as objects for their patronage. See Brook 1997, pp. 179-180.
54 It is well known that the founder of Ming dynasty, Ming Taizu, in building powerful institutions at the same time drew on the popular traditions of Buddhism, Daoism, and Manichaeism. See Langlois and Sun 1983, pp. 97-117; with regard to the distinction between syncretism and eclecticism see Berling 1980, pp. 9-10.
55 See Hertzer 1996. The discussions on the appropriate usage of the *Yijing* is based on the critique by Wang Bi (226–249). See Bauer 2001, pp. 142-149.
56 On the perception of the *Yijing* by Ming and Qing scholars see Smith 1991, pp. 108-109.
57 See Elman 2000, p. 307.
58 This has to be seen in connection with the flourishing of a print culture and with the prevalence of a new medical scholarly orthodoxy in the 13th and

tistic world-views into scholarly Confucian reasoning are mirrored by a special emphasis on *qi*. This emphasis on *qi* united an otherwise disparate group of Qing thinkers.[59] To them techniques for "self-cultivation for nourishing life" (*yangsheng*) gained importance, and *yangsheng* became a mainstream cultural activity in the 16th and the 17th centuries.[60]

Admittedly, most of the ancient Confucians had paid attention to the regulation of the physical body: dietary regulations and warnings were quite common[61] which, furthermore, are to be found in the ancient medical canon.[62] However, the major Neo-Confucian concern for a life-long study of the classics (*gewu zhizhi*, investigating things to extend knowledge) provoked the criticism by Wang Yangming and his followers.[63]

By now, in the 16th century, next to previously integrated Buddhist conceptualizations — which included body techniques such as silent sitting and meditation (*jing zuo*) as well as respectful attitude (*jing*) — other techniques of self-cultivation for nourishing life (*yangsheng*) became integral parts of self-cultivation (*xiu shen*) practices[64]: *daoyin* (lit. "guiding and pulling") practices, breathing practices (*tugu naxin*, lit.: "expelling the old and taking in the new"), abstention from grains (*quegu*), sexual practices (*fangzhong*), clapping the teeth (*kou chi*), clenching the fists (*wo gu*) — only to mention the most prominent body techniques for daily practice. Ultimately, all these techniques were concerned with orderly *qi*-flow through the body and within the whole cosmos. It is important to note that these practices were not newly invented at this time. But by now, more and more people who could afford to become acquainted with pleasure and entertainment, such as writing, reading and playing musical instruments, also became attracted to the practices of self-cultivation for respecting and nourishing life (*yangsheng*). At the same time, these practices still included ethical refinement through the focus on benevolence.

    14th centuries, which in turn was related to the rise of Neo-Confucianism. See Leung 2003, pp. 374-398.

59 This group included Huang Zongxi (1610–1695), Gu Yanwu (1613–1682), Wang Fuzhi (1609–1692), and Yan Yuan (1635–1704). See Bloom 1979, p. 76. For a discussion of Huang Zongxi see also the article by Dennis Schilling in this volume.

60 See Zheng Jinsheng 1999 and Liu Wengang 2002.

61 See Linck 2001, pp. 128-152.

62 See Unschuld 2003, pp. 294-301 and pp. 303-305; Stein 1999b.

63 See the detailed discussion of this issue in Epstein 2001, pp. 13-28, and pp. 69-87.

64 See Engelhardt 2000, p. 81; Stein 1999a, pp. 41-52.

Moreover, *ren* (humaneness and benevolence) advanced to the utmost virtue in the newly constituted field of engagement for many scholars in the 17th century.

Medicine: The Art of Humaneness and Benevolence

In order to be able to cure their old and ill parents, Confucian scholars have conventionally considered medicine as an important part of the practice of filial piety. Yet, as scholars chose medicine as a main profession, and the flourishing book market made medical knowledge accessible to everyone able to read, the hereditary physicians (*shiyi*), who had traditionally accumulated specialized experience (e.g. in pediatrics) and who were often illiterate, felt threatened by those emerging scholarly physicians.[65] The 17th century saw the tension between the classical canon and its norms on the one hand and a specific style of constituting authority on the other hand in a newly emerging sphere: that of *medicine as part of the higher culture*.

The medical landscape in the 17th century was populated with common physicians (*zhongyi*), temporary physicians (*shi yi*), incompetent physicians (*yong yi*), famous physicians (*mingyi*), illustrious physicians (*mingyi*), itinerants (*liuyi*), virtuous physicians (*deyi*), monk physicians (*sengyi*), hidden, reclusive physicians (*yinyi*), female physicians (*nüyi*), wounds and skin infection physicians (*yangyi*), devious physicians (*jianyi*), immoral, licentious physicians (*yinyi*), hereditary physicians (*shiyi*) and scholar physicians (*ruyi*).[66] The high diversity of medical practitioners and the mere absence of any institutionalized standards led to the compilation of guidelines for patients and physicians alike, in order to evaluate competence and reliability.[67]

Among the aforementioned surplus of scholars, whose chances to receive an official post were diminished in the 17th century (in addition to Ming loyalists who refused to serve under the Manchu), many chose medicine as an alternative career. Medical engagement as a substitute for being an official is a known practice reaching back to the Song dynasty. In the 17th century, however, the new medical practice is specifically connected

---

65 On the issue of ethics and medicine in the Chinese historical context see Unschuld 1975. For the discussion of this issue in late Imperial China see Chao 1995.
66 The term *ruyi* firstly appeared in the early 12th century, referring to doctors who behaved like gentlemen, and to those who abandoned Confucian studies to become doctors. See Liu Boyi 1974, p. 269; Chen Yuanpeng 1997, pp. 39-40; Hymes 1987, pp. 9-76.
67 See the reprint from 1644 of the "Xuanqi qiu zheng lun 6" in Xiao Jing 1983, pp. 509-577.

to the shaping of Ming loyalist identities, and this provoked attempts to increase the overall status of the medical field in society.

These developments formed the background to the develoment of argumentative strategies to elevate medicine from a minor profession (*xiao dao, jian ye*) to a higher status. Conventionally, medicine had been considered as a kind of handcraft, as a skill (*shu*). As such the physician, by imperial decree, was labeled as artisan (*gong*).[68] Physicians' biographies in the local gazetteers, and dynastic histories were placed under the craft categories (*yishu* or *fangji*), and they were forbidden to travel[69] in the Late Ming.

By now, as more and more scholars entered the medical field, *ren* (humaneness, benevolence) came to play a crucial role in identity-shaping processes on the part of scholars who turned to work as physicians in 17th century. By introducing the formula "medicine is humaneness, benevolence" (*yi renshu ye*), medicine was branded as part of the higher culture. By blending skill[70] and benevolence (*ren*), as the paramount virtue of the Song Neo-Confucian agenda of self-cultivation, medicine became more than a skill.

The relation between medical skills and the way of a superior man (*junzi*) had already been established in the 14th century,[71] when medicine was claimed as an integral part of the Neo-Confucian scholarly agenda along with its emphasis on "investigating things and thereby extending knowledge" (*gewu zhizhi*)[72] as an important instrument for achieving learning and extending knowledge. In addition to the conventional practice of filial piety, medicine, as it was supposed to become a profession, had to be *re-invented* epistemologically as a scholarly field. Through negotiating the boundaries

---

68 The Hongwu emperor in 1386 issued a decree defining the four classes: scholars (*shi*), farmers (*nong*), artisans (*gong*), and merchants (*shang*). This was to observe their proper status. Physicians and geomancers were considered to be local agents and thus forbidden to travel. But, as the society experienced changes in economy, this fixed status was also modified. Officially, during the Ming times, the physicians' status was considered to be an inherited, professional one. In the three categories of commoners (*min*), military (*jun*), and craftsmen (*jiang*), they were part of the latter.
69 See Chao 1995, pp. 30-31.
70 We find notions of basic virtues such as compassion and also benevolence as important for healing practice from the 7th century on. See Unschuld 1975, pp. 18-31. The propagation of medicine as an integral part of "investigating things in order to extend knowledge" (*gewu zhizhi*) was already put forward by Zhu Zhenheng (1281–1358).
71 Zhu Zhenheng, who appears within several biographies in the official annals as a prominent scholar physician (*ruyi*). See *Siku quanshu, zongmu, juan* 103, *zibu* 13, *yijilei*. See also Rall 1970, p. 70.
72 See the "Abstract" (*tiyao*) of the discussion by Zhu Zhenheng, in *Siku quanshu* 1974, pp. 637-746. See Bol 1992, pp. 300-341; Ma Boying 1994, pp. 466-469; Elman 1999, p. 11; Furth 1999, pp. 146-148.

and the relation between medical skills (*yishu*) and benevolence (*ren*), medicine should become part of the higher culture, i.e. of the great way (*da dao*).

What did *ren* refer to in the realm of the medical practice? A physician (as a Confucian scholar) should practice self-cultivation (*xiu shen*) in order to achieve refinement and accomplishment. In addition to the knowledge of diseases and therapeutic remedies, medicine's inherent power to save lives required its responsible handling and a high sensibility for the specific situation of the patient. Humanity and benevolence here referred to the conscious and responsible usage of one's medical instruments and to refrain from working for profit.[73]

Transforming the Body: Shifting Cartography of the Inner Visceral Order

The *Thoroughgoing Knowledge on Medicine* (*Yiguan*) from 1617 by the scholar physician Zhao Xianke (ca. 1567–1644) claims that the heart was not the ruler of the human body but something else:

The *Neijing*[74] says that the heart is the ruler of the human body. But I say, there exists another ruler within the human body which is not the heart. I tell you that the heart is [in his ranking] at the same level as the [other 12 organs]… (*dangyu shi er guan pingdeng*).[75]

With these words, Zhao contextualizes a changed geography of the human body. By referring to a high ranking Buddhist monk (*gao seng*) who told him the real place of the ruler in the body[76] he defines the *mingmen* (the life gate between the kidneys) as the real centre within the human body. Thus, in contrast to the classic view, this would not be the heart but a place amidst the kidneys in the lower part. This newly introduced cartography of the human body with the focus on the *mingmen* was part of a re-cosmologisation of the human being and can be seen as a direct expression of the aforementioned philosophical and religious syncretism in the late 16th early 17th centuries. The life gate between the kidneys, understood as the *concrete* locus of the celestial fire, takes the position of the *concrete* place of heaven within the human body, the self.

---

73 Cf. for instance the paratext apparatus of the writings of Chen Shiduo (1627–1707), in Liu Zhanghua 1999.
74 The Classic of the Yellow Emperor (ca. 200 BC–100 AD).
75 He hereby refers to a passage within the *Huangdi neijing suwen* 1982, 3, 8, p. 131: "When the ruler is not bright, this means danger for the 12 officials." See Zhao Xianke, *Yiguan* 1982, 1.
76 Cf. Zhao Xianke, *Yiguan* 1982, 1-2.

Conclusion

Since the 13th century self-cultivation (*xiu shen*) has represented the idea of steadily reading and memorizing the canonical texts. As early as the 16th century and throughout the 17th century, scholars openly proposed alternative practices. Besides meditation (*jing zuo*) and the correct guiding of the *qi* through the body, various other bodily techniques to preserve the body from crises and diseases had been contextualized and became part of the cultural mainstream in that time in wealthy places in the Southeast of China. As we have seen, the practice of *ren* (humaneness and benevolence) in late Ming-early Qing times gradually shifted towards a specific feature for all those who turned to explore and celebrate their emotions, passions and sentiments.

This perspective on the emotions can be seen as a major attack on conventional views put forward within Neo-Confucian contexts, which in turn shaped the understanding of *ren* (humaneness) and elevated the status of emotions and passions to a higher epistemological level by subtly altering their former perception as dangerous features of the human nature.

The perception of human nature as basically good is bound to an old narrative elaborated by Mencius stating that everybody would feel commiseration at seeing a child about to fall into a well.

In the 15th and 16th centuries Wang Yangming went beyond Mencius' notion by connecting his narrative with the formula that one's humaneness would extend the self to form one body with all things. Here, empathy is defined by humaneness, which in turn is not restricted to human beings but includes animals and to all matter, and which serves as an all-embracing link to society.

Furthermore, humaneness (*ren*) has also gained significance in the medical field. It is obvious that as many scholars chose the medical field as an alternative career in the 17th century, they urgently needed the conceptual elevation of the former low status of medical practice. Through negotiating the boundaries between medical skills (*yishu*) and benevolence (*ren*) medicine became part of higher culture.

This article mainly dealt with the question of how the abstract cultural concept "humaneness" was mapped into and onto the human body. The controversial claim that the heart (*xin*) is not the ruler of the human body served as a fundamental source for the observation of a newly elaborated cartography of the human body. This, on the other hand, was supplemented by the observation of a general emphasis on bodily practices and techniques for nourishing life (*yangsheng*) as a mainstream cultural activity in the 16th and 17th centuries.

The shifting medical cartographic views on the human body had its roots in the 14th century; however, in the 17th century they became supported by a manifest syncretism of the three teachings (*sanjiao he yi*) Confucianism, Buddhism, and Daoism. The ways in which these cultural (philosophical and political) borrowings have been applied in medical perspectives on the human body provide a fragmentary insight on how man acquires cultural concepts in terms of material, i.e. a bodily logic.

Human Equality in Modern Chinese Political Thought

DENNIS SCHILLING

Introduction

Human equality is one of the most important ideas in modern political theory, demarcating the change from older conceptions based on the excellence of certain individuals in accordance with metaphysical, religious or traditional beliefs. Human equality, however, is still a highly disputed idea. From a logical point of view, the uncertainty results from both the polyvalent logical structure of the concept of equality and its prescriptive usage. Equality is a tripartite relation. Two (or more) individuals are equal with regard to distinct features — the *tertium comparationis* of the equation — while differing in others.[1] If we say — in a descriptive sense — that human beings are equal, we suppose that there are certain properties in human nature with high ethical significance which all human beings share. The prescriptive usage of the idea demands various ways of realization such as social, political, legal, or economic equality.[2]

Already in ancient Greek and Roman thought, equality was considered to be an important term for the substantiation of political and ethical claims, for example for the exercising of justice; but not until recent times has equality advanced to a fundamental idea in political and social theory. The intellectual shift in European political theory is largely due to the increasing importance of the idea of a human natural right which acknowledges an

---

1 Cf. Brennan 2002–2003, p. 106.
2 Cf. Nagel 1978, p. 3.

equal dignity among all humans. This also can be analyzed as a shift from a mere descriptive usage of the idea of human equality to its prescriptive usage.[3]

In modern China, the French Revolution and the American *Declaration of Independence* evoked great admiration from progressive political thinkers. Kang Youwei (1858–1927) was one of the first scholars who developed a social and political theory based on the idea of human equality. Tan Sitong (1865–1898), the famous essayist and political activist at the end of the Qing dynasty (1644–1912), followed him. In the eyes of the intellectuals of the latter half of the 19th century like Kang and Tan, human equality is a universal idea common in every culture. Although Western society put the idea into practice first, the idea of human equality is not absent from China's own intellectual tradition. Kang and Tan both recognize distinct "humanistic" traditions in Chinese thought, Kang in the so-called Confucian *Gongyang* School, Tan in Buddhism, Mohism, Mencian Confucianism and in the philosophy of Zhuangzi.[4] Their historical outlook was seriously questioned by contemporary thinkers, but exerted tremendous impact on later writings about Chinese thought.

Some political thinkers in the Chinese tradition, nevertheless, accused their social and political order of injustice and inequality and supported their accusation by referring to concepts resembling human equality. Thinkers like Huang Zongxi (1610–1695) focused their critiques on the conception that the "human way" (*rendao*) mirrors the "way of heaven" (*tiandao*) and authority rests in natural predispositions. The theory criticized by Huang goes back to ancient Confucian thought and was completed in the Song dynasty (960–1279) by scholars like Cheng Yi (1033–1107) and Zhu Xi (1130–1200). I will refer to this theory as the "traditional Confucian social theory" or as the "(Confucian) naturalistic view (of society)".

The naturalistic view proposes a very sound theory of how conditions of human nature determine the stratification of human society. Although the naturalistic view was subject to much criticism in modern times, it is still alive in China and other Confucian societies in Asia and functions in contemporary discourse as the theoretical fundament in the defense of cultural relativism, proposing indigenous Chinese concepts of social welfare and human policy (*rendao*) against foreign concepts of human rights (*renquan*) and individuality.

---

3   Cf. Dann 1975, pp. 1009-1011; Gosepath 2007.
4   Tan Sitong 1998, p. 293.

In the present paper, I will not debate the naturalistic view in detail or its impact on contemporary discussions, but ask how the idea of human equality was adopted in modern Chinese political discourse. To do this, I will show how progressive thought in China targets the traditional naturalistic view. This confrontation is complicated by the fact that human equality and the naturalistic view are not necessarily mutually exclusive or contradictory. Human equality refers to both human nature and social conditions, partly resembling partly opposing the traditional naturalistic view. Modern progressive thought, therefore, has to be selective as well as creative in its refutation of traditional beliefs. Traditional beliefs have to be refined and reshaped to certain claims which oppose progressive ideas. Therefore, in the eyes of its opponents, the traditional naturalistic view became reduced to certain dogmas like the ancient social doctrine of the "five bonds" (*wu lun*) or to the doctrine of ruling a state in a authoritarian manner by creating a hierarchy of fixed positions and limited functions termed "names" (*ming*) according to ancient political theory. Although these ancient conceptions of social stratification do not have much in common with social reality and social policies either in 17th or 19th century China, society was still conceptualized in the terms of traditional Confucian ethics and ancient political philosophy.

In this paper, I will first give an overview of the traditional naturalistic view with regard to the conception of human equality and then go on to briefly discuss some distinct characteristics of the ideas on human equality in the late 16th and 17th century while taking Huang Zongxi as example. I will continue with a discussion of the ideas of the 19th century by referring to the works of Kang Youwei and Tan Sitong. All these thinkers held different conceptions of human equality, in a communitarian sense or individual sense;[5] all of them, however, identify the naturalistic view as the main source of inequality. Moreover, the concept of human equality has an intrinsic force which demands social change. This force rests in its prescriptive use, demanding the realization of social communitarian ideals, the redistribution of power and wealth, and the abolition of unequal limitations and differences. Tan Sitong identifies the prescriptive usage of the idea of human equality with soteriological beliefs in rescuing man from suffering. Therefore, in Tan's political thought, equality has significance beyond the realm of an ideal human society, but acts as a guiding principle for human action. I will conclude with a brief discussion of the ethical and political function of human equality.

---

5   Cf. Nagel 1978, p. 5.

The Equation of Nature and Society

"Equality" as a basic condition in human nature can bear different meanings. "Humans are equal" may be a claim for equity, meaning humans are equal regarding their rights and dignity and should therefore be treated with equal respect. However, "humans are equal" may permit the opposite conclusion: that social inequality should rather be accepted than denied, as social inequality, not natural equality, is the necessary condition for social wealth and diversity. This argument was common in both traditions, in Europe and in China. In the last centuries, however, more weight is given to the claim that equality can secure social peace and public welfare.[6]

In the Chinese tradition, humans are not equal. Human inequality, however, does not so much rely on the excellence of certain individuals and of a certain social class, but on the fact that one human being is born and raised by two others. This fact can be treated both as a natural condition of all human beings as well as a basic condition for human society.

Therefore, social hierarchy is naturally given. The life-creating forces bring forth their fruits in sequence, thereby producing strata and differences.[7] Some living beings are born first, others next. Humans are born and brought up by their parents. The simple facts of seniority and reproduction separate the positions of father and son clearly. What a newborn child possesses — his life, his body and mind — is given by his parents and ancestry. The responsibility of the child to his elder generation lasts forever and cannot become subject to change. The principles of ancestry and seniority were written down in the Confucian ritual scriptures, comprised in a doctrine of the so-called "five human bonds" (*wu lun*) and explained as the different obligations toward the senior or junior members of the family and society. These "unequal" hierarchical principles are given to all human beings by nature, and were considered as fundamental principles of human society, whereas clan distinction and individual excellence rank second in importance for social distinction.

Thus, to be human means to act as a human, that is, to fulfill all the social and familial duties respectfully. To act as a human means to act according the principles of the natural way of succession and creation called the way of heaven (*tiandao*). What is called the "human way" (*rendao*) is conceptualized as nothing other than the application of the principles of the way of heaven to the conditions of human life, thereby regulating the

---

6 Cf. Rawls 1999; Dworkin 2000.
7 The *locus classicus* for this view is the *Great Treatise* (*Dazhuan*; chapter A1), a late Warring State or early Han commentary (3rd century BC) on the *Book of Changes* (*Yijing*; cf. Lynn 1994, p. 47).

transmission of demands, property and merits from the past life into the present and from the present life into the future, letting the ancestral line and its glory persist through the ages.

Therefore, human society is unequal, because human nature which every human being equally possesses attains its full realization in social hierarchy. Traditional Confucian social theory (the "naturalistic view") equates human nature and society and describes man as a social being who has social rôles and has to fulfil his obligations towards his family members. In this view, human nature (*xing*) has the status of a potential source and is described as a command (*ming*) demanding his realization in social affairs. The naturalistic view holds a twofold equation of human nature and society: society is based on natural causes, just as human nature contains the basic roots of social organization.

By equation of the hierarchies of nature and society, Chinese traditional social philosophy has brought forth a very durable and popular theory. This theory was propagated by the Confucian schools, but was not unrivalled by other social theories. Already, in antiquity, the Mohists explained social organization solely on the basis of social positions and functions, thereby opposing the Confucian explanation of social structure in terms of a natural order.

Chinese traditional views of society do distinguish between political authority and clan authority, as both rest on the authority of heaven. Political authority belongs to the same logical category as social authority and can be discussed in the same terms: rule over the empire is given by heaven, succeeding natural creation by spreading forth the fruit-bearing powers of heaven and earth towards every human being. Enjoying the magnificence of the great authority of the "son of heaven," the life of the Chinese people is blessed by his fortune and power. Not to acknowledge the social and political order means not only to resist them, but to make a fault against the natural order and to fail to make use of nature's most productive and fertile powers.

The naturalistic view was re-affirmed and re-shaped in early modern China (11th century, Song dynasty) by strengthening the equation of nature and society by recognizing a universal "humanity" in nature and society. Human beings are formed by one and the same kind of "breath" (*qi*) that forms human corporeal and mental constitution.[8] All human beings, there-

---

8 This view became extreme popular with the "Western Inscription" (*Ximing*) of Zhang Zai (1020–1077), which also introduces the last chapter of his book *Zhengmeng* (*Correction of Obstruction*), see Zhang Zai 1985, pp. 62-63.

fore, share the same natural predisposition.[9] Human action may individually differ, but in order to guarantee security and prosperity, human beings have to adopt the pattern of heaven for their own action. In the modern reformulation of this concept, first articulated by philosophers of the Song dynasty, humans are able to bring forth the same order (*li*) which underlies the action of heaven. The "ten thousand things" (*wan wu*) may differ in their behavior and in the different properties; their differences, however, form only part of an overall cosmic order which everyone has to follow to secure wealth and prosperity. According to their theory, moral excellence should be the criterion for social stratification and authority, which is given by nature to the ruling dynasty, as can be seen in the heavenly command, and to the ministers by education and moral perfection, as is proved by the system of recruitment.

By attesting to an equal human nature, Confucian thinkers in Song China appeal to the universality of their claims, while holding to social stratification and to political authority in the hands of certain human beings in possession of excellence by nature (the ruling dynasty; authority is decreed by heaven, *tianming*) or by education (the ministers). Before the Ming dynasty (1368–1644), the universal predisposition of human nature, therefore, was not considered as an argument for human dignity. The reason lies in the fact that for the Chinese thinkers the question of "being human" is not only a question of nature, but a question of social conduct and social duties.

To sum up, humans are naturally unequal because nature follows an unequal sequence of reproduction. Social organization has to follow this natural pattern, building up social hierarchy and authority. By equalizing the ways of action of nature and society, traditional Chinese social philosophy recognizes the same values and meaning in human action as well as in the processes of nature (the way of heaven). The productive powers of heaven and earth are self-less, impartial and just. On the other side, society is settled in a state of harmony with the natural order as there is no other foundation of society besides the natural order of reproduction. However, at the end of the Ming dynasty, some thinkers question the equation of nature with society because this equation still argues for a naturally given impartial political authority. Moral excellence should be the lone criterion. To achieve this, society and authority have to be based on different grounds.

---

9   A short description of the early modern Confucian view of the Song scholars on the creation of man can be found in Zhu Xi's (1130–1200) explanations to the *Doctrine of the Mean* (*Zhongyong*), see Zhu Xi 1986, p. 17.

On Friendship

To introduce the culture and values of their own tradition, Jesuits missionaries translated passages and moral stories from Greek and Latin in literal Chinese.[10] Matteo Ricci (1552–1610) chose friendship as the subject of his collection titled *De amicitia* (1595) providing a Chinese translation of 72 proverbs of European antique literature.[11] The subject was well chosen, and father Ricci's little book enjoyed a warm welcome by the Chinese literati. Friendship, being regarded as an ethical value since antiquity in both cultures, serves as an ideal go-between in the encounter of the two traditions — on equal terms.

The Jesuits utilize friendship as a means to get into a closed system of society, conjuring up the famous phrase of the *Analects* (*Lunyu*) of Confucius. Friendship was the fifth and last "bond" in the doctrine of the "five bonds". In contrast to the other four, friendship was considered as a "non clan-bound" relation and contains no prescription for exercising or obeying authority. Therefore, friendship can be seen as concept of equality disregarding clan privilege.

Friendship, however, is nothing other than a concept of an "open society" and joins with the concept of equality a selective function: including certain individuals by excluding others. In Imperial China, friendship was important for social identity, fixing the social strata of the scholar class in Chinese society and securing the influence of certain individuals, and was much esteemed as a favorite subject in the long and enduring Chinese poetical tradition. Therefore, the Jesuit extension of the idea of friendship, passing beyond the four seas and making friends with foreigners, can convey two totally different connotations. On a conceptual level, it claims nothing more than the expansion of familiar ethical norms over the borders of culture and nations. On a functional level, however, this extension means to open up solidified structures of managing authority.

Contemporaneously with the early Christian mission, Chinese thinkers began to write on friendship in order to express their views on social unity and human equality. He Xinyin (1517–1579), for example, wrote an essay titled "On Friendship" (*Youlun*) claiming that "all human beings under heaven are closely related to each other".[12] He Xinyin, therefore, forces his

---

10 Ad Dudink and Nicolas Standaert provide a short description of these writings (cf. Standaert 2001, pp. 604-620).
11 The Chinese title usually is given as "Jiaoyou lun," "On the Intercourse with Friends," according to the Zikawei-edition. The book collection of Chen Jiru (1558–1639), *Baoyan tang Miji guanghan*, includes the book under the title "Youlun," "On Friendship". Ricci's book makes use of Andreas Eboscuris' (1498–1573) *Sententiae et Exempla* (cf. Standaert 2001, p. 605).
12 He Xinyin 1960, p. 28.

reader to "see all under heaven as one family" (*shi tianxia wei yijia*),[13] combining several common sayings on moral excellence and on the impartial attitude of the ruler to his subjects and turning them into an argument for human equality.[14] To "see all under heaven as one family" argues against the excellence of dynastic or aristocratic structures. To call this egalitarian view "friendship" implies developing a social community beyond clan distinctions. Social rôles should be defined on principles of equity and equality while excluding a naturally given authority.

He Xinyin's writings, however, were not much known during his time, but the eccentric thinker Li Zhi (1527–1602) extolled He Xinyin's views on friendship. It was Li, too, who discovered a kind of familiarity in the ideas of Father Ricci's *De amicitia* with He Xinyin's claims for human equality.[15] By identifying the Jesuit literature with political protest, Li gives the Christian treatises much more social concern than they deserve.[16]

After the downfall of the Ming empire (1368–1644), Confucian writers like Huang Zongxi (1610–1695) continue to proclaim human equality, criticizing the priority which is given to the ruler. Besides Huang, Tang Zhen (1630–1704) and Fu Shan (1607–1684) are noted as thinkers who claim a kind of equality between the sovereign and his subject. For both thinkers, all human beings, although belonging to different social strata, still share the same "dignity" or "respect" (*zun*). Fu Shan remarks that the famous poet Li Bo (701–762) treated the emperor as a close friend. Tang Zhen recognizes that "respect" should be given as equally to a farmer as to the emperor.[17] After one hundred years, at the end of the Ming rule and the beginning of the Manchu empire (Qing, 1644–1912), the discourse on friendship, the single "equal" relation in Chinese traditional society, became a discourse on equality and social status.

---

13 He Xinyin 1960, p. 28.
14 This common phrase in the political philosophy of Confucianism was reaffirmed by Wang Yangming (1472–1529) on the first page of his "Questions on the 'Great Learning'" ("Daxue wen*)* laying out the idea of how to become a sage (Wang Yangming 2006, p. 968). Wang only slightly altered the phrase from the chapter "Li yun" of the *Book of Rites* (*Liji*), in which it is said that "the sage is able to consider all under heaven as one family" (*Liji zhengyi* 22, in Ruan Yuan 1980, p. 1422, 2nd column).
15 Li Zhi in his "Essay on He Xinyin" (1936, pp. 99-101).
16 Some contemporary Chinese historians see in the Jesuit treatises a stimulus for the late Ming progressive political thought, for example Li Zhijun (2004, pp. 201-216) who, however, quite deliberately combines statements from various Jesuit sources to build an argument. Ricci's reasons for writing a book on friendship were as concerned with his own status in Chinese society as with the status the Chinese people enjoyed.
17 Cf. Li Zhijun 2004, pp. 207-208.

The Distinctness of Nature and Society: Huang Zongxi (1610–1695)

Huang Zongxi is the author of the *Records while Waiting for Appointment* (*Daifang lu*), which became popular under the title *Records [while] Waiting for Appointment in a Time of Obscured Light* (*Mingyi Daifang lu*) in Chinese intellectual history. His *Records [while] Waiting for Appointment in a Time of Obscured Light* belong to a genre of political literature written down as advice for an enlightened ruler in future. Although the first publication of Huang's *Records* did not reach a wide audience, some of its tractates were known in political circles, some of them still inclined to loyalty to the former Ming dynasty.[18]

Huang starts his discussion with a re-definition of the relationship between lord and subject. By doing this, he introduces the concept of the common good ("common benefit," *gongli*) as a common and universal principle for everyone, guiding the different interests and actions of the people of different rôles and strata:

In the beginning of human life each man lived for himself and looked to his own interests. There was such a thing as the common benefit, yet no one seems to have promoted it; and there was a common harm, yet no one seems to have eliminated it. Then someone came forth who did not think of benefit on term of his own benefit but sought to benefit all-under-Heaven, and who did not think of harm in terms of harm to himself, but sought to spare all-under-Heaven from harm. Thus his labors were thousand or ten thousand times greater than the labors of ordinary men. Now to work a thousand or ten thousand times harder without benefiting oneself is certainly not what most people in the world desire. [...] However, with those who later became princes it was different. They believed that since they held the power over benefit and harm, there was nothing wrong in taking for themselves all the benefits and imposing on others all the harm. They made it so that no man dared to live for himself or look to his own interests. Thus the prince's great self-interest took the place of the common good of all-under-Heaven.[19]

In Huang's view, there was once a natural state of human life which differs from the later states of humankind in that point that social action (a common good and a common harm) was not be recognized. The step from the natural state to a society is described as a step from individual action to social action.

---

18 The wooden printing blocks of the first publication were destroyed by fire, no copy preserved. Although Huang's writings were proscribed during the Qianlong era (1736–1795), there were several printings during the 18th century (Wu Guang 1990, pp. 1-10; Wu Guang in Huang Zongxi 1985, pp. 423-427).
19 Huang Zongxi 1985, pp. 2-3, the translation given is taken from de Bary 1993, pp. 91-92.

According to the traditional Confucian view, human society was created by the sages applying the order of heaven to the natural state of human community, thereby producing an ideal social order.[20] Huang, in contrast, discusses society in terms of individual action ("labor") which is not done for oneself but in respect for others (social action) whereby bringing forth benefit and repelling harm (social life). Huang's idea of social action does not possess an example in the order of heaven but proceeds from the realization of a common life. In Huang's society, at the base level of the common good, societal grades exist, but all human beings equally share its benefit — at least in proportion to status and labor. Thus, the idea of distribution must be very important. In Huang's argument, the idea of a proportional equality is inherent in his description, where the equal distribution of the common benefit became distorted and was monopolized exclusively by the lord.

Huang's view on social organization breaks with two traditional views. First, he denies the simple equation of nature and society by separating individual and social action. Individual action arises from the natural tendencies of human beings, whereas social action needs cognition and action against the natural disposition. Individual action as a state of nature is prescribed as human ignorance, whereas social action springs forth from the awareness of the limits of natural behavior. Second, Huang abandons the "five bonds" as principles of authority. Action ("labor") is not ruled by duty with regard to an authority but by common interest in a common good.

In Huang's view, human equality becomes important to sustain his claim that collective labor is the fundament of society. Everyone takes part in it. Furthermore, Huang favors a kind of proportional equality for defining authority. Authority is derived from action which is done for the common interest, and should be defined as being proportional to social action.

However, Huang's descriptions of the distribution of authority and the justification of the status of emperor are not very clear, but he sees the point that the traditional concept of authority is a formation by analogy from the natural relationship between father and son. In the view of Huang, this analogy is false for two reasons: social authority qualitatively differs from any patriarchal system, and the analogy between nature and society is impractical, because social authority has to govern the whole state while patriarchy is limited to the family. Therefore, Huang calls for another social hierarchy ("ministers") to govern the state.[21]

To make the difference between natural and social authority clearer, Huang draws a distinction between nature and society, between "heaven"

---

20 Cf. *Mengzi*, 3A.4.
21 De Bary 1993, p. 94; Huang Zongxi 1985, p. 4.

(*tian*) and that which is "under heaven" (*tianxia*). Discussing the difference between the relationship between lord and subject and the relationship between father and son, he says:

> It may be asked, is not the term "minister" always equated with that of "child"? I say no. Father and child share the same vital spirit. The child derives his own body from his father's body. Though a filial child is a different person bodily, if he can draw closer each day to his father in vital spirit, then in time there will be a perfect communion between them. An unfilial child, after deriving his body from his father's, drifts farther and farther from his parent, so that in time they cease to be kindred in vital spirit. The terms "prince" and "minister" derive from their relation to all-under-Heaven. If I take no responsibility for all-under-Heaven, then I am just another man on the street. If I come to serve him without regard for serving all-under-Heaven, then I am merely the prince's menial servant or concubine. If, on the other hand, I have regard for serving the people, then I am the prince's mentor and colleague, Thus with regard to ministership the designation may change. With father and child, however, there can be no such change.[22]

The natural relationship between father and son is a relation based on of the same vital spirit or "breath" (*qi*). Father and son are sharing an identical part of nature. This relationship is extraordinary, and cannot serve as an example for society. Identity regulates the relation between father and son, and in regard to this relation, seniority may be accepted as an apt principle to define authority. To strengthen his argument for the particularity of this natural relation, Huang provides a utilitarian argument: because the natural material disposition of father and son possesses a special communicative potential, sons can foreshadow the wishes of the father. The relationship between ruler and subject, however, has to make use of other forms of communication: exercising mutual education, instruction and critique. Furthermore, a great difference in the aims of acting underlies the pattern of nature and the pattern of society. According to the pattern of nature, the aim of the action of the son is to achieve a maximum of identity with his father, but according to the pattern of society, the aim of the actions of the minister is not directed toward the person of the lord, but toward the common good. The two patterns have a different logic. The relation between father and son is a twofold relationship, stressing similarity or identity. Father and son are related to each other. The relation of lord and minister, however, is a tripartite relation, and this fact stresses their equality: the lord and his ministers are equally related to the common good, "all under heaven". To sum up, in

---

22 Huang Zongxi 1985, pp. 5-6; the translation given is taken from de Bary 1993, p. 96.

Huang's view, nature and society stand in different relation to one another and cannot be taken interchangeably.

Huang comes to the conclusion that there are different kinds of authority. He defines ministership as a concern with the prospering of the state. Ministers do not fulfill orders from the lord but act on behalf of the common good, that is to say, the rule of the state. Ministers enjoy authority but seem to be exempted from an obligation to a higher authority. On the contrary, the lord is like a guest of the empire. He enjoys the products and the wealth the country will offer to him. His authority results in a granted position and can be seen as purely symbolic.

At the end, Huang's view of authority is very unusual and radical, but lacks any further explanation of how to define the symbolic authority of the guest rôle of the emperor. Huang's solution, however, can also be seen as a solution of an immanent uncertainty in the naturalistic view, in which authority rests upon either an unequal natural predisposition or upon moral excellence and education. His use of the term "guest" allows a choice as to which person should be honored by the highest, to some degree symbolic, position in the state.

In Ming Chinese thought, the concept of equality aims to distribute authority among a certain class of well-trained scholars with high moral standards who, in an altruistic way and with selfless ambitions, take the affairs of "that under heaven" (*tianxia*; meaning the empire) as their own affairs. Huang pleads for equity in the recruitment of scholars and argues against clan authority as the base of political authority. Huang's theory had a great impact on later generations, more so than in his own time. Progressive thinkers at the end of the Qing dynasty take up the idea of the "guest emperor" in a very literal sense, considering Manchu rule as transient and the Manchu emperors rather as parasites. The polemic reading of Huang's treatise, however, loses sight of Huang's effort to rebuild a society which excludes conditions of authority based on clan structure and tries to dissolve the common equation of nature and society.

The Inequality of Nature and Society: Kang Youwei (1858–1927)

To express his new social outlook, Huang uses traditional vocabulary. Chinese thinkers at the end of the 19th century, however, operated with new terms. For expressing the meaning of equality, the Buddhist term *pingdeng* became prominent. The solitary term *ping* denotes the even level of water. In ancient political texts, the term is used in an active sense meaning "bringing something to peace," that is to secure a country, a nation, or a revolting state. *Deng* denotes a relation: two things belong to the same class or have the same value. The combination of *pingdeng* was coined by the Buddhists to describe the mind at rest in the process of meditation. In this state of mind, distinctions of the characteristics of the visualized objects disappear, and *samatā*, "sameness," becomes manifest. In a negative definition, *samatā* connotes the absence of all characteristics.

The terms *ping* and *deng* become popular through Jesuit translations of Euclidian geometry in China, as well. *Ping* denotes the quality of being "even" like in *pingmian*, "plain surface," or *pinghang*, "parallel lines".[23] Here, to be even means to share common characteristics, therefore all points of a plain surface can be described by one identical algebraic function. *Deng* is the special term for "equation" or "is equal to".

Taking *ping* and *deng* in their algebraic sense, the compound *pingdeng* is not very meaningful and rather tautological. The idea of equality as an algebraic and geometrical function became very popular in 19th century China, and the discourse on equality using the Buddhist compound *pingdeng* makes use of the mathematical imagination.

The Chinese vocabulary for expressing equality is different: equal distribution is usually expressed by *jun*, as in *jun tian,* "the equal distribution of land". As seen above, Ming tractates borrow the term of friendship for discussing human equality or equal social status. The meaning "community" and "co-existence" are expressed by *tong*. The word for peaceful coexistence among different nations, *hetong*, became familiar in modern China with the propagation of international law.[24] In traditional Chinese philosophy, the vocabulary for different kinds of equality varies, and claims for social equality are therefore not necessarily linked with claims for material equality, as can be seen in the thought of Huang Zongxi. The modern term *pingdeng*, applied to socio-political discourse, however, covers a broad spectrum of meanings. Transferred from Buddhist meditation practice to society and applied to abstract geometrical problems, the term is not bound to traditional pragmatics and is freed for every kind of use. *Pingdeng* denotes equality in social status and social authority, human natural equality, as well as equal distribution of land and wealth, peace and security. With the term *pingdeng*, different aspects of equality can be treated together.

The new political scene imperial China was faced with in the 19th century stimulated a new discussion on equality. Having become an agent on the stage of international politics, China had the need to develop a new framework to manage contacts with other political powers and with her partners in foreign trade. Traditional principles based on patterns like the

---

23   Cf. Engelfriet 1998, pp. 282, 284.
24   Article in the *Shenbao* 26th February 1888, cf. Svarverud 2007, pp. 146-147.

ruler and his subordinate or on the imperial tribute system could no longer be employed. The introduction of the American concept of international law proclaimed by the *Shenbao* and other journals[25] received a great audience.

On the other hand, the forces of the Heavenly Kingdom of Great Peace (*Taiping tianguo*)[26] cast aside traditional social hierarchies, thereby building up a new authoritative structure. Human equality was seen as an eschatological goal. Equality was seen as a feature of peace and harmony (*ping*). Furthermore, the French Revolution and the American Declaration appear in China in the last decades of the 19th century and had a great impact on concepts of society. Political participation and political representation by congregations (*hui*) become common issues in the political debates of the last decade and led to a great number of activities at a local level. Ideas from the French Revolution of the civil virtues of the individual instead of the nation as the common good become popular. Traditional society was blamed for the oppression of women; political activists fought for the equal status of women in society.

Social pressure and social inequality, however, treated in various treatises about statecraft, seemed not to have a great impact on the discussions of social equality. Traditional conceptions of social welfare and how to adjust the nation's resources to urgent needs of poverty seemed to be still effective enough to settle ongoing uprisings and social unrest.

Kang Youwei became known as a supporter of the great political reform in 1898, rebuilding new institutions with the emperor in the centre after the model of Meiji Japan, thereby downgrading the existing bureaucracy.[27] The reform failed and Kang became famous in the intellectual history of modern China as one of the first great intellectuals who had to leave the country and to live in exile.[28] Before Kang became active in court policies he lectured and wrote in the south of China, gradually extending his influence in scholarly circles.

Before engaging in the reform movement, Kang set out his ideas for a future society in several writings. In the present paper, I will discuss Kang's *Comprehensive Writings on the Common Laws [based on] the Principles of Reality* (*Shili gongfa quanshu*), which only became known quite recently.[29]

---

25 Cf. Svarverud 2007, pp. 140-150.
26 The popular revolt began in southern Guangxi province in early 1851 and secured control of the central and lower Yangtse area between 1853 and 1864.
27 Cf. Zarrow 2004.
28 Cf. Wordern 1972.
29 The date of completion of the *Common Laws* may be the beginning of the last decade of the 19th century. In Kang's autobiographical writings he describes

Most material for the study of modern progressive Chinese thought first gets published in a much later date or even after the death of their authors. Kang's ideas, although unknown to most contemporary scholars, circulated through various networks at the end of the Qing dynasty.

In his sketch of society, Kang distinguishes between the natural conditions of man called "principles of reality" (*shili*) and their social application called "common laws" (*gongfa*).[30] Kang clearly sees nature and society as two different realms, each of them possessing its own set of norms and rules. The ideal society has to be based on both, on social as well as natural conditions. The equation of both sets of rules, however, does not always succeed. It requires a third standard whereby differences can be regulated. This third standard is called "proportion" (*bili*) by Kang, perhaps better understood as "lesser alternatives" (according to Li San-pao).[31]

In Kang's view, as society comprises different phenomena, different approaches should be chosen, for them he divides his book into several "entrances" (*men*) in accord with Buddhist dogmatic literature. The first and most basic entrance is the "entrance of mankind" (*renlei men*). Kang lays down four principles of reality which define the humans' natural condition:

---

his earlier works as steps on his path to his master piece, the *Book of Great Unity* (*Datong shu*) which he drafted during his exile. Although the *Common Laws* resemble in some way the *Great Unity*, sketching out a plan of an ideal society, the main idea is quite different, and the book lacks the utopian and radical spirit of the *Great Unity*. Kang's *Common Laws* seem to be more notes of his own ideas which became subject to re-formulating and re-writing. In his autobiography, Kang mentions a piece titled *Universal Principles of Humankind* (*Renlei gongli*) which he has written during his time as a recluse in Yunnan and Guangdong provinces in 1885. The *Universal Principles* are lost. The *Common laws* may represent a later re-written version of this early treatise; see Tang Zhijun in his foreword to the edition of the *Datong shu* (Kang Youwei 2009, p. 4). The title "*Shili gongfa quanshu*" dates from the edition of Kang's manuscripts published by Jiang Guilin, a late pupil of Kang, in Taiwan in 1976. Jiang's publication goes back to holdings of Kang's work in the Hoover Institute of the Stanford University. Completed with other holdings of Kang's writings conserved in the Shanghai Museum, a more complete version of the *Shili gongfa quanshu* was published nine years later in Shanghai (cf. Weizheng Zhu's foreword in Kang 1998, p. 27 notes 6 and 7). See also Li San-pao 1978, who provides an English translation of Kang's *Common Laws*; Sakade 1985, pp. 91-92; Wu Xizhao 1988; Zang Shijun 1997, pp. 60-77.

30 For Kang "principles of reality" are "empirically by scientific investigation" (Kang Youwei 1998, p. 5; compare Li San-pao's translation (1978, p. 693, cf. also p. 697)); Li San-pao translates *shili* as "substantial truths" and *gongfa* as "universal principles".

31 Li San-pao, 1998, p. 700.

(1) Each man takes part in the raw matter of heaven and earth to become man.
(2) Each man has one soul, whereby he has knowledge and perception, what is called "intellect". The quality of the spiritual soul, however, differs in each man.
(3) Man at the time of his birth has the two [emotional] attributes of loving and hating. When he grows up, and has contacts with other people, his emanation of his loving attribute must be useful for others and his emanation of his hating attribute must be helpful for others. Furthermore, loving and hating can only be mutually productive, but cannot be used together.
(4) Man at time of his birth has "confidence," but no actual intent to defraud others. Humans come to defraud others because of their habits.[32]

The first principle is a mere reformulation of the common Confucian anthropological view: each human is part of the stuff of heaven and earth (in analogue to the "breath" (*qi*) in the traditional vocabulary). In opposition to the naturalistic view, Kang does not acknowledge different grades of similarity in the composition of "breath" according to different clans. The second principle is a refinement of the first one; Kang accepts the Christian doctrine of a single soul in man's body. At the first glance, the second principle resembles the traditional view of the intellectual capacity and moral disposition in human beings. Kang's conclusion, however, is not difference in intellectual capacity or moral excellence, but a human's individuality. Each human being is unique in his composition of the cosmic stuff. Individual difference, however, does not result in moral superiority or inferiority, as is stated in traditional Chinese anthropology. Human beings should not be privileged over other kinds of thing. The individual natures of human beings are equally good; if born in ideal circumstances human beings do not develop bad habits and aggressiveness.

Human nature comprises two emotional tendencies which are basic in social communication. Human nature tends to association with each other, thus fixing social structures, and human nature tends to regulate or educate each other, thus, dispelling bad habits and influences and protecting the good. In Kang's view, human nature can be seen as naturally inclined to be social, although the social tendencies of human nature easily can become subject to bad habits and lose their natural orientation.

The first three conditions for a society ("common laws," *gongfa*), are related to the four principles of reality (here translated with Kang's own comments):

---

32 Kang Youwei 1998, p. 7; cf. Li San-pao 1978, p. 699.

(1) Man has the right of being his own lord.
   Comment: This is a law which stems from the axioms of geometry. As one man shares with other men the matter of heaven and earth to become man and as every man combines the real principle of one soul, this [principle] is the most fruitful one for the human way.
(2) The laws which man establish have to been made in the spirit of equality.
   Comment: Human equality is an axiom of geometry. Laws made by men, however, cannot be effective if they are [made by] all [of them]; only if they are made [by some men] in the spirit of equality, they can be effective.
(3) Laws [should] be made in such a way that people could restrain one another. For all men of the whole world in antiquity and contemporary times, there should not be one single man who is exempt from being restrained.
   Comment: This is a principle derived from geometrical axioms and is most beneficial to the human way.[33]

Natural individuality requires social autonomy. Common law and social norms, on the other hand, require authority besides individual autonomy. Kang provides two solutions to this problem. A presumption of equality should be the guiding principle in the legislative act, while equal access to authority and equal participation in authority should guarantee people's equal social status.

Kang considers the common laws as derivations from so called "axioms of geometry".[34] This proposition is a little bit puzzling. I suggest an analogical reading. Kang sees society as a construction of individuals like the (idealized) construction of a line from individual points. Therefore, the autonomy of a human being is analogous to the idealized incommensurability of the point in Euclidean geometry. Points are the basis of lines, and every other figure is constructed by using them. No point can take the place of another point; points are not mutually interchangeable. No entity (line, figure, society) can be construed without every single autonomous point. Thus, in the construction of the whole figure every point enjoys equal dignity. Giving each point a different value would destroy the whole figure.

There is still another aspect to Kang's argumentation which needs to be pointed out. In his comment on the first law, Kang mentions a utilitarian principle explaining why every individual should enjoy autonomy. As each man equally shares heaven and earth, it must be the exploitation of the fruitfulness of heaven and earth if each man can contribute the maximum of his share to the common good.

---

33 Kang Youwei 1998, pp. 7-8; cf. Li San-pao's translation (1998, pp. 699-700).
34 Compare the important role of geometrical proportion in Aristotle's discussion of justice (Nic. Eth. V.iv).

To conclude, Kang Youwei starts his discussion with a separation of nature and society, which had been equated in former traditional social theory. This separation does not allow an implantation of the norms of nature into the social realm. Therefore, there must be a principle of transfer, which Kang calls "equality" (*pingdeng*), which, however, is better understood as "adequacy". Social norms as a whole should adequately reflect the natural conditions of man: natural individuality requires social autonomy, human equality requires political participation. Principles in the construction of geometrical figures are seen as guidelines for this transference. Besides this, Kang, in line with the scholars in Ming dynasty and with the naturalistic view, acknowledges natural human equality, as every human being possesses the same kind of material stuff. Kang, however, does not draw the conclusion of human dignity or respect resulting from a common dignity towards the creative forces of nature, as late Ming thinkers had. According to Kang, human equality defines individuality through utilitarian and functional reasons. Individuality demands principles of equality in order to secure the whole welfare of nature. Here, Kang's conclusion is far away from Huang Zongxi's common good which serves as a principle of social action. For Huang, human social action differs from human natural conditions, which only result in individual action. By contrast, for Kang, social action is a function resulting from individual actions by giving individuality equal value. Inequality in value would destroy the whole function. Therefore, although Huang and Kang both agree in separating nature and society they provide quite different solutions for how nature and society should be organized as two distinct domains of human action.

The Learning of Humanity:
Tan Sitong (1865–1898)

Tan Sitong, formerly engaged in the reform movement in Hunan province around the Academy of Actual Affairs (*Shiwu xuetang*) in 1898,[35] was recommended to the reform-minded officials at court in August 1898. As the reform party and the emperor himself was threatened by a revolt of conservative and military forces under the influence of the empress dowager, Tan unsuccessfully made an attempt to win over the assistance of the military leader Yuan Shikai (1859–1916), who officially became the first president of the Republic of China in 1916. In October 1898, Tan was sentenced to death. His friend Liang Qichao (1873–1929), who succeeded in escaping to

---

35 Cf. Lewis 1969, pp. 35–42.

Japan, painted Tan's death in the colors of martyrdom, making Tan known as one of the six martyrs of the "Hundred Day Reform Movement".

Tan left a manuscript titled *Learning of Humanity* (*Renxue*) explaining his ideas on a "new learning" (*xinxue*) for mankind, which Liang Qichao published in Japan after his death.[36] Tan's "new learning" is designated to serve as a new religion and ideology for a global society combining basic and common ideas in the religions and societies in East and West. It is rather unlikely that Tan ever read Kang's *Common Laws* — Tan did not know Kang Youwei personally[37] —, but Tan was at least familiar with Kang's messianic theory of a future society developed in accordance with a schema of historical decay mentioned in the chapter "The Transformation of the Rites" ("Li yun") of the *Book of Rites* (*Liji*).[38]

Although he finished writing the *Learning of Humanity* in summer 1897, Tan did not publish his major work as he originally intended to do. Instead, he distributed his work to some friends, for example, to his Hunanese compatriot Tang Caichang or to his friend Liang Qichao. At the Academy, Tan became well known for his work and earned some literary and political recognition, but the people who saw the *Learning of Humanity* were few and Tan himself rarely mentions it in 1898. And where he did, he distanced himself from it, claiming that the time for the realization of his "new learning" was not ripe yet.

The significance of Tan's "new learning" in modern Chinese philosophy is still a very controversial issue: readings differ widely. One question arises from Tan's use of the concept of *ren*. According to the traditional meaning, *ren* is an ethical value applied to human action, human ideas or to a social government.[39] In traditional Confucian ethics, human actions, to which *ren* is assigned, do not pursue selfish goals, are neither unjust nor partial. Therefore, "to act in a selfless way" (*ren*) exposes the true value of man (*ren*, a homophone). *Ren* as a term of moral excellence is seen as the most distinct feature of mankind, unfolding what makes man human, namely his "humanity". Confucian thinkers stress the point that everyone — being a human being — equally has the opportunity to develop this excellence, even if intellec-

---

36 Tan's *Learning of Humanity* first became published after his death by Liang Qichao in a serial which Liang founded in Japan, and shortly afterwards, in Shanghai; Tang Caichang (1876–1900) began to publish Tan's major work in a serial financed and organized by a Japanese secret society, as well. Manuscripts or bromides for the several editions are not known. Corrections of the editors can not be verified. Cf. Tang Zhijun 1984; Schilling 2002.
37 Zhang 1962, pp. 81-85; Chan 1984, pp. 15-16.
38 Cf. Tan Sitong 1998. pp. 367-368.
39 For a discussion on the pivotal term *ren* see also the article by Achim Mittag in this volume.

tual capacity and social conditions may differ.[40] By acting in a selfless way (*ren*), man can exhaust his moral capacity to the utmost, transcending the limits of his inborn natural tendencies, creating a just and humane society, unlike other living beings which only can exist according to their natural design and functions. In this sense, humanity (*ren*) connotes a good social establishment against the forces of a raw and blind nature.

In an attempt to expose the uniform pattern underlying nature and society, Song Confucians conceptualize *ren* as a quality of the life-giving forces of "heaven" and "earth". "Heaven" and "earth" are altruistic in their spreading of fertility and productiveness. The human way modeled after the way of heaven should be productive and fertile, as well. Human society called *ren* is a fruitful society securing peace and wealth for everyone. In the naturalistic view, *ren* prescribes good government for all people disregarding their difference in social status.

There is a great discrepancy among traditional Confucian views about the manifestation of *ren* in human natural disposition, but there is a common view that humanity is based on social activity at least and that human beings are considered as social entities. Tan follows the traditional meaning, recognizing *ren* as the basic characteristic of mankind, as man's "humaneness" or "humanity". In his view, *ren*, however, is not only a quality of moral excellence, which makes man humane, but a force which overcomes any boundaries, partitions, and terminations. As such a force, *ren* follows the laws of nature, conceptualized by Tan as geometrical and algebraic equations. *Ren* is ubiquitous: as "attraction" (*aili, xili*) *ren* exercises power in chemical reactions.[41] As a "mental force" (*xinli*), *ren* overcomes the fundamental distinction of self-perception ("I") and outer-world ("You").[42] For Tan, a selfless act (*ren*) is not merely an act with a high moral quality but a kind of existential transformation. Tan calls this transformation "communication" (*tong*),[43] a term which was first used in the *Great Commentary* (*Dazhuan*; 3rd century BC) to the oracle book *Book of Changes* (*Yijing*) to explain the effect of the oracle as a connection between man and the gods. In the middle ages, *tong* describes the experience of Buddhist enlightenment. According to Tan, if "communication" is realized an individual has lost his perception to be a distinct person but is part of a single common "consciousness".[44]

Tan gives two explanations of why selfless action is not only morally good but performs an existential transformation.

---

40 Cf. *Mengzi*, 6B.2.
41 Tan Sitong 1998, p. 294.
42 Ibid., pp. 296, 364-365.
43 Ibid., pp. 291, 296.
44 Ibid., pp. 295-296, 365.

First, selfless action overcomes the insensibility in present cognition to see oneself as a distinct person from another person. Selfless action meets a deeper structure of consciousness because the basic substance of every entity possesses a kind of intrinsic sensibility which is obstructed by false cognition. Thus, selfless action re-establishes a primary native knowledge or awareness of man.[45] According to the 19th century physical concept of overall luminiferous ether Tan calls this substance *yitai*, a phonetic transliteration.[46]

Second, selfless action forces others to clear themselves of their own limited self-perception. Selfless action transforms the self and transforms the other. The reversal of perceptions is explained by the Buddhist conception of mind. Self-perception and the perception of other individuals are illusionary acts of a mind divided in several capacities which — mutually alluding to each other — conjointly produce a flux of perceptions. Neither an independent outer world nor an independent thinking subject is given. Perceptions are the result of a solipsistic and idealistic functioning of mind.[47]

There is a great discussion concerning Buddhist Vijñānavada theory (the "Mind Only school" which claims that phenomena exist only as activities of the mind). Tan is referring to how individual minds are interrelated to each other and how individual mind is receptive of other minds.[48] He develops a theory of his own, claiming that the individual mind is a result of historical development. The universal mind once stirred up by ignorance (*wuming*, *avidyā*) ceaselessly continues to produce illusionary perceptions.[49] Tan calls false cognition "karmic cognition" (*yeshi*).[50] "Karmic cognition" denotes both a collective mental activity which is responsible for the existence of individual mental activity and the inherent dynamic of individual mental activity which determines future individual mental activity.

Moreover, Tan explains karmic cognition as a shared collective mentality. Individuals share certain perceptions and construct collective mentality in turn. In this view, habits, tradition, values, and social behavior are all reflections of karmic cognition. Mentality defines social behavior and organization. Distinctions like the "five bonds" originate from karmic cognition. Like many other progressive thinkers during his time, Tan regards the mentality of the Chinese people as the main source of China's actual political misery and seeks to awaken the mind of the people.[51]

---

45 Tan Sitong 1998, pp. 295-296.
46 Ibid.; cf. Schäfer 2001; Wright 1994; Talbott 1960.
47 Tan Sitong 1998, pp. 363-365.
48 Cf. Piatigorsky 1983.
49 Tan Sitong 1998, p. 330.
50 Ibid.
51 Ibid., pp. 323-325, 341-342.

Blending individual and collective thinking together, Tan considers mentality as historically constructed and originated from a continuous irregular psychological function of mind. At the end, social mentality is conditioned by psychological facts such as self-perception. Consequently, selfless actions, which disregard interest arousing from self-perception, are able to cease the mechanics of karmic cognition. In Tan's explanation, every individual mental activity is a "machine mind" (*jixin*) which can be analyzed as a "mind force" (*xinli*) sharing common features with other physical forces. Mind force acts like vibrations, vibrating up and down, or like elasticity, springing to and fro. Vibrating mental activity is considered by Tan as irregular and irregularity is the reason for the continuity of false cognition. Consequently, the mechanism of false cognition has to be altered by releasing irregularity, which means to avoid thinking in distinctions like "I" and "You".[52]

To sum up, a selfless action transforms the self into a deeper reality marked by a new identity. The mental force will be directed against the "machine mind" and the vibrating mechanism will calm down its dynamism, discontinuing the sequence of illusory perceptions. Tan calls the result of such selfless action *pingdeng*, "equality". *Pingdeng* can be understood in the Buddhist context as the balanced and equally leveled mind. Tan, however, views the equalized mind as better understood through the mechanistic metaphor and refers to the psychological explanations of Henry Wood (1834–1908), an author with close filiations to the American New Thought movement in the 19th century.[53]

Interestingly enough, in the *Learning of Humanity*, *pingdeng* is not only a principle or a rule for how to organize a just society and how to distribute rights and goods; *pingdeng* describes to a certain degree whether a single action can succeed or fail. The mental activity of the enlightened mind is considered as to be "equal," the activity of the unenlightened mind is unequal and irregular. On the other hand, if individual mental activity became "equal," individuality would be diminished. The activity of mind is replaced by other forms of communication and sensibility.

Tan's concept of *pingdeng*, "equality," abolishes individually oriented cognition by creating a unified cognition. Thus, *pingdeng* consists of two different functions, equating and unifying. In a strict sense, if two individuals are unified in a single entity, equality as a relation between two distinct entities no longer exists. However, according to Tan, the unified entity pro-

---

52 Tan Sitong 1998, pp. 363-365.
53 Henry Wood's book *Ideal Suggestion Through Mental Photography* was translated into Chinese by the missionary John Fryer in Shanghai 1896 (cf. Shek 1976).

duced by equation is not a single entity. The former entities still continue to exist in some manner although they do not possess an individual identity any more. Tan's conception can be interpreted such in a way that *pingdeng* destroys individual identity by producing collective identity. In my view, what Tan calls "communication" (*tong*) — being the aim or the result of a selfless act (*ren*) — can be considered as an act executed by a joint identity or collective mind. Tan's explanation that *pingdeng* is the specific characteristic of "communication" can be understood in the sense that the cognitive activity of several individuals performs uniform acts, thereby realizing a kind of collective identity.

The pragmatics of Tan's philosophic vocabulary in the *Learning of Humanity* — for example, the terms *ren*, "selfless humane action," *tong*, "communication," *ming*, "name," or *pingdeng*, "equality" — are not restricted to one single context. On the contrary, context shifting is a fundamental method of his philosophy. Only concepts with an equivalent meaning applied to various contexts convey the task of Tan's "new learning" to integrate distinct disciplines within a unit. Tan's "new learning" constitutes itself through three disciplines: physics, society, and religion. Therefore, the concept "communication" (*tong*) refers to the effects of electricity or of the etheric medium in the physical context; in the social context it denotes telegraphic systems and railway connections; in the spiritual context it means a form of community of minds. *Ming*, "name," equally refers to mental concepts and social hierarchical positions, both of which obstruct equality.[54] The usage of *ming* in the sense of social position is an anachronism coming from the vocabulary of ancient political discourse, which was re-introduced in the 19th century with the revival of ancient non-Confucian textual traditions. In Tan's terminology, the "five bonds" are "names," as well.[55] Likewise, distinct perceptions like "I" and "You" are "names," leading one to believe in an individual identity. Consequently, the meaning of *pingdeng*, equality, can be found in different contexts in the *Learning of Humanity*, as well: *pingdeng* demands the abolition of social distinctions, for example, the distinction between man and woman or between political classes. It qualifies physical primal matter as well as the principles behind evolution: the shape of earth, for example, changes from irregular formations to a more regular form. As Tan regards intellectuality as a necessary requisite for com-

---

54 The eighth chapter begins with the statement "Names are responsible for the confusion of benevolence" (citing Chan Sin-wai's translation, 1984, p. 77); see also subsequent *Renxue*, chapters 8, 9 for Tan's refutation of names (Tan Sitong 1998, pp. 299-302).
55 Tan Sitong 1998, p. 348.

passion and empathy, the steadfast increase of human intellectuality displays the evolution of man.[56]

The logic of Tan's theory rests on basic concepts used as universal patterns. The principles of physics are not different from the principles of society or of religion, or vice versa. Acting according to these patterns or principles means evoking universal results. Acting in the social realm has an effect on physical nature. An effect on psychological qualities changes social and physical conditions. All these patterns converge in the basic relation of distinct perceptions, in the prejudiced view of self as an independent reality. *Ren* as selfless action, therefore, is in Tan's soteriology the starting point of universal change.

The universal function of *ren* asks for a precise universal meaning. *Ren* in the sense of what makes man human is both part of nature (material and spiritual) and society but is not, however, restricted to a specific human action or moral quality but to an abstract concept of action or reality. This abstract meaning of *ren* can be summarized as the act by which equation (*pingdeng*) produces identity ("communication," *tong*). This interpretation has some support from various connotations in Tan's etymology of the character *ren* in the Introduction to his book:[57] according to Tan, the character for the word *ren* 仁 is written with the character for the word "man" 人 and the character for the word "two" 二. The basic definition of *ren* as an act of equation is conserved in the character for "two". Moreover, Tan identifies in the characters of *yuan* 元, "primal source," and *wu* 无, "nothingness," the same construction in their writing forms as being a compound of the single characters for "man" (written by the alternative form 儿) and "two". Tan's etymology can be interpreted to mean that the meaning and function behind the three characters 仁, 元 and 无 are essentially the same. As the three characters represent the three disciplines,[58] the definition of *ren* as an act of equation is true not only for the human realm of society but for the principles behind all the material and spiritual phenomena in nature.

In this sense, Tan's theory of humanity can be understood as a strong re-affirmation of the claims of the naturalistic view, that is, that nature and society not only follow identical principles but display a common structure. The structure underlying nature and society according to Tan, however, is not defined by hierarchies but by equality. On the other side, in Tan's view, society enjoys only ephemeral value. In the natural evolution from coarseness to fineness and from material complexity to spiritual equality social

---

56 Tan Sitong 1998, pp. 330-331.
57 Ibid., p. 289.
58 Physics is represented by *yuan*, the primal source of all matter, society by *ren*, humanity, and religion by *wu*, nothingness as the spiritual realm.

organization is merely a transient being. It is evident that Tan's concept of equality breaks with the continuity of intellectual efforts using equality as a principle to construct a society based on human effort and common interest (Huang Zongxi) or on equal organization, individuality and free will (Kang Youwei).

In my view, Tan's interest in a re-construction of a theory of human action which is largely deterministic is due to his interest in political activism. Tan argues in two ways: human action which comes from "karmic knowledge" is predetermined, and therefore the effects of human action can be predicted. Selfless action like compassion, however, breaks out of the karmic continuity and offers a choice for realizing an unpredicted event. Due to the laws of determinism, this event will have unchangeable effects on future events.

Following this logic, Tan delineates a program of "converting others" (*du ren*) in the last two chapters of his book that can be read as a program to motivate others for political activism. Tan's language, however, is the language of Buddhist soteriology, and the political significance of his phrases largely has to be decoded. The phrase "converting others," literally "to ferry others across," is derived from the metaphor for the converting and liberating power of the bodhisattva. According to Tan's conception of individual solipsistic minds, "converting others" can not be considered an action which exerts direct influence on an individual mind, but every individual mind has to become enlightened by his own effort and spontaneously. Therefore, there must be the condition that the individual mind can become enlightened by itself. Tan locates this condition in the flux of events. He explains his theory of "converting others" by citing a phrase from the commentary of the *Book of Changes*:

The *Book of Changes* says, "The empire is such that the same destination can be arrived at by different paths, and the same conclusion arrived at by a hundred thoughts."[59]

His explanation is as follows:

The reason why it does not say that different paths arrive at the same destination, or that a hundred thoughts arrive at the same conclusion is that being different, they can no longer be the same. Not that there is any harm in their being the same; of course, there is no need to make them the same either. Being a hundred, they can no longer be one. Not that there is any harm in their being one; and of course, they certainly cannot be made to be one by force. Alas, the situation of the world can be

---

59 Tan Sitong 1998, p. 372; the translation cited is taken from Chan Sin-wai (1984, p. 225).

compared to the flowing of a river. Once it has passed, it is never the same again. This is why the *Book of Changes* begins with the Hexagram "*ch'ien*" (create) and ends with the Hexagram "*wei chi*" (incomplete).[60]

The expressions "same destination" and "a hundred" in the soteriological context mean the function of the individual mind as an enlightened mind. The individual is converted but still continues to exist as an individual mind, therefore, his conversion was not "made [...] by force". To enlighten others cannot be an act of instruction. Applied to the context of political activism, political aims are collective beliefs, but a belief requires personal appreciation, an intimate identification with its content and a selfless willingness for its realization. In Tan's view, this can be achieved by creating an event which will change all subsequent events at one moment. Tan's program of political activism tries to convert others by an event which wins over the estimation of others.

In this context, *ren* should be read in the specific meaning of "to commit suicide" as in the phrase "to die for a noble cause" (*chengren quyi*).[61] In the eyes of Tan, martyrdom seems to be the most effective way to change the flux of events and to change the thinking of other individuals. In a list of "Definitions" ("Jieshuo") in front of his "new learning" — whereby imitating Euclid's *Elements* — Tan defines martyrdom by the term *pingdeng*, "equation".[62] Tan first defines *pingdeng* in a negative way as "not to have any opposite" (*wu duidai*). Since life is the opposite of death, an act which achieves *pingdeng* transcends the limits of life and death. The further consequences of martyrdom equally can be predicted by the principles of equation:

Because there is equality between "not to be born" and "not to die," there is equality between "to be born" (life) and "to die" (death), and also equality between "to be born and to die" (life and death) on the one hand and "not to be born and not to die" on the other.[63]

The consequences are given by several equations: "not to be born" and "not to die" do not belong to an individual life. Consequently, they are equal. On the contrary, "to be born" and "to die" equally qualify individual life. Since the two equations both evolve "equality," the two equations can be equated once more. The principle of equation first defines the concepts mortal "individuality" ("to be born" and "to die") and "immortality" ("not to be born"

---

60 Chan Sin-wai 1984, p. 225. The Wade Giles transliteration of Chan Sin-wai was corrected.
61 Tan Sitong 1998, p. 309.
62 Ibid., pp. 291-292.
63 Ibid., p. 292; cf. Chan 1984, p. 63.

and "not to die"), then how the two concepts are interrelated to each other. I suggest the following reading of the "Definitions" by decoding Tan's language in the context of his aim for political martyrdom: "To die for a noble cause" makes the noble cause reality, thereby altering all future events and individual actions. Such an act bestows upon an individual ("to be born and to die") immortality ("not to be born and not to die"). The immortal noble cause ("not to be born and not to die"), therefore, will be preserved in every individual human action ("to be born and to die") in future. In Tan's program for political action the meaning of *pingdeng* underwent a radical change from equality to identity.

Conclusion

The use of the concept of equality in modern Chinese political thought originates from the denial of any innate authority in the naturalistic view. At the end of the Qing dynasty, while radicalism is growing, distribution or regulating access and possession of authority clear the way for a radical denying of any authority and for acting against any authority.

Since the end of the Ming dynasty in the middle of the 17th century, political thought tries to define authority beyond the traditional naturalistic view that social distinctions are manifestations of natural inequality. To do this, thinkers in the Ming dynasty separate nature and society and recognize equality as a basic condition for human living, while inequality may continue to be a distinct feature of the natural human condition. In the social thought of Huang Zongxi the concern for the common good should regulate access to and possession of authority. Huang defines this concern as equally shared by a certain ruling class of moral excellence. Equality, here, becomes a crucial factor which underlies Huang's social organization. At the end of the Qing dynasty at the turn of the19th/20th centuries, Kang Youwei recognizes equality as a natural principle of organizing and providing unequal entities. Therefore, a just society should manifest the variety of nature as widely as possible. In his social design, this principle should be reflected in the social organization as clearly as possible. Kang's use of equality in a prescriptive sense, for society is justified by its descriptive sense in human nature. A return to a more naturalistic view and deterministic theory of action occurs in the thought of Tan Sitong. This reversal can be explained by Tan's interest in building up a program for political activism. In his *Learning of Humanity*, the concept of equality advances to a religious dogma highly promoted by a broad range of connotations and analogies and expressed in an ambiguous and encoded language. Tan's *Learning of Humanity*, therefore, marks a shift in political literature towards the function of mass propaganda.

It is noteworthy that modern Chinese thinkers rarely refer to the idea of natural rights to justify claims of equality. Huang and Kang both appeal to utilitarian reasons, Kang and Tan to mathematical conditions. Human dignity, which became an idea early in the thought of some thinkers at the end of the Ming dynasty, was not at that time further developed into a theoretical basis for the equality of individuals.

Inventing Humanism in Modern China

KE ZHANG

When the young Chinese botanist Hu Xiansu (1894–1968) first used the term *renwen zhuyi* in 1922 to translate the American critic Irving Babbitt's (1865–1933) concept of "humanism," he did not expect that for later generations, this term would become so divergent in meaning.[1] Some ten years later, the renowned Chinese scholar Hu Shi (1891–1962) used the term "humanist movement" in a lecture delivered in Chicago University to define the cultural movement taking place in the first two decades of the 20th century in China, which he considered similar to the humanist movement during the European Renaissance.[2] We may see it as the beginning of the journey of "humanism" in modern China, which has not yet ended.

In the 1990s, there was a nationwide discussion in China on contemporary humanism. Most of the authors engaged in the discussion considered it a fundamental problem to find a proper definition of "humanism" in Chinese.[3] Although the term they used was "humanistic spirit" (*renwen jingshen*) which differed subtly, both in literalness and implication, from the term *renwen zhuyi*, almost all of them traced the concept back to the English word "humanism" or the German word "*Humanismus*". However, with very few exceptions, no one in this discussion regarded humanism merely as a certain movement during and after the Renaissance period in Europe, nor *renwen zhuyi* as a certain movement before the 1930s in China, as Hu Shi asserted. Moreover, while the general assumption in the discussion was that humanism is a universally valid concept, it never acquired a settled

---
1 See Wu Mi 1995, p. 233. Both Wu Mi (1894–1978) and Hu Xiansu were Irving Babbitt's students.
2 See Hu Shi 2001, p. 79. The lecture was delivered in July, 1933.
3 Nearly all the articles in this discussion were collected in Wang Xiaoming 1996.

meaning. In some scholars' eyes the meaning of humanism was obvious and widely approved, but other scholars did notice the confusion that arose from the terminological inconsistency within the discussion. In his introduction to Alan Bullock's (1914–2004) book *The Humanist Tradition in the West*, the noted translator Dong Leshan (1924–1999) criticized some Chinese scholars for their ignorance of the connotation of the term "humanism" and the confusion of ideas they had brought on.[4]

In this case, probably one cannot help asking why the simple term *renwen zhuyi* could be so ambiguous in meaning in the past eighty years. Therefore, this article will take it as the starting point and try to track the shifting meaning of "humanism" in Chinese contexts. As is well known from postmodernist theory, the fixed hypothetical equivalence between words and their meanings has been doubted. If we take Jacques Derrida's (1930–2004) view of language as "an infinite play of signification," which implies that every time the word is uttered, its relation with other words in the semantic system changes,[5] we may deepen our understandings of the term "humanism". However, I shall not go further and deny the existence of the transcendental signified, which determines meaning in itself, as Derrida did.

Moreover, I think it is more reasonable to regard the concept "humanism" as an interpretative, rather than a substantiative term referring to the past. The Dutch philosopher Franklin Ankersmit (born 1945) proposed the important notion "narrative substance" in his early book *Narrative Logic*. He took the term "Renaissance" as an example of narrative substance, and argued that terms like this "do not refer to things in or aspects of, the past, but exclusively to narrative interpretations of the past".[6] Some scholars have already pointed out that humanism can also be viewed as a narrative substance whose meaning is determined by different interpreters, not directly by the historical facts.[7] Therefore, the term humanism is more open and uncertain in the field of meaning, as it is often used to fulfill the needs of different narrations.

Compared to the English term humanism, the Chinese renderings are by far more complicated when speaking of the translation *renwen zhuyi*, let alone the alternative ones such as *rendao zhuyi*. As we will see below, in the past eighty years, the word *renwen zhuyi* is clearly used in various texts by different authors. Therefore, I propose to consider *renwen zhuyi* as a narrative substance as well. However, my emphasis on this does not presuppose that *renwen zhuyi* was deliberately employed with a specific indication on

---

4 See the introduction by the translator Dong Leshan in Bullock 1997, p. 3.
5 See Derrida 1978, pp. 278-294.
6 Ankersmit 1981, p. 104.
7 Chinese historians also recognized this, see Chen Xin 2003, pp. 74-85.

every occasion. What I try to do here is to reveal the subtle and often unconscious shifts of the signified in different contexts. It is noted that, the diversity of signification within the term in the source language is, often magnified in the target language. Scholars like Lydia Liu are not satisfied with the distinction between source language and target language; instead Liu proposed the notions "host language" and "guest language". When a concept is translated from guest language into host language, as Liu observes, the meaning is invented in the local context of the host language, rather than merely changed.[8]

In this regard, the meaning of *renwen zhuyi* should not be seen as an equivalent of humanism, since the word *renwen zhuyi* in Chinese not only referred to a certain Western trend of thought, but was also tied to a specifically "Chinese humanism" or "Confucian humanism". Initially, the word *renwen* just happened to be taken from the ancient Chinese classics to translate "humanism," but as time went by, an essential equation was built between these two words in most Chinese scholars' minds. In this case, some scholars have recently pointed out that it is dangerous to fix the equivalence between "humanism" and *renwen zhuyi*.[9]

The aim of this article is twofold. Firstly, I will discuss the different translations of humanism and the associated controversies. Secondly, I will delineate the four stages of the invention of humanism in modern China. I will argue that both translations — *renwen zhuyi* and *rendao zhuyi* — arose from different discourses which bore specific realistic motives or academic intentions. When speaking of *renwen zhuyi*, a certain targeted audience and rivals, whom the authors bore in mind, matter. Not only the word "humanism," but also those to whom it was addressed, determine the meaning of *renwen zhuyi* in different contexts. Many of them added new connotations to the term *renwen zhuyi* and thus made it increasingly difficult to understand.

Different Chinese Translations of the Term "Humanism"

The term "humanism" in Western contexts is rich in meaning. It originates from the German term "*Humanismus*" which was first used by the German scholar Friedrich Immanuel Niethammer (1766–1848) in 1808.[10] Many historians in the 19th century, such as Georg Voigt (1827–1891) and Jacob

---

8 Lydia Liu 1995, pp. 25-27.
9 Li Guangbo 2001, p. 101.
10 Niethammer 1808.

Burckhardt (1818–1897), used this term to denote a certain intellectual phenomenon in Italy from the 14th through the 16th centuries, while philosophers like Arnold Ruge (1802–1880) and Karl Marx (1818–1883) used it in a much broader sense.[11] The 19th century also saw the English term "humanism" being broadened to denote human self-development and self-perfection.[12] The contemporary usage of humanism is even more generalized, "denoting a focus on human agents as the dominant and central actors in the world".[13]

However, historically, humanism bears the mark of the philosophical and literary movement in early modern Europe, in an effort to reclaim a position for humans in the hierarchy of the universe. The term "humanity" has usually been contrasted with "divinity" since the late 15th century.[14] Thus, the relationship between humanism and Christian thinking in early modern Europe has to be taken into account when studying the original meaning of humanism.

The Chinese intellectuals first noticed that the humanistic culture of the Italian Renaissance, or at least parts of it, could be traced back to the 17th century, in wake of the arrival of the Jesuit missionaries. The Jesuits introduced quite a few humanistic ideas in their works.[15] For instance, one aphorism from Erasmus was recorded in the Jesuit Matteo Ricci's (1552–1610) first Chinese composition "On Friendship" (Jiaoyou lun).[16] Nevertheless, since the Jesuits and their readers obviously knew no such thing as an integrative idea of humanism, therefore it would have been anachronistic for them to have marked what they discussed explicitly as "humanism". For the Jesuits and their European counterparts, the key controversy for centuries to come remained the conflicting ideas between Catholicism and traditional Chinese morality.[17]

The first known Chinese translation of the word "humanism" is the one in the 1901 book *European History* (*Ouluoba tongshi*). The original translation was written in Japanese. The term "humanism," which came up in the chapter about Renaissance, was rendered ideographically as *rendao pai* in Chinese, and the Chinese version kept this rendering.[18] Later on, many different translations of "humanism" emerged in Chinese.

---

11 Bödeker 1982, p. 1121.
12 Williams 1976, p. 151.
13 Bennett et al. 2005, p. 166.
14 Williams 1976, p. 150.
15 See Masini 1996.
16 Ricci 1965, p. 304.
17 See Gernet 1985.
18 Xu Youcheng et al. 1901, vol. 2, p. 63.

Although the earliest emergence of the term *renwen zhuyi* was detected in a Japanese-Chinese dictionary published in 1908,[19] it was not accepted by Chinese scholars until 1922 when Hu Xiansu introduced Babbitt's concept of Humanism. However, another translation, *rendao zhuyi*, came up in Chinese much earlier. According to recent studies, *rendao zhuyi* was first used in the dictionary *The New Approaching Correctness* (*Xin Erya*) published in 1903.[20] In 1918, when the writer Zhou Zuoren (1885–1967) published his article "Human Literature" (Ren de wenxue) in the magazine *New Youth* (*Xin qingnian*), he called for a new style of literature which should be based on the human being; he summarized this kind of literature as *rendao zhuyi*:

> The new literature we should now advocate, in short, is a human literature, and what we should exclude is the opposite. [...] The so-called humanism [*rendao zhuyi*], is not feeling of commiseration or philanthropy, but a kind of individualism focusing on human life. [...] The new literature should be based on this humanism [rendao zhuyi].[21]

Here Zhou Zuoren used the word *rendao zhuyi* to denote the direction of the new literature, and Zhou further suggested that we can hardly find any "human" literature in ancient China and that the literature coming from Confucianism and Daoism was not admissible as human literature. His article was influential as it indicated the rediscovery of the problem of human being in modern China, in the contemporary intellectual mainstream, that is, the "New Culture Movement" (*Xinwenhua yundong*).[22] Although most intellectual historians see this article as the first claim of Chinese humanism, Zhou himself used the term mainly in the field of literary criticism, and did not define it explicitly. Later in his own memoirs, he revealed his attempt to trace the origin of modern *rendao zhuyi* back to the Western Christian tradition of that time.[23]

The rendering of the English term "humanism" as *renwen zhuyi* in Chinese was perhaps achieved by sheer chance. In January 1922, when Hu Xiansu and Wu Mi discussed how to translate the term "humanism" in Irving Babbitt's article "Humanistic Education in China and in the West," Wu first proposed another term, *renben zhuyi*, which implies all the thoughts based on a human being. But Hu Xiansu, the acting translator of that article,

---

19 Ji Yuancheng et al. 1908, p. 71.
20 See Huang Heqing et al. 2001, p. 209. For the entries in the dictionary *Xin Erya* see Wang Rongbao and Ye Lan 1903, pp. 57, 70.
21 Zhou Zuoren 2002b, pp. 11-12.
22 Li Yi 2006, p. 78.
23 Zhou Zuoren 1982, p. 373.

had a different choice in mind: the term *renwen zhuyi*. And the latter finally was "adopted by all".[24] Meanwhile, Hu chose *rendao zhuyi* as the translation of "humanitarianism". Although the distinction of these two terms seems to be widely accepted by the succeeding scholars, or at least by most of the editors of dictionaries, it has been challenged from time to time. Up till now, it is still under dispute which term should be appropriate for translating humanism, especially in philosophical studies.

Before I go on to analyze the difference between *rendao zhuyi* and *renwen zhuyi*, first let us look into the etymology of the words *renwen* and *rendao* in Chinese, leaving out the shared suffix *zhuyi*, which means "-ism". Both terms have their origins in the Chinese classics. The word *renwen* was defined in the Confucian classic *The Book of Changes* (*Zhou Yi*),[25] while *rendao* was defined in the classic *The Commentary of Zuo* (*Zuozhuan*).[26] In these texts, *renwen* and *rendao* are respectively opposite to *tianwen* and *tiandao*, in which *tian* means "heaven" or "transcendental power" in ancient Chinese philosophy. In fact it is difficult to differentiate the meanings of *renwen* and *rendao* in Confucian classics, because what these ancient texts exactly meant remains debatable. Nevertheless, a subtle difference can perhaps be perceived in the signification of the words *wen* and *dao*, as the former indicates "cultivation," thus *renwen* refers to the "intellectual pursuit," while the latter means the "ultimate way," thus *rendao*, the "moral principle".

The strong implication of cultivation in the word *renwen* had been considered by the early 20th century translators. In the third edition of the Japanese dictionary *Dictionary of Philosophy* (*Tetsugaku jii*) which was published in 1912, the compilers picked up *renwen* as one of the equivalents to the word "culture".[27] This was not an exception in Meiji Japan. The Meiji Japanese dictionary compilers frequently resorted to the Chinese classics to coin new terms in Japanese when translating Western ideas and a considerable amount of these new terms were imported to China, many of which are still used in contemporary China.[28] This implication of cultivation in humanism is also noticed by Hu Shi who used "humanists" to denote the participants in the Chinese Renaissance in early 20th century.[29]

---

24 Wu Mi 1995, p. 233.
25 See *Zhou Yi* 2007, p. 117.
26 See Zhu Dongrun 2007, p. 158.
27 Inoue Tetsujirō et al. 1912, Quoted from Feng Tianyu 2004, p. 352. The first and second editions published in 1881 and 1884, both of them did not include *renwen* under the entry word "culture".
28 See Feng Tianyu 2004, pp. 350-353.
29 Hu Shi 2001, p. 79.

The debate about a proper translation for the term humanism arose again among Chinese scholars in the 1980s. Some scholars insisted that *renwen zhuyi* only indicated the humanist education in the Renaissance. They argued that if *renwen zhuyi* is considered equivalent to "humanism," the moral significations of the term humanism would probably be neglected. Therefore, they suggested *rendao zhuyi* which is assumed to bring out the meaning of "humanism" in a broader sense. "All thoughts in history which are based on the human can be interpreted as *rendao zhuyi*," said the philosopher Zhou Fucheng (1911–2009); thus the definition is broad enough to include the humanist culture of the Renaissance.[30]

Afterwards the debate reached its climax among philosophers. Noticing the dual (narrow and broad) senses of the term "humanism," scholars in favor of *rendao zhuyi*, like Wang Taiqing (1922–2000), suggested that logically the term *renwen zhuyi* cannot exhaust the whole idea of humanism. Moreover, Yang Shi (born 1932) even chose *rendao*, without *zhuyi*, to translate "humanism". On the other hand, philosophers like Zhang Chunnian criticized Wang, arguing that he misunderstood the meaning of *wen* in *renwen*. Zhang suggested that *renwen zhuyi* is more appropriate an equivalent for the term "humanism" while *rendao zhuyi* is better for the term "humanitarianism".[31]

The seemingly endless dispute about *renwen zhuyi* and *rendao zhuyi* indicates the dilemma of translation. This is not only due to the various interpretations of *renwen* or *rendao* in the Chinese context, but is also a consequence of the complexity of their assumed Western equivalents "humanism" and "Humanismus". Nevertheless, it is still fair to say that the unconscious and heedless uses of *rendao zhuyi* or *renwen zhuyi* were, to a large extent, responsible for this very confusion. The following section will show that translating the term humanism into Chinese is not merely about picking up a substantial equivalent. Rather, the translingual practice brought up new meanings and interpretations. To make it clearer, "humanism" was, in a sense, used as a conceptual tool in certain intellectual discourses. Since the different interpretations of humanism in the Chinese context even pointed to utterly contrary ideas, it is not surprising that humanism became such an equivocal concept in modern Chinese writings.

---

30 Zhou Fucheng 1984, pp. 8-9.
31 On these discussions see Lai Huiliang 2004, pp. 59-65.

Four Stages of Modern Chinese Humanism

1 The May Fourth Movement

The historian Chow Tse-tsung (1916–2007) detected two critical issues in the May Fourth Movement which shaped modern Chinese thought. One is the literary revolution; the other is the importing of Western thought and the revaluation of traditional Chinese culture.[32] They laid the ground for modern Chinese humanism. The first issue, the most heated controversy in the revolution between the old and new literature, focused on the language of literature: Classical Chinese or Vernacular Chinese (*baihua*). Hu Shi and his colleagues claimed that the only medium for present-day Chinese literature would be *baihua*. In an article from 1918, Hu Shi even declared "the death of Classical Chinese," although it was actually not the case.[33]

Zhou Zuoren was one of the earliest writers to use *baihua* during the literary revolution. As mentioned above, in 1918 Zhou established *rendao zhuyi* as the main foundation of the new literature. However, what did this abstract idea *rendao zhuyi* mean? At first, Zhou Zuoren claimed that *rendao zhuyi* would pave the way to a self-realization as an individual human being, and that human literature should be based on human morality. In this case, Zhou criticized those literary works which "obstruct the growth of human nature and destroy human harmony".[34] Thus, this sort of human literature, i.e. Zhou's concept of *rendao zhuyi*, had a strong moral signification.

But mere moral signification was not enough for the new literature. If the new literature simply found its basis in a new kind of morality, then it was merely another version of the traditional notion "literature as the vehicle for the ultimate doctrines" (*wen yi zai dao*). However, Zhou did not agree with the opinion that literature should be based on its own intrinsic values, either. Two years later in 1920, Zhou Zuoren articulated his idea of human literature and argued publicly against what was opposite to it. In a public speech, he criticized the argument that "art exists for its own sake" (*wei yishu er yishu*) and advocated the alternative notion, "literature for the sake of human life" (*wei rensheng er wenxue*).[35] In this speech, Zhou suggested that all types of art should find their values in human affairs as well as in themselves. Moreover, he enlarged the foundation of human literature, the literature of *rendao zhuyi*, from the topic of morality to that of human life. It is noteworthy that Zhou, whether consciously or not, made human

---

32 Chow 1960, p. 270.
33 Hu Shi 1918; see also Chow 1960, p. 278.
34 Zhou Zuoren 2002b, pp. 11-12.
35 Zhou Zuoren 2002c, pp. 18-23.

self-development the purpose of *rendao zhuyi*, yet he did not develop his argument any further. Generally speaking, Zhou Zuoren's calling for a "human literature" was somewhat idealistic. And it was closely linked to his religious ideas, as he revealed that *rendao zhuyi* derives from the Western Christian tradition.

Again in the article "Human Literature" (*Ren de wenxue*), Zhou Zuoren observed that in Europe the discovery of the value of the individual human being can be traced back to the 15th century, but in China the problem of "human" has never been solved.[36] This observation reflected the attitude of many May Fourth intellectuals who reevaluated traditional Chinese culture according to Western culture and values. At the end of 1919, Hu Shi explicitly expressed this idea as the main purpose of the movement:

The priority of the new movement is a new kind of attitude. This attitude can be called "an attitude of evaluating," and the best interpretation of this attitude is "to revaluate all values".[37]

When Hu Shi borrowed the idea of "revaluating all values" from the German philosopher Friedrich Nietzsche (1844–1900), he still supported the radical position of his colleagues. They fiercely attacked old literature, together with traditional culture, particularly the political and ethical doctrines of Neo-Confucianism. In this sense, the May Fourth Movement is often characterized as a movement of totalistic iconoclasm. In the following years, Hu Shi began to reevaluate the former revaluations. He retreated to a more moderate and pragmatic attitude. When he commented on the Chinese Renaissance in the 1930, he had a comparison with the Western Renaissance in mind. Therefore, he insisted that the Chinese Renaissance should never be an utter iconoclasm; rather, the proponents of the Chinese Renaissance should examine tradition, and look for instructive elements within it. Furthermore, he used the term "humanist" with great caution, as if he had foreseen the confusion it would bring about. In 1933, when he intended to epitomize the past twenty years and bridge the May Fourth Movement and the Chinese Renaissance, he described characters of a genuine "humanistic" movement:

First, it was a conscious movement to promote a new literature in the living language of the people to take the place of the classical literature of the old. Second, it was a movement of conscious protest against many of the ideas and institutions in traditional culture, and of conscious emancipation of the individual man and

---

36 Zhou Zuoren 2002b, p. 9.
37 Hu Shi 1919, p. 552.

woman from the bondage of the forces of tradition. It was a movement of reason versus tradition, freedom versus authority, and glorification of life and human values versus their suppression. And lastly, strangely enough, this new movement was led by men who knew their cultural heritage and tried to study it with the new methodology of modern historical criticism and research. In that sense it was also a humanist movement.[38]

Hu Shi defined a "humanist movement" only at the very end, that is, a certain attitude towards one's own cultural heritage. And when we take the other three definitions into account, it is clear that for Hu Shi, they actually indicated the uniqueness of the Chinese humanist movement in comparison with its European counterpart. The Chinese humanist movement is more critical towards its cultural heritage. If a movement is meant "to promote a new literature," "to protest against many of the ideas and institutions in traditional culture," "to emancipate the individual man and woman from the bondage of the forces of tradition," "as reason versus tradition, freedom versus authority, and glorification of life and human values versus their suppression," how can we identify it with the humanist culture of the Western Renaissance? Hu Shi himself was also aware of this self-contradictory argument, and that was the reason why he had advocated a Chinese Renaissance for many years, but only defined it as "humanist movement" once and in such a strict and critical sense, as present-day scholars observed.[39]

Although Hu Shi and Zhou Zuoren slightly differed in their arguments, both of them, in the course of the May Fourth Movement, targeted the old literature or the whole traditional culture. In this regard, the emergence of *rendao zhuyi* can not be separated from the revaluation of traditional literature and culture. This revaluation often started with a comparative view of China and the West. The interpretation of humanism, in fact, became one of the weapons with which to criticize traditional doctrines, when traditional culture was found to be suppressing human self-development.

2 The *Kexuan* Debate and the *Xueheng* School

The early 1920s saw the collapse of the old regime and traditional doctrines. Following the May Fourth Movement, Chinese intellectuals were eager to create a new modern Chinese culture. Those who attempted to inaugurate the New Culture began to split. Many scholars have noticed the fragmentation of the Chinese intelligentsia in the 1920s. One of its hallmarks was the "Debate over Science and Metaphysics" (*kexuan lunzhan*).

---

38 Hu Shi 2001, p. 79.
39 Zhu Weizheng 1996, pp. 135.

In 1919, the two renowned scholars Liang Qichao (1873–1929) and Zhang Junmai (1887–1968) accompanied some Chinese officials to attend the Paris Peace Conference at the end of the First World War. After the conference, they had a flying visit through Europe. Observing the postwar social and cultural crisis, particularly the pessimism which overwhelmed Europe, they devoted themselves to the study of its origins. Liang Qichao later ascribed the crisis to "scientism" (*kexue wanneng lun*). In his influential travelogue "Impressions of a Voyage to Europe" (Ouyou xinying lu), he argued that the development of science and technology in Europe did not bring welfare to human beings; however, it brought all the human life under material or mechanical rule and therefore acted as the foundation of utilitarianism and power politics. What Liang Qichao criticized most about scientism was that it denied and suppressed the free will of human beings, and made it increasingly difficult to maintain righteousness in human society.[40] Although Liang only criticized the viewpoint which regarded science as omnipotent, and did not entirely deny the role of science in the modern world, his attitude easily invited misunderstandings among his readers. Some Chinese cultural conservatives thought their dreams of European science smashed after reading the book, as Hu Shi observed.[41]

The debate was complicated by Zhang Junmai's lecture on "The View of Human Life" (Rensheng guan) delivered in February 1923. In fact, Zhang Junmai's view of science and the human mind mainly came from the French philosopher Henri Bergson (1859–1941), rather than Liang Qichao. After stating a five-fold distinction between science and the view of human life, he claimed that science could not solve its problems. Later, both of his opponents in the debate, Ding Wenjiang (1887–1936) and Hu Shi, doubted the distinction Zhang made, pointing out that Zhang's understanding of modern science was more or less mechanical or material, and that his view of human life was ambiguous. Furthermore, they defended science, as it should not bear the responsibility for the war.[42]

I see the *kexuan* Debate as a part of the discussion of modern Chinese humanism, because it took the New Culture to another stage where the Chinese intellectuals began to dispassionately examine the Confucian tradition. Zhang Junmai and other scholars discovered a profound view of human life in Confucian thought, and pointed out the possibility of a new spiritual culture based on that. As we will see below, it laid the theoretical grounding for the modern Chinese "New Confucianism" (*Xin rujia*) in the

---

40 Liang Qichao 1989b, pp. 11-12.
41 Hu Shi 1997, p. 12.
42 Later Zhang Junmai also gave several responses. Nearly all his articles (more than thirty) are found in Zhang Junmai et al. 1997.

1950s. Moreover, although none of the scholars in the debate used the term *renwen zhuyi*, their attempts to re-define human and human life under the dominant discourse of scientism marked a critical shift in the meaning of humanism in modern China.

Besides the "Debate over Science and Metaphysics," the "*Xueheng* School" (*Xueheng pai*), which advocated *renwen zhuyi* in the 1920s, contributed greatly to the acceptance of the term among the Chinese intelligentsia. Wu Mi and Hu Xiansu were among the leading members of this school. The academic journal *Xueheng* was their platform.[43] Although it was never outspoken, the *Xueheng* School endeavored to rival those advocating New Culture.

As mentioned above, Hu Xiansu first consciously translated the term "humanism" as *renwen zhuyi*, and his idea of humanism was borrowed from the American critic Irving Babbitt. The introduction of Babbitt was not by sheer chance, since most of the members of the *Xueheng* School had an American-educated background. Although most of the present-day scholars recognized Babbitt's criticism of modern culture as the academic resources of the *Xueheng* School, it should be stressed that Babbitt's Chinese students accepted his thoughts in a rather selective manner. When Babbitt's critique towards the materialism and relativism in American life as well as the claim for moral idealism was transplanted into the Chinese intellectual realm, it bore the mark of the nationalism of the *Xueheng* scholars. If we recall the fierce criticism of traditional Chinese literature and culture in the course of the New Culture Movement, it is clear that the *Xueheng* School intended a counteraction against the former. It was epitomized by the efforts to turn the term "humanism" (*renwen zhuyi*) into an instrumental concept to reinterpret traditional Chinese culture. As Irving Babbitt had insisted,

> [...] at present, we need to defend the humanities from the invasion of natural science, just as we defended it from the invasion of theology before.[44]

The members of the *Xueheng* School were also considering the relationship between scientism and humanism, taken to an extreme by one of its members, Zhang Qiyun (1900–1985), who advocated "a scientific humanism" (*kexue renwen zhuyi*) in his later years.[45] Wu Mi seemed to think more profoundly. He stressed the necessity of a principle of humaneness in the process of industrialization and the development of science and technology. He

---

43 See Shen Weiwei 2005.
44 Irving Babbitt 2003b, p. 20.
45 Zhang Qiyun 1988, vol. 10, p. 5062.

felt that China was in bad need of the "spirit of religion and the will of morality" which could be found in *renwen zhuyi*, he concluded.[46]

Then where would this religion or morality come from? The *Xueheng* scholars looked into their own interpretation of the Confucian tradition. Babbitt once compared and identified Confucius' discourse of virtue with that of Aristotle (384–322 BC), praising Confucius as a "moral realist".[47] His argument greatly inspired the members of the *Xueheng* School to connect Confucianism with humanism. Zhang Qiyun went as far as to directly claim that "the doctrines of Confucius and humanism (*renwen zhuyi*) could be regarded as the same," and that "Confucius was the founder of Chinese humanism".[48] On other occasions, he also stated that Confucianism is only one form of humanism, but is not humanism itself. He argued that the "doctrine of the mean" (*zhongyong*) in Confucianism could contribute to humanism, through which the virtue of *zhongyong* explained by Confucius could "combine sentiment and reason in a harmonious way".[49]

At that time, the idea of *zhongyong* played a crucial role in connecting Confucianism to humanism; another *Xueheng* scholar, Lin Yutang (1895–1976), once translated *zhongyong* as "religion of commonsense". Lin did agree with Babbitt and found no trouble claiming *renwen zhuyi* and defining humanism as the spirit of Chinese culture. In his Oxford lecture delivered in 1933, Lin said "the first principle of humanism is having a fair understanding of the purpose and meaning of human life". In order to reach such an understanding, "we should adopt the idea of *zhongyong* from Confucianism, which also can be named 'religion of commonsense'".[50]

It is reasonable for present-day scholars to doubt whether the idea of *zhongyong* would, in fact, promote human self-development. They may even think the opposite, wondering whether the former would suppress the latter. Whatever the case, Lin Yutang fully endorsed *zhongyong* in his interpretation of humanism. On the whole, the key issue in the interpretation of Chinese humanism by the *Xueheng* School was what Confucianism could contribute to humanism, mainly in a spiritual sense, yet they hardly considered the status of individuals under the doctrines of Confucianism on a practical level. When the term *renwen zhuyi* was invented in the 1920s, it was utilized by the cultural conservatists, and the discourse on humanism dramatically became the weapon with which to defend traditional Chinese culture.

---

46 See Wu Mi 1998, vol. 3, pp. 364-365: entry for July 3rd, 1927.
47 Babbitt 1919; the Chinese translation is in Babbitt 2003a, p. 8.
48 Zhang Qiyun 1988, vol. 21, p. 11297.
49 Ibid., vol.10, p. 5061.
50 Lin Yutang 2007b, p. 189.

3 The New Confucianism

The most profound invention Chinese scholars ever made in their understanding of humanism perhaps comes from the overseas Chinese advocates of the "New Confucianism" (*Xin rujia*). In a sense, the New Confucianism can be regarded as the successor of the cultural conservatism of the 1920s. Zhang Junmai, who doubted scientism in the above-mentioned "Debate over Science and Metaphysics" (*kexuan lunzhan*), became one of the founders of the New Confucianism. On January 1st, 1958, Zhang, along with the philosophers Mou Zongshan (1909–1995), Xu Fuguan (1903–1982) and Tang Junyi (1909–1978), published a manifesto reappraising Chinese culture in Hong Kong.[51] This manifesto is generally regarded as the first conscious expression of New Confucianism in 20th century China, although up till now it is still debatable who could, in fact, be counted as the members of New Confucianism.

The New Confucianists claimed the necessity and significance of Confucianism (or reformative Confucianism) in modern Chinese society, especially in the spiritual realm. The reason why they chose spiritual issues as their starting point might be related to the social transformation taking place in 20th century China. The intellectual historian Yu Yingshi (born 1930) once gave a brilliant analysis of the predicament of modern Chinese Confucianism. In ancient China, Confucianism was not merely a philosophy or a religious idea, as he argued, but a system of thought comprehensively arranging the order of the human world. So it did not dominate Chinese traditional culture directly, but indirectly, in an institutionalized way, by certain social structures which were based on moral doctrines. Since the collapse of the Qing Empire in 1911, or even shortly before that, namely since the abolition of the civil service examination system in 1905, the social institution on which Confucianism relied fell apart. That was the main cause of the unprecedented predicament Confucianism encountered in the 20th century. Yu even named modern Confucianism as "a drifting soul" (*youhun*), since it lost its institutional foundation.[52]

Although it is difficult to institutionalize Confucianism again in modern Chinese society, the New Confucianists still insisted that Confucianism can be reformed to meet the demand of the modern world. In two chapters of the 1958 manifesto, the authors argued that nothing in Confucianism or Chinese culture fundamentally contradicted modern science and democracy. They even argued that the moral spirit of the Chinese culture is in con-

---

51　Mou Zongshan, Xu Fuguan, Zhang Junmai and Tang Junyi 1958. The manifesto was mainly composed by Tang Junyi.
52　Yu Yingshi 2004b, pp. 53-58.

flict with monarchism, and that, in fact, a constitutional democracy is its inherent demand.⁵³ This mysterious concept of the "moral spirit of Chinese culture", among other similar concepts they used, can be viewed as a vehicle invented for their arguments. How can we imagine a civilization that developed so tightly bound with monarchism over more than two thousand years, and yet suddenly found a "moral spirit" which was against monarchism? Although there are some elements in traditional culture which accord with modern science or democracy, they still cannot represent Confucianism to its fullest extent. The New Confucianists' selective interpretation of Confucianism is an effort to legitimize Confucianism in a globalized world whose yardstick is modernity. Moreover, they found humanism to be a good platform with which to establish the moral (or ethical) discourse of Confucianism.

Almost all of the members of the New Confucianism School believed that there was a fundamental characteristic of Chinese culture named *renwen* or *renwen zhuyi*. For instance, one of the New Confucianists, Qian Mu (1895–1990), wrote that "Chinese culture is based on the concept of humaneness, and its focus is *renwen*".⁵⁴ Tang Junyi also shared the opinion that "Chinese culture, from the beginning, is a human-centered culture".⁵⁵ However, like *Xueheng* intellectuals in the 1920s, the New Confucianists mainly focused on the ethical or transcendental aspects of Confucianism in a rather abstract way, and hardly considered the role of the individual within the Confucian tradition on a more practical and social level.

However, from the perspective of modern individualism, one is less likely to agree with the New Confucianists that Confucianism is a type of humanism. As some scholars have pointed out, Confucianism only regards the individual as a "moral individual," but does not prescribe any personal right or freedom in the realistic social order. From the point of view of social history, after Confucianism was institutionalized and became the official ideology in Imperial China, it mainly stressed the responsibility of ordinary people towards the governor.⁵⁶ However, this article will not expand on the relation between Confucianism and modern individualism. The concept of individualism, like humanism, serves as an instrumental concept for the sake of some specific interpretation. Whereas the intellectuals in the New Culture Movement criticized the Chinese tradition for oppressing the value of the individual, the New Confucianists attempted to emphasize the idea of moral self-development in Confucianism.

---

53 Mou Zongshan, Xu Fuguan, Zhang Junmai and Tang Junyi 1958, pp. 33-34.
54 Qian Mu 1987, p. 12.
55 Tang Junyi 1984, p. 14.
56 Gu Hongliang and Liu Xiaohong 2004, p. 10.

This interpretation of connecting Confucianism with humanism in effect changed both terms conceptually. On the one hand, the invention of Chinese humanism or Confucian humanism added new connotations to the concept of humanism. Xu Fuguan among others, clearly distinguished between European and Chinese humanism, and focused on "how these two respectively consider human nature".[57] On the other hand, the invention of Chinese humanism will probably lead Confucian thinking towards a humanistic orientation. Maintaining Confucianism as a kind of humanism would make scholars consider that Confucianism, with all its moral doctrines and religious institutions, only focuses on the practical world of real life, and thus ignores the transcendental dimensions within Confucianism. The New Confucianists were also aware of these possible misunderstandings. They attempted to distinguish Confucian humanism from Western humanistic thinking which developed under and conflicted with the domination of Christianity. The New Confucianist Tu Weiming (born 1940) criticized the Western type of humanism for its anthropocentric tendency which leant towards instrumental rationality and argued against the divine. On the contrary, he expected Confucian humanism to be an open concept which could cover both religious thoughts and ultimate concerns, as well as the pursuit of harmony in the human world.[58]

4 The Discussion on *Renwen Jingshen* in the 1990s

After the heated discussion on Chinese and Western cultures in the 1980s, another discussion on *renwen jingshen* ("humanistic spirit") arose in the People's Republic of China in the mid 1990s. This discussion on humanism was unprecedented in the history of the People's Republic of China. It began with two symposiums on *renwen jingshen* held by the journals *Review (Dushu)* and *Shanghai Literature (Shanghai wenxue)*, yet quickly went far beyond the literary circle. It seemed ironic that when intellectuals began to frequently mention the word "humanism," they became worried about the decline or a crisis of literature and humanism.[59] Many scholars in the discussion found that all subjects of humanities at colleges were marginalized and in crisis ever since the economic reform and the advent of the market economy at the beginning of the 1990s. As most of the participants seemed to express their own opinions respectively and passionately, they reached no

---

57 Xu Fuguan 1996, p. 165.
58 Tu Weiming 1999, pp. 28-40.
59 Wang Xiaoming et al. 1993.

agreement, and indeed the discussion was not as productive as the participants had expected.

Basically, the anxiety of the participants in the discussion came from the de-centering of the Chinese humanities in and out of the academic compound. Although it has not been explicitly revealed, the occasion for this discussion was that the old Marxist paradigm in the academy was doubted and partly abandoned, thus causing the absence of the standard and object. Moreover, according to the contemporary critic Wang Xiaoming (born 1955), Chinese literature in the 1980s was full of inferior taste, and lacked fine imagination. He also pointed out the poverty of academic studies and described it as aphasia.[60]

However, many intellectuals in the 1990s did not reconcile themselves to such "aphasia". Above all, the claim of *renwen jingshen* indicates the attempt to employ a general and universal perspective to judge literature and academic studies. Some scholars in the discussion proposed the crucial question: "What kind of humanism do we need today?"[61] The question inspired people to consider iconoclastic humanism and Confucian humanism in a more critical way, and moreover, motivated them to search for the universality of *renwen jingshen* and the humanities. What is interesting here is that the idea of "enlightenment" (*qimeng*) was brought up again (for the second or third time). It indicates that some intellectuals dared to self-consciously to go beyond the boundary of a debate which continued for eighty years and start to reevaluate the intellectual movements in 20th century China.

The recall of *renwen jingshen* aimed at the reconstruction of values in the Post-Mao era, and found as its very opponent the dominant instrumental rationality in the cultural life. It was brought forth by the market economy, as many people thought. The embarrassment of studying humanities came from an ever more commercialized society, at the beginning of the social transformation, and discussions on issues of values were regarded as meaningless and useless. Very few scholars in the discussion admitted that the logic of commercial society and consumptive culture could assort with the idea of humanism, or *renwen jingshen*. In fact, the contradiction between humanism and instrumental rationality only represents the predicament of the humanities in an era of transition. As the philosopher Zhang Rulun (born 1957) has pointed out incisively, the decline of *renwen jingshen* should not only be ascribed to the market economy, but also be traced back to the be-

---

60 Wang Xiaoming 1996, p. 272.
61 Wu Xuan et al. 1994.

ginning of modern times, even before the May Fourth Movement.[62] In a sense, it indicates that the invention of humanism in modern China is subject to different purposes of interpretation, with its meaning remaining uncertain. Another philosopher, Qu Weiguo (born 1958), has argued in the context of the discussion that as long as human beings exist, the consideration of and reflection on human nature or human destiny will not end. In this sense, humanism could not decline. What will really decline are some specific forms or discourses of humanism.[63]

Conclusion

The four stages of the invention of humanism in modern China indicate that there has never been a fixed meaning of "humanism" in modern Chinese texts. The term serves as an instrumental concept which could be used as a weapon to attack or defend certain ideas. In a conference held in 1986 in Shanghai, on the revaluation of Chinese tradition, the historian Liu Zehua (born 1935) drew a conclusion as follows:

> The ancient Chinese thinking of *renwen* on the whole led to the suppression rather than liberation of the individual: it made most people inhuman.[64]

It should be asked why we still name it *renwen* if it made people inhuman. However, this question indicates the predicament Chinese scholars will probably be trapped in when they use Western concepts, especially such complex concepts as humanism, to study Chinese history. The British historian Alan Bullock (1914–2004) remarked that humanism is a word "that no one has ever succeeded in defining to anyone else's satisfaction".[65] In fact, humanism, or renwen in the Chinese context is often taken merely as a topic or subject which encompasses different interpretations, rather than a concept with one single and fixed meaning.

Therefore, with regard to the Chinese translations of humanism, it is more important to examine the context or the narrative framework in which the term is situated, and to detect the audience and potential opponents of a certain discourse, rather than merely defining it. The British critic Tony Davies (born 1940) argued,

> [... t]he meanings of a powerful and complex word are never a matter for lexicography alone. They are tied inescapably to the linguistic and cultural authority, real, ab-

---

62 Zhang Rulun and Lin Hui 1996, p. 164.
63 Qu Weiguo 1996, pp. 101-102.
64 Liu Zehua 1987, p. 72.
65 Bullock 1985, p. 8.

sent or desired, of those who use it. The important question, over and above what the word *means* in a particular context, is why and how that meaning *matters*, and for whom.[66]

Thus the various discourses of modern Chinese humanism are closely related to specific authorities interpreting Chinese tradition and contemporary culture. It is reasonable to give "humanism" or *renwen zhuyi* a meaning in Chinese, but we have to examine the implications of the terms in a more critical way.

---

66 Davies 1997, p. 6.

Bibliography

Ames, Roger T. and Henry Rosemont Jr. (1998): *The Analects of Confucius: A Philosophical Translation,* New York: The Random House Publishing Group.

Ankersmit, Franklin (1981): *Narrative Logic. A Semantic Analysis of the Historian's Language,* Groningen: University of Groningen.

Atwell, William (1982): "International Bullion Flows and the Chinese Economy circa 1530-1650." In: *Past and Present* 95, pp. 68-90.

Babbitt, Irving (1919): *Rousseau and Romanticism,* Boston: Houghton.

—— 白璧德 (2003a). *Lusuo yu langman zhuyi* 卢梭与浪漫主义 (Rousseau and Romanticism), translated by Sun Yixue 孙宜学, Shijiazhuang: Hebei jiaoyu chubanshe.

—— 白璧德 (2003b), "Shenme shi renwen zhuyi 什么是人文主义？(What is Humanism?)", in: *Renwen zhuyi: quanpan fansi* 人文主义：全盘反思 (Humanitas: Rethinking it all), translated by Wang Chen 王琛, Beijing: Sanlian shudian, 2003. pp. 1-21.

Bauer, Wolfgang (1971): *China und die Hoffnung auf Glück. Paradiese, Utopien, Idealvorstellungen,* München: Karl Hanser Verlag.

—— (2001): *Geschichte der chinesischen Philosophie: Konfuzianismus, Daoismus, Buddhismus,* edited by Hans van Ess. München: Verlag C.H. Beck.

Bennett, Tony et al. (eds.) (2005): *New Keywords, A Revised Vocabulary of Culture and Society,* London: Blackwell.

Berg, Daria (1993): "Die Heilkunde im Spiegel des Romans *Xingshi yinyuan* aus dem 17. Jahrhundert." In: *China Med* 6, pp. 59-61.

Berling, Judith A. (1980): *The Syncretic Religion of Lin Chao-en,* New York: Columbia University Press.

Bloom, Irene (1979): "On the 'Abstraction' of Ming Thought: Some Concrete Evidence from the Philosophy of Lo Ch'in-shun." In: W. T. de Bary and Irene Bloom (eds.), *Principle and Practicability,* New York: Columbia University Press.

Bödeker, Hans Erich (1982): "Menschheit, Humanität, Humanismus." In: Brunner, Conze and Koselleck 1972–1997, vol. 3, pp. 1063-1128.

Bol, Peter K. (1993): "Government, Society, and State: On the Political Visions of Ssu-ma Kuang and Wang An-shih." In: Robert P. Hymes and Conrad Schirokauer (eds.), *Ordering the World. Approaches to State and Society in Sung Dynasty China*, Berkeley, Los Angeles, Oxford: University of California Press, pp. 128-192.

Brennan, Patrick McKinley (2002-2003): "Arguing for Human Equality." In: *Journal of Law and Religion* 18/1, pp. 99-149.

Brook, Timothy (1997): "At the Margin of Public Authority: The Ming State and Buddhism." In: Huters, Theodore, R. Bin Wong and Pauline Yu (eds.), *Culture & State in Chinese History. Conventions, Accommodations, and Critiques*, Stanford: Stanford University Press, pp. 161-181.

—— (1999): *The Confusions of Pleasure. Commerce and Culture in Ming China,* Berkeley and Los Angeles: University of California Press.

Brunner, Otto, Werner Conze and Reinhart Koselleck (eds.) (1972–1997): *Geschichtliche Grundbegriffe: Historisches Lexikon zur politisch-sozialen Sprache in Deutschland*, Stuttgart: Klett-Cotta.

Bullock, Alan (1985): *The Humanist Tradition in the West*, London: Thames and Hudson.

—— (1997): *Xifang renwen zhuyi chuantong* 西方人文主义传统 (The Humanist Tradition in the West), translated by Dong Leshan 董乐山, Beijing: Sanlian shudian.

Chan, Sin-wai (1984): *An Exposition of Benevolence. The Jen-hsüeh of T'an Ssu-t'ung*, Hongkong: Chinese University Press.

Chan, Wing-tsit (1970): "The Ch'eng-Chu School of Early Ming." In: Wm. Theodore de Bary (ed.), *Self and Society in Ming Thought,* New York: Columbia Press, pp. 29-51.

—— (1975): "The *Hsing-li ching-i* and the Ch'eng-Chu School of the Seventeenth Century." In: Wm. Theodore de Bary (ed.), *The Unfolding of Neo-Confucianism*, New York: Columbia University Press, pp. 543-579.

——, (transl. and comp.) (1963): *A Source Book on Chinese Philosophy*, Princeton: Princeton University Press.

Chang, Gene H. (2002): "The Cause and Cure of China's Widening Income Disparity." In: *China Economic Review* 13/4, pp. 335-340.

Chao, Yüan-ling (1995): *Medicine and Society in Late Imperial China: A Study of Physicians in Suzhou,* Ph.D. University of California, Los Angeles and Ann Arbor: UMI Dissertation Services.

Chen Xin 陈新 (2003): "Renwen zhuyi de xingqi: yige youguan shixue renshi de ge'an fenxi 人文主义的兴起：一个有关史学认识的个案分析 (The Rise of Humanism, a Case Study of Historical Thinking)." In: *Shijie lishi* 世界历史 (World History) 1, pp. 74-85.

Chen Yuanpeng 陳元朋 (1997): *Liangsongde shangyishiren yu ruyi* 兩宋的商醫士人與儒醫 (The Gentlemen who Learnt Medicine and Gentlemen Doctors in the Northern and Southern Song), Taibei: National Taiwan University Press.

Cheng Shide 程士德 et.al. (eds.) (1982): *Suwen zhushi huicui* 素问注释汇粹 (The Basic Questions with Selected Commentaries), Beijing: Renmin weisheng chubanshe.

Cheng Shude 程樹德 (1988): *Jiuchao lü kao* 九朝律考 (A Study of the Laws of the Nine Dynasties), Beijing: Zhonghua.

Ch'ien, Edward T. (1986): *Chiao Hung and the Restructuring of Neo-Confucianism in the Late Ming,* New York: Columbia University Press.

Chow, Kai-wing (1993): "Ritual, Cosmology, and Ontology: Chang Tsai's Moral Philosophy and Neo-Confucian Ethics." In: *Philosophy East and West* 43/2, pp. 201-228.

Chow, Tse-tsung (1960): *The May Fourth Movement: Intellectual Revolution in Modern China,* Cambridge: Harvard University Press.

Cullen, Christopher (1993): "Patients and Healers in Late Imperial China: Evidence from the Jingpingmei." In: *History of Science* 31, pp. 99-150.

Dann, Otto (1975): "Gleichheit." In: Brunner, Conze and Koselleck 1972–1997, vol. 2, pp. 995-1046.

Darga, Martina (transl. and comm.) (1999): *Das alchemistische Buch von innerem Wesen und Lebensenergie Xingming guizhi,* München: Diederichs.

Davies, Toni (1997): *Humanism.* London: Routledge.

De Bary, Wm. Theodore (1970): "Individualism and Humanitarianism in Late Ming Thought." In: Ibid. (ed.), *Self and Society in Ming Thought,* New York: Columbia Press, pp. 145-247.

—— (1975): "Neo-Confucianism and the Seventeenth-Century 'Enlightenment'." In: Ibid (ed.), *The Unfolding of Neo-Confucianism,* New York: Columbia Press.

—— (1993): *Waiting for the Dawn: A Plan for the Prince. Huang Tsung-hsi's Ming-i-tai-fang lu,* New York: Columbia University Press.

Derrida, Jacques (1978): "Structure, Sign and Play in the Discourse of Human Sciences." In: *Writing and Difference*, translated by Alan Bass, London: Routledge.

Ding Shouhe 丁守和 (1996): "Guanyu ren'ai yu renzheng de sikao 關於仁愛與仁政的思考 (Reflections on Caring for Others (*ren'ai*) and on benevolent government (*renzheng*))". In: *Chuantong wenhua yu xiandaihua* 傳統文化與現代化 (Traditional Culture and Modernity) 1/19, pp. 7-15.

Dworkin, Ronald (2000): *Sovereign Virtue: The Theory and Practice of Equality*, Cambridge, Mass.: Harvard University Press.

Elman, Benjamin A. (1990): *From Philosophy to Philology: Intellectual and Social Aspects of Change in Late Imperial China*, Cambridge, Mass.: Harvard University Press.

—— (1993): "The Revaluation of Benevolence (Jen) in Ch'ing Dynasty Evidential Research." In: J. Smith and D.Q. Y. Kwok (eds.), *Cosmology, Ontology, and Human Efficacy. Essays in Chinese Thought*, Honolulu: University of Hawaii Press, pp. 59-80.

—— (1994): "Changes in Confucian Civil Service Examinations from the Ming to the Ch'ing Dynasty". In: Benjamin A. Elman and Alexander Woodside (eds.), *Education and Society in Late Imperial China, 1600-1900*, Berkeley, Los Angeles and London: University of California Press, pp. 111-149.

—— (2000): *A Cultural History of Civil Examinations in Late Imperial China*, Berkeley and Los Angeles: University of California Press.

Elvin, Mark (1996): "Was There a Transcendental Breakthrough in China?" In: Ibid., *Another History. Essays on China from a European Perspective*, Broadway: Wild Peony, pp. 261-301 [originally in Shmuel Noah Eisenstadt (ed.), *The Origins and Diversity of Axial Age Civilizations*, Albany: State University of New York Press, 1986].

Engelfriet, Peter (1998): *Euclid in China. The Genesis of the First Chinese Translation of Euclid's Elements Books I-VI (Jihe yuanben; Beijing, 1607) and its Reception up to 1723*, Leiden: Brill.

Engelhardt, Ute (2004): "Longevity Techniques and Chinese Medicine". In: Livia Kohn (ed.), *Daoism Handbook*, 2 vols., Leiden: Brill.

Epstein, Maram (2001): *Competing Discourses. Orthodoxy, Authenticity, and Engendered Meanings in Late Imperial Chinese Fiction*, Cambridge/Mass. and London: Harvard University Press.

Esherick, Joseph W. (1976): *Reform and Revolution in China. The 1911 Revolution in Hunan and Hubei*, Berkeley: University of California Press.

Fa yan 法言 (Exemplary Sayings), by Yang Xiong 揚雄 (53 BC–18 AD), cf. *Fayan yishu*.

Fayan yishu 法言義疏 (Commentary of Exemplary Sayings), by Wang Rongbao 汪榮寶 (died 1933), punctuated and edited by Chen Zhongfu 陳仲夫, Beijing: Zhonghua shuju, 1987.

Feng Menglong 馮夢龍 (1993): "Qingshi 情史 (History of Love/ Emotions)". In: *Feng Menglong quanji* 馮夢龍全集 7 (The Complete Works of Feng Menglong), Jiangsu: Guji chubanshe.

Feng Tianyu 冯天瑜 (2004): *Xinyu tanyuan* 新语探源 (*Studies on New Terms*), Beijing: Zhonghua shuju.

Fung, You-lan / Feng Youlan 冯友兰 / 馮友蘭 (1948): *A Short History of Chinese Philosophy. A Systematic Account of Chinese Thought from its Origins to the Present Day*, New York: The Free Press.

—— (1952–1953): *A History of Chinese Philosophy*, translated by Derk Bodde, 2 vols., Princeton: Princeton University Press.

—— (1980): *Zhongguo zhexueshi xinbian* 中国哲学史新编 (New Edition of A History of Chinese Philosophy), Beijing: Beijing Xinhua Publishing.

Furth, Charlotte (2007): "Introduction. Thinking with Cases." In: Charlotte Furth, Judith T. Zeitlin and Ping-chen Hsiung (eds.), *Thinking with Cases. Specialist Knowledge in Chinese Cultural History*, Honolulu: University of Hawai'i Press, pp. 1-27.

Gernet, Jacques (1985): *China and the Christian Impact: A Conflict of Cultures*, translated by Janet Lloyd, Cambridge: Cambridge University Press.

Gongyang zhuan zhushu 公羊傳注疏 (Gongyang Commentary, with Annotations and Subcommentary). In: *Shisan jing zhushu*, vol. 7.

Gosepath, Stefan (2007): "Equality." In: Edward N. Zalta (ed.), *The Stanford Encyclopaedia of Philosophy*, June 27, 2007 edition (http://plato.stanford.edu/entries/equality).

Graham, Angus C. (1989): *Disputers of the Tao. Philosophical Argument in Ancient China*, Chicago: Open Court.

—— (2001): *Chuang Tzu. The Inner Chapters*, Indianapolis: Hackett Publishing Company.

Gu Hongliang 顾红亮 and Liu Xiaohong 刘晓虹 (2004): *Xiangxiang geren* 想象个人 (Imagining the Individual), Shanghai: Shanghai guji chubanshe.

Hanshu 漢書 (History of the Former Han Dynasty), Beijing, Zhonghua shuju, 1962.

Harbsmeier, Christian: *Thesaurus Linguae Sericae* (http://www. tls.uni-heidelberg.de).

Hartwell, Robert M. (1971): "Historical Analogism, Public Policy, and Social Science in Eleventh- and Twelfth-Century China." In: The *Amerian Historical Review* 76, pp. 690-727.

He Xinyin ji 何心隱集 (The Collected Works of He Xinyin [1517–1579]), edited by Rong Zhaozu 容肇祖, Beijing: Zhonghua shuju, 1960.

Hertzer, Dominique (1996): *Das alte und das neue Yijing: Die Wandlungen des Buches der Wandlungen,* München: Diederichs.

Hirsch, Alfred (2010): "Different Cultures and Universality of Human Rights." In: Meinert and Zöllner 2010, pp. 21-39.

History Department of Fudan University 复旦大学历史系 (ed.) (1987): *Zhongguo chuantong wenhua de zaiguji* 中国传统文化的再估计 (The Revaluation of the Chinese Traditional Culture), Shanghai: Shanghai renmin chubanshe.

Hostetler, Laura (2001): *Qing Colonial Enterprise: Ethnography and Cartography in Early Modern China*, Chicago and London: The University of Chicago Press.

Hsu, Pi-ching (2000): "Courtesans and Scholars in the Writings of Feng Menglong: Transcending Status and Gender." In: *NAN NÜ — Men, Women and Gender in Early and Imperial China* 2/1, pp. 40-77.

—— (2006): *Beyond Eroticism. A Historian's Reading of Humor in Feng Menglong's Child's Folly,* Lanham and Oxford: University Press of America.

Hu Shi 胡适 (1918): "Jianshe de wenxue geming lun 建设的文学革命论 (On Constructive Literature Revolution)." In: Hu Shi 1998, vol. 2, pp. 44-57.

—— (1919): "Xinsichao de yiyi 新思潮的意义 (The Significance of the New Movement)." In: Hu Shi 1998, vol. 1, pp. 551-558.

—— (1997): "'Kexue yu renshengguan' xu 《科学与人生观》序 (Foreword to *Science and the View of Human Life*)", in: Zhang Junmai 1997, pp. 9-32.

—— (1998): *Hu Shi wen ji* 胡适文集 (*The Works of Hu Shi*), 12 vols., Beijing: Beijing daxue chubanshe.

—— (2001): *Zhongguo de wenyi fuxing* 中国的文艺复兴 (The Chinese Renaissance), Beijing: Waiyu jiaoxue yu yanjiu chubanshe.

—— (2003): *Hu Shi quanji* 胡適全集 (The Complete Works of Hu Shi): vol. 37, Anhui: Jiaoyu Press.

Huangdi neijing suwen 黃帝內經素問 (The Inner Classic of the Yellow Emperor. Basic Questions)," cf. Cheng Shide 1982.

Huang Heqing 黄河清 et al. (eds.) (2001): *Jinxiandai hanyu xinci ciyuan cidian* 近现代汉语新词词源词典 (An Etymological Glossary of Selected Modern Chinese Words), Shanghai: Hanyu dacidian chubanshe.

Huang Zongxi 黃宗羲 (1985): *Huang Zongxi quanji* 黃宗羲全集 (The Complete Works of Huang Zongxi), vol. 1, Hangzhou: Zhejiang guji chubanshe.

Huang, Chun-Chieh (2009): *Konfuzianismus: Kontinuität und Entwicklung. Studien zur chinesischen Geistesgeschichte*, translated and edited by Stephan Schmidt, Bielefeld: transcript.

Huang, Martin W. (2001): *Desire and Fictional Narrative in Late Imperial China*, Cambridge: Harvard University Press.

Hung, Ho-fung (2003): "Orientalist Knowledge and Social Theories. China and the European Conceptions of East-West Difference from 1600 to 1900." In: *Sociological Theory* 21/ 3, pp. 254-280.

Hymes, Robert (1987): "Not Quite a Gentleman? Doctors in Sung and Yuan." In: *Chinese Science* 8, pp. 9-76.

Inoue Tetsujirō 井上哲次郎 et al. (eds.) (1912): *Kaitei zoho tetsugaku jii* 改訂增補哲學字彙 (Revised and Enlarged Dictionary of Philosophy), Tokyo: Toyokan Shoten.

Ivanhoe, Philip J. (2009): *Readings from the Lu-Wang School of Neo-Confucianism. Translated, with Introductions and Notes,* Indiananapolis and Cambridge: Hackett Publishing Company, Inc..

Ji Yuancheng 戢元丞 et al. (eds.) (1908): *Dongzhong dacidian* 东中大辞典 (A Japanese-Chinese Dictionary), Shanghai: Zuoxin she.

Ji, Xiao-bin (2004): "Mirror for Government: Ssu-ma Kuang's Thought on Politics and Government in *Tzu-chih t'ung-chien*". In: Lee 2004a, pp. 1-31.

Jingxue lishi 經學歷史 (History of Classical Studies), by Pi Xirui 皮錫瑞 (1850–1908), originally published Changsha: Sijian shuju, 1907; annotated by Zhou Yutong 周予同, Shanghai: Shanghai Commercial Press, 1930; repr. Beijing: Zhonghua shuju, 1959.

Kang Youwei 康有為 (1998): *Kang Youwei Datong lun er zhong* 康有為大同論二種 (The Book of Great Unity by Kang Youwei in Two Versions), edited by Zhu Weizheng 朱維錚, Beijing: Sanlian shudian.

—— (2009): *Datong shu* 大同書 (The Book of Great Unity), Shanghai: Shanghai shiji chuban jituan.

Knoblock, John and Jeffrey Riegel (2000): *The Annals of Lü Buwei: A Complete Translation and Study*, Stanford: Stanford University Press.

Kubny, Manfred (1995): *Lebenskraftkonzepte in China: Definition, Theorien, Grundlagen*, Heidelberg: Karl F. Haug Verlag.

Lai Huiliang 赖辉亮 (2004): "Renwen zhuyi haishi rendao zhuyi 人文主义还是人道主义 (Humanism: *renwen zhuyi* or *rendao zhuyi*)." In: *Zhongguo qingnian zhengzhi xueyuan xuebao* 中国青年政治学院学报 (Journal of China Youth College for Political Science) 6, pp. 59-65.

Langlois, John D. Jr. and Sun K'o-K'uan 孫克寬 (1983): "Three Teachings Syncretism and the Thought of Ming T'ai-tsu." In: *Harvard Journal of Asiatic Studies* 43/1, pp. 97-139.

Lau, D.C (trans.) (2001): *Tao Te Ching*. Hong Kong: Chinese University Press.

Lee, Thomas H. C. (ed.) (2004a): *The New and the Multiple: Sung Senses of the Past*, Hong Kong: The Chinese University of Hong Kong.

—— (2004b), "Introduction." In: Lee 2004a, pp. vii-xxxii.

Legge, James (1960): *The Chinese Classics. With a Translation, Critical and Exegetical Notes, Prolegomena, and Copious Indexes*, 5 vols., repr. Hongkong: Chinese University Press.

Leung, Angela Ke-che (2003): "Medical Learning from the Song to the Ming." In: Smith, Paul Jakov and Richard von Glahn (eds.): *The Song-Yuan-Ming Transition in Chinese History,* Cambridge and London: Harvard University Press, pp. 374-398.

Lewis, Charlton M. (1969): "The Hunanese Elite and the Reform-Movement, 1895–1898." In: The *Journal of Asian Studies* 29/1, pp. 35-42.

Li Guangbo 李广柏 (2001): "Zhongguo lishi shang de renwen zhuyi sichao 中国历史上的人文主义思潮 (The Thought of Humanism in Chinese History)." In: *Huazhong shifan daxue xuebao* 华中师范大学学报 (Journal of Central China Normal University) 40/4, pp. 100-108.

Liji zhushu 禮記注疏 (*The Book of Rites* with Annotations and Subcommentary). In: *Shisan jing zhushu*, vol. 8.

Li Yi 李怡 (2006): "Renwen zhuyi yu wusi xinwenhua yundong 人文主义与五四新文化运动 (Humanism and the May Fourth New Culture Movement)." In: *Fujian luntan* 福建论坛 (Fujian Forum) 1, pp. 76-80.

Li Zhi 李贄 (1936): *Li shi Fenshu* 李氏焚書 (Writings to Burn by Li Zhi), edited by A Ying 阿英, Shanghai: Bei ye shan fang.

Li Zhijun 李志军 (2004): *Xixue dongjian yu Ming Qing shixue* 西学东渐与明清实学 (The Introduction of Western Knowledge in China and the Studies on Statecraft in Ming and Qing China), Chengdu: Sichuan chubanshe.

Li Zhongzi 李中梓 (1997): *Yizong bi du* 醫宗必讀 (Essential Readings of Medical Lineage), reprint from 1637 (first imprint), Beijing: Zhongguo Zhongyiyao chubanshe.

Li, San-pao (1978): "K'ang Yu-wei's Shih-li kung-fa chuan-shu (A Complete Book of Substantial Truths and Universal Principles)." In: *Zhongyang yanjiuyuan jindai shi yanjiusuo jikan* 中央研究院近代史研究所集刊 (Bulletin of the Institute of Modern History, Academia Sinica) 7, pp. 683-722.

Liang Qichao 梁启超 (1989a): *Yinbingshi heji* 饮冰室合集 (The Complete Works of Liang Qichao), 12 vols., Beijing: Zhonghua shuju.

—— (1989b), "Ouyou xinying lu 欧游心影录 (Impressions of a Voyage to Europe)." In: Liang Qichao 1989a, vol. 6, no. 23, pp. 1-162.

Lin Yutang 林语堂 (2007a): *Lin Yutang ji* 林语堂集 (The Works of Lin Yutang), Guangzhou: Huacheng chubanshe.

—— (2007b): "Zhongguo wenhua zhi jingshen 中国文化之精神 (The Spirit of Chinese Culture)." In: Lin Yutang 2007a, pp. 185-196.

Linck, Gudula (2001): *Leib und Körper: Zum Selbstverständnis im vormodernen China*, Frankfurt am Main: Peter Lang.

Liu Boyi 劉伯驥 (1974): *Zhongguo yixue shi* 中國醫學史 (History of Chinese Medicine), Tabei: Huagang chubanbu.

Liu Wengang 劉文剛 (2002): "Su Shi de yangsheng 蘇軾的養生 (Su Dongpo's Art of Nourishing Life)." In: *Zongjiao xue yanjiu* 宗教學研究 56/13-18, p. 113.

Liu Zehua 刘泽华 (1987): "Zhongguo chuantong de renwen sixiang yu wangquan zhuyi 中国传统的人文思想与王权主义 (The *renwen* Thoughts and Kingship in Chinese Tradition)." In: *History Department of Fudan University* (1987), pp. 56-80.

Liu Zhanghua 柳長華 et al. (eds.) (1999): *Chen Shiduo yixue quan shu* 陳士鐸醫學全書 (The Complete Works on Medicine by Chen Shiduo), Beijing: Zhongguo zhongyiyao chubanshe.

Liu, Lydia (1995): *Translingual Practice: Literature, National Culture and Translated Modernity-China 1900-1937*, Stanford University Press.

Lunyu jizhu 論語集注 (Collected Glosses to the *Analects*); cf. *Sishu zhangju jizhu*.

Lunyu zhengyi 論語正義 (The Correct Readings of the *Analects*). By Liu Baonan 劉寶楠 (1791–1855), 2 vols., Beijing: Zhonghua shuju, 1990.

Lunyu zhushu 論語注疏 (The *Analects* with Annotations and Subcommentary). In: *Shisan jing zhushu*, vol. 8.

Lynn, Richard John (1994): *The Classic of Changes. A New Translation of the I Ching as Interpreted by Wang Bi*, New York: Columbia University Press.

MacIntyre, Alasdair (1966): *A Short History of Ethics*, New York: Macmillan Publishing.

Mao Shi zhengyi 毛詩正義 (The Correct Readings of the *Shijing* in the Mao School Tradition). In: Ruan Yuan 1980.

Marks, Robert B. (1998): *Tigers, Rice, Silk, and Silt. Environment and Economy in Late Imperial South China,* Cambridge: Cambridge University Press.

Masini, Federico (ed.) (1996): *Western Humanistic Culture Presented to China by Jesuit Missionaries (XVII–XVIII centuries),* Rome: Institutum Historicum SJ.

Meinert, Carmen and Hans-Bernd Zöllner (2010) (eds.): *Buddhist Approaches to Human Rights. Dissonances and Resonances,* Bielefeld, New Brunswick, and London: Transcript, and Transaction.

Mengzi zhushu 孟子注疏 (*Mencius* with Annotations and Subcommentary). In: *Shisan jing zhushu,* vol. 8.

Metzger, Thomas (1977): *Escape from Predicament. Neo-Confucianism and China's Evolving Political Culture,* New York: Columbia University Press.

Mittag, Achim (1993): *Das Shi-jing-Studium in der Song-Zeit (960–1279). Vorstufen zu einer Neubetrachtung der Song-Klassikergelehrsamkeit,* Nördlingen: Steinmeier.

—— (1996): "Wang Anshis posthumer Aufstieg im Konfuziustempel: Zur konfuzianischen Ideologiegeschichte des 11. und 12. Jahrhunderts." In: *Bochumer Jahrbuch zur Ostasienforschung* 20, pp. 29-66.

Moeller, Hans-Georg (2006): *The Philosophy of the Daodejing,* New York: Columbia Press.

Mou Zongshan 牟宗三, Xu Fuguan 徐复观, Zhang Junmai 张君劢, and Tang Junyi 唐君毅 (1958): "Wei zhongguo wenhua jinggao shijie renshi xuanyan 为中国文化敬告世界人士宣言 (A Manifesto on the Reappraisal of Chinese Culture)." In: Feng Zusheng 封祖盛 (1989) (ed.): *Dangdai xinrujia* 当代新儒家 (Contemporary New Confucianism), Beijing: Sanlian shudian, pp. 1-52.

Mowry, Hua-yuan Li (1983): *Chinese Love Stories from "Ch'ing-shih",* Hamden: The Shoe String Press.

Nagel, Thomas (1978): "The Justification of Equality." In: *Crítica: Revista Hispanoamericana de Filosofía* 10/28, pp. 3-31.

Ng, On-Cho (1993): "Toward an Interpretation of Ch'ing Ontology." In: Richard J. Smith and D.W. Y. Kwok (eds.): *Cosmology, Ontology, and Human Efficacy. Essays in Chinese Thought,* Honolulu: University of Hawaii Press, pp. 35-58.

Nienhauser, William Jr. (ed.) (1994): *The Grand Scribe's Records,* vol. I: *The Basic Annals of Pre-Han China.* Bloomington: Indiana UP.

Niethammer, Friedrich Immanuel (1808): *Der Streit des Philanthropinismus und Humanismus in der Theorie des Erziehungs-Unterrichts unserer Zeit*, Jena: Frommann.

OECD (2004): *Income Disparities in China. An OECD Perspective*, Paris: OECD Publishing.

Piatigorsky, A. (1983): "Some Remarks on 'Other Stream'." In: Philip Denwood and Alexander Piatigorsky (eds.), *Buddhist Studies. Ancient and Modern*, London: Curzon Press, pp. 124-152.

Qian Mu 钱穆 (1987): *Zhonghua wenhua shi'er jiang* 中华文化十二讲 (Twelve Lectures on Chinese Culture), Taibei: Dongda Book Company.

Qu Weiguo (1996): "Weiji? Jinbu? 危机？进步？ (Crisis or Progress?)." In: Wang Xiaoming 1996, pp. 100-105.

Rall, Jutta (1970): *Die vier großen Medizinschulen der Mongolenzeit. Stand und Entwicklung der chinesischen Medizin in der Chin- und Yüan-Zeit*, Wiesbaden: Franz Steiner Verlag.

Rawls, John (1999 [1971]): *A Theory of Justice*, Cambridge, Mass.: Harvard University Press.

Reckwitz, Andreas (2008): "Praktiken und Diskurse. Eine sozialtheoretische und methodologische Relation." In: Herbert Kathoff, Stefan Hirschauer and Gesa Lindemann (eds.), *Theoretische Empirie. Zur Relevanz qualitativer Forschung*, Frankfurt am Main: Suhrkamp Taschenbuch Wissenschaft, pp. 188-209.

Ricci, Matteo (1965): "Jiaoyou lun 交友論 (On Friendship)", in: Li Zhizao 李之藻 (ed.): *Tianxue chuhan* 天學初函 (On Tianxue), Taibei: Xuesheng shuju, vol. 1, pp. 299-320.

Roetz, Heiner (1992): *Die chinesische Ethik der Achsenzeit. Eine Rekonstruktion unter dem Aspekt des Durchbruchs zu postkonventionellem Denken*, Frankfurt/M.: Suhrkamp.

—— (1995): *Konfuzius*, München: Beck.

—— (2009): "China und die ‚Harmonische Gesellschaft': Die Welt als Garten." In: Deutsche China-Gesellschaft (ed.), *Mitteilungsblatt der Deutsche China-Gesellschaft*. Bochum, in print.

Ruan Yuan 阮元 (ed.) (1980): See *Shisanjing zhushu (fu jiaokanji)*.

Rummel, Stefan M. (1992): *Der Mönche und Nonnen Sündenmeer. Der buddhistische Klerus in der chinesischen Roman- und Erzählliteratur des 16. und 17. Jahrhunderts. Mit einer vollständigen Übersetzung der Sammlung Sengni niehai*, Bochum: Brockmeyer.

Sakade Yoshinobu 坂出祥伸 (1985): *Kō Yūi. Yūtopia no kaika* 康有為. ユートピアの開花 (Kang Youwei's Development of Utopia), Tōkyō: Shūeisha 集英社.

Sanguo zhi jijie 三國志集解 (Collected Annotations of the *Record of the Three Kingdoms*), ed. by Lu Bi 盧弼 (1876–1967), repr. Taipei: Xinwenfeng chubanshe, 1975.

Santangelo, Paolo (1994): "Emotions in Late Imperial China. Evolution and Continuity in Ming-Qing Perception of Passions." In: Vivienne Alleton and Alexei Volkov (eds.), *Notions et perceptions du changement en Chine. Textes présentés au IX Congrès de l'Association Eurpénne d'ètudes chinoises*. Paris: Collège de France, pp. 166-186.

Schäfer, Ingo (2001): "Natural Philosophy, Physics and Metaphysics in the Thought of Tan Sitong: The Concepts of *Qi* and *Yitai*." In: Michael Lackner, Iwo Amelung and Joachim Kurtz (eds.), *New Terms for New Ideas. Western Knowledge and Lexical Change in Late Imperial China*, Leiden: Brill, pp. 257-269.

Schilling, Dennis (2002): "The Making of the Jên Hsüeh." In: *Asiatische Studien* 61/3, pp. 677-704.

Schmidt, Stephan (2009): "Vorwort des Übersetzers und Herausgebers." In: Huang 2009, pp. 9-27.

Schmidt-Glintzer, Helwig (2003): "China im Wandel im 17. Jahrhundert." In: Klaus E. Müller (ed.): *Historische Wendeprozesse. Ideen, die Geschichte machten*, Freiburg, Basel and Wien: Herder Verlag, pp. 128-145.

Schucher, Günter (2007): "Harmonie ist Pflicht. China vor dem 17. Parteitag". In: *GIGA Focus Asien* 10/2007, 1-8 (http://www.giga-hamburg.de/dl/download.php?d=/content/publikationen/pdf/f_asien_0710.pdf).

Shek, Richard (1976): "Some Western Influences on T'an Ssu-t'ung's Thought." In: Paul A. Cohen and John E. Schrecker (eds.), *Reform in Nineteenth Century*, Cambridge, Mass.: Harvard University, East Asian Research Center, pp. 194-207.

Shen Weiwei 沈卫威 (2005): *Xuehengpai xipu* 学衡派系谱 (The Genealogy of the Xueheng School), Nanchang: Jiangxi jiaoyu chubanshe.

Shiji 史記 (Records of the Grand Historian), by Sima Qian 司馬遷 (ca. 145 – ca. 90/85). Beijing: Zhonghua shuju, 1959.

Shijing 詩經 (Book of Odes): See *Mao Shi zhengyi*.

Shin, Leo K. (2006): "The Last Campaigns of Wang Yangming." In: *T'oung Pao* 42, pp. 101-128.

Shi sanjia yi ji shu 詩三家義集疏 (Collected Glosses to the Three Shijing Schools and their Interpretations), by Wang Xianqian 王先謙 (1842–1917), punctuated and edited by Wu Ge 吳格, 2 vols., Beijing: Zhonghua shuju, 1987.

Shisanjing zhushu 十三經注疏 (*The Thirteen Classics*, with Annotations and Subcommentary), 1821 reprint of Song editions, repr. in 8 vols., Taipei: Yiwen yinshuguan, 1965.

Shisanjing zhushu (fu jiaokanji) 十三經注疏（附校勘記）(*The Thirteen Classics* with Commentarries, Subcommentaries and with Critical Notes Appended), 1816 standard edition of the *Thirteen Classics* prepared by Ruan Yuan 阮元 (1764–1849), repr. in 2 vols., Beijing: Zhonghua shuju, 1983.

Shi Zhiru (2010): "Buddhist Responses to State Control of Religion in China at the Century's Turn." In: Meinert and Zöllner 2010, pp. 125-157.

Shuowen jiezi 說文解字 (Explanations of Pictographs and Characters), compiled by Xu Shen 許慎 (2nd century AD), Shanghai: Shanghai guji chubanshe, 1981.

Siku quanshu zongmu tiyao 四庫全書總目提要 (Abstract to the Register of the *Complete Collection of Books in the Four Treasuries*), comp. by Ji Yun 紀昀 (1724–1805) et al., repr. Taibei: Yiwen yinshuguan.

Siku quanshu zongmu tiyao. Yijia lei ji xubian 四庫全書總目提要．醫家類及續編 (Abstract to the Section on Medicine of the Register of the *Complete Collection of Books in the Four Treasuries*), Shanghai, Shanghai kexue jishu chubanshe, 1992.

Sishu zhangju jizhu 四書章句集注 (*The Four Books* with Commentaries by Sections and Sentences and Collected Glosses), by Zhu Xi 朱熹 (1130–1200), Beijing: Zhonghua shuju, 1983.

Skinner, William (ed.) (1977): *The City in Late Imperial China,* Stanford: Stanford University Press.

Smith, Richard J. (1991): *Fortune-tellers and Philosophers: Divination in Traditional Chinese Society,* Boulder, San Francisco and Oxford: Westview Press.

Standaert, Nicolas (2001): *Handbook of Christianity in China. Volume One: 635–1800,* Leiden: Brill.

Stein, Stephan (1999a): "'Die wesentlichen Prinzipien zur Kultivierung der Langlebigkeit' (*Xiuling yaozhi* 修齡要旨), ein mingzeitliches Kompendium zur Kultivierung des Lebens (*yangsheng* 養生)." In: *Zeitschrift für Qigong Yangsheng. Berichte aus Theorie und Praxis, Medizin, Psychologie, Kunst, Kultur, Bildung,* pp. 41-52.

—— (1999b): *Zwischen Heil und Heilung. Zur frühen Tradition des Yangsheng in China,* Uelzen: Medizinische Literarische Verlagsgesellschaft.

Struve, Lynn A. (transl. and ed.) (1993): *Voices from the Ming-Qing Cataclysm: China in Tigers' Jaws,* New Haven and London: Yale University Press.

Sung, Z. D. (1935): *The Text of Yi King (and Its Appendixes). Chinese Original with English Translation*, Shanghai: China Modern Education.

Svarverud, Rune (2007): *International Law as World Order in Late Imperial China. Translation, Reception and Discourse, 1847–1911*, Leiden: Brill.

Talbott, Nathan (1960): "T'an Ssu-t'ung and the Ether." In: Robert Sakai (ed.), *Studies on Asia*, Lincoln: University of Nebraska, pp. 20-30.

Tan Sitong 譚嗣同 (1998 [1981]): *Tan Sitong quan ji (zeng ding ben)* 譚嗣同全集 (增訂本) (The Complete Works of Tan Sitong, enlarged and corrected edition), edited by Cai Shangsi 蔡尚思 and Fang Xing 方行, Beijing: Zhonghua shuju.

Tang, Chün-i / Tang Junyi 唐君毅 (1970): "The Development of the Concept of Moral Mind from Wang Yang-ming to Wang Chi." In: Wm. Theodore de Bary (ed.), *Self and Society in Ming Thought*, New York: Columbia Press, pp. 145-247.

—— (1984): *Zhongguo renwen jingshen zhi fazhan* 中国人文精神之发展 (The Development of Chinese Humanism), Taibei: Xuesheng shuju.

Tang Yi-jie (1991): *Confucianism, Buddhism, Daoism, Christianity and Chinese Culture*, Washington: The Council for Research in Values and Philosophy.

Tang Zhijun 湯志鈞 (1984 [1963]): "*Renxue* banben tanyuan 仁學版本探源" (Studies on the Editorial History of the *Learning of Humanity*). In: Tang Zhijun (ed.), *Kang Youwei yu Wuxu bianfa* 康有為與戊戌變法 (Kang Youwei and the Reform Movement of 1898), Beijing: Zhonghua shuju, pp. 301-321.

Tessenow, Hermann (1991): *Der chinesische Moralbegriff 'i'. Analyse von Texten aus Philosophie und Geschichtsschreibung*, Frankfurt/M.: Verlag Peter Lang.

Tu Weiming 杜维明 (1999): "Renwen jingshen yu quanqiu lunli 人文精神与全球伦理 (Humanism and Global Ethics)." In: *Renwen luncong* 人文论丛 (Humanities), pp. 28-40.

Unger, Ulrich (2000): *Grundbegriffe der altchinesischen Philosophie. Ein Wörterbuch für die Klassische Periode*, Darmstadt: Wissenschaftliche Buchgesellschaft.

Unschuld, Paul U. (1975): *Medizin und Ethik. Sozialkonflikte im China der Kaiserzeit*, Wiesbaden: Franz Steiner Verlag.

—— (2003): *Huang Di nei jing su wen. Nature, Knowledge, Imagery in an Ancient Chinese Medical Text. With an Appendix. The Doctrine of the Five Periods and Six Qi in the Huang Di nei jing su wen*, Berkeley, Los Angeles and London: University of California Press.

Volpp, Sophie (2003): "The Literary Consumption of Actors in Seventeenth-Century China." In: Judith T. Zeitlin and Lydia H. Liu with Ellen Widmer (eds.), *Writing and Materiality in China. Essays in Honour of Patrick Hanan,* Cambridge/Mass. and London: Harvard University Asia Press, pp. 133-183.
von Glahn, Richard (1996): *Fountain of Fortune. Money and Monetary Policy in China, 1000–1700,* Berkeley: University of California Press.
von Zach, Erwin (1939): *Yang Hsiung's FA-YEN (Worte strenger Ermahnung). Ein philosophischer Traktat aus dem Beginn der christlichen Zeitrechnung,* Batavia: Drukkerij Lux [repr. San Francisco: Chinese Materials Center, 1976].
Wakeman, Frederic, Jr. (1986): "China and the Seventeenth-Century Crisis." In: *Late Imperial China* 7/1, pp. 1-26.
Wang, Huangsheng and Wugong Hu (eds.) (2003): *Humanism in China (Zhongguo renben). A Contemporary Record of Photography,* Hong Kong: Anno Domini Publishing Company.
Wang, Hui, "Humanism as the Theme of Chinese Modernity". In: *Surfaces* 5.202 (01/11/1995): http://www.pum.umontreal.ca/revues/surfaces/vol5/hui.html.
Wang Jinggong wenji jianzhu 王荊公文集箋注 (Collected Works of Wang Jinggong [Wang Anshi 王安石, 1021–1086], with Brief Annotations), by Li Zhiliang 李之亮, 3 vols., Chengdu: Ba Shu shushe, 2005.
Wang Rongbao 汪荣宝 and Ye Lan 叶澜 (eds.) (1903): *Xin Erya* 新尔雅 (The New Approaching Correctness), Shanghai: Mingquan she.
Wang Xiaoming et al. (1993): "Kuangye shangde feixu: wenxue he renwen jingshen de weiji 旷野上的废墟：文学和人文精神的危机 (The Ruin on the Weald: The Crisis of Literature and Humanism)." In: Wang Xiaoming 1996, pp. 1-17.
Wang Xiaoming 王晓明 (ed.) (1996): *Renwen jingshen xunsilu* 人文精神寻思录 (Reflections on Humanism), Shanghai: Wenhui chubanshe.
Wang Yangming 王陽明 (1978): "Daxuewen 大學問 (Questions on the *Great Learning*)." In: *Wang Yangming xuanji* 王陽明選集 (Selected Works of Wang Yangming), Taibei: Zhongguo xueming zhujichengbian yinji jinhui.
—— (1992): "Chuanxi lu quanshi 傳習錄全譯 (*A Record for Practice*: A Complete Translation)," translated and edited by Bao Xifu 鮑希福, Chengdu: Ba Shu shushe.
—— (2006 [1992]): *Wang Yangming quanji* 王陽明全集 (The Complete Works of Wang Yangming), Shanghai: Shanghai guji chubanshe.
—— (1963): *Instructions for Practical Living and Other Neo-Confucian Writings by Wang Yangming,* translated, with notes, by Wing-tsit Chan, New York: Columbia University Press.

Watson, Burton (1993): *Records of the Grand Historian*, Hong Kong: Columbia UP.
Williams, Raymond (1976): *Keywords: A Vocabulary of Culture and Society*, London: Fontana Press.
Williamson, H[enry] R[aymond] (1935–1937): *Wang An Shih. A Chinese Statesman and Educationalist of the Sung Dynasty*, 2 vols., London: A. Probsthain.
Wong, Siu-kit (1969): *Ch'ing in Chinese Literature*, Ph.D. thesis, Oxford University.
—— (1978): "Ch'ing in Chinese Literary Criticism." In: Adele Rickett Austin (ed.), *Chinese Approaches to Literature from Confucius to Liang Ch'i-ch'ao*, Princeton: New Jersey, pp. 121-150.
Wood, Henry (1894): *Ideal Suggestion Through Mental Healing*, Boston: Lee and Shepard Publishers.
Wordern, Robert Leo (1972): *A Chinese Reformer in Exile: the North American Phase of the travels of K'ang Yu-wei, 1899–1909*, Ph.D. Diss. Washington, D.C., Georgetown University.
Wright, David (1994): "Tan Sitong and the ether reconsidered." In: *Bulletin of the School of Oriental and African Studies* 57, pp. 551-575.
Wu Guang 吳光 (1990): *Huang Zongxi zhuzuo huikao* 黃宗羲著作彙考 (A Comprehensive Investigation into the Writings of Huang Zongxi), Taipei: Taiwan xuesheng shuju.
Wu Mi 吳宓 (1995): *Wu Mi zibian nianpu 1894-1925* 吳宓自編年譜 (Wu Mi's Chronicle Autobiography 1894–1925), Beijing: Sanlian shudian.
—— (1998); *Wu Mi riji* 吳宓日記 (The Diaries of Wu Mi), 10 vols., Beijing: Sanlian shudian.
Wu Xizhao 吳熙釗 (1988): "Cong 'Jihe dingli' dao 'Renlei gongli' de tuiyan. 'Shili gongfa quanshu' jianlun 從「幾何定理」到「人類公里」的推演──《實理公法全書》簡論 (From the Axioms of Geometry to the Universal Principles of Humankind: A Preliminary Discussion of *The Comprehensive Writings on the Common Laws [based on] the Principles of Reality* (*Shili gongfa quanshu*))." In: Huang Mingtong 黃明同 et. al. (eds.), *Kang Youwei zaoqi yigao shuping* 康有為早期遺稿述評 (Critical Review of Early Manuscripts of Kang Youwei), Guangzhou: Zhongshan daxue chubanshe, pp. 43-57.
Wu Xuan 吳炫 et al. (1994): "Women xuyao zenmeyang de renwen jingshen? 我们需要怎样的人文精神？(What kind of Humanism We need?)." In: Wang Xiaoming 1996, pp. 59-71.
Xiao Jing 肖京 (1983): "Xuan qi jiu zheng lun 軒歧救正論 (A Treatise on the Rescue [of Life] According to Huangdi and Qi Bo)," repr. from the 1644 imprint, Beijing: Zhongyi guji chubanshe.

Xu Fuguan 徐复观 (1996): *Zhongguo renwen jingshen zhi chanyang* 中国人文精神之阐扬 (Interpreting Chinese Humanism), Beijing: Zhongguo guangbo dianshi chubanshe.

Xu Youcheng 徐有成 et al. (eds.) (1901): *Ouluoba tongshi* 欧罗巴通史 (European History), 2 vols., Shanghai: Dongya yishuhui.

Xunzi jianshi 荀子簡釋 (*The Book of Master Xun*, with a Short Commentary), edited by Liang Qixiong 梁啟雄. Beijing: Zhonghua shuju, 1983.

Yang Liuqiao 杨柳桥 (ed.) (2007): See *Zhuangzi yizhu*.

Yantie lun jiaozhu 鹽鉄論校註 (*Discourses on Salt and Iron*, with Commentary), edited by Wang Liqi 王利器, 2 vols., Beijing: Zhonghua shuju, 1992.

Yu, Ning (2009): *From Body to Meaning in Culture. Papers on Cognitive Semantic Studies of Chinese,* Amsterdam and Philadelphia: John Benjamins Publishing Company.

Yü, Ying-shih / Yu Yingshi 余英时 (2001): "Neither Renaissance nor Enlightenment: A Historian's Reflections on the May Fourth Movement." In: Milena Doleželová-Velingerová and Oldřich Král (eds.), *The Appropriation of Cultural Capital. China's May Fourth Project*, Cambridge/Mass. and London: Harvard UP, pp. 299-324.

—— (2004a): *Xiandai ruxue de huigu yu zhanwang* 现代儒学的回顾与展望 (*Modern Confucianism: Retrospect and Prospect*), Beijing: Sanlian shudian.

—— (2004b): "Xiandai ruxue de kunjing 现代儒学的困境 (The Predicament of Modern Confucianism)." In: Yu Yingshi (2004a), pp. 53-58.

Zang Shijun 臧世俊 (1997): *Kang Youwei Datong sixiang yanjiu* 康有為大同思想研究 (Studies on Kang Youwei's Philosophy of Great Unity), Guangzhou: Guangdong gaodeng jiaoyu chubanshe.

Zarrow, Peter (2004): "Late-Qing Reformism and the Meiji Model: Kang Youwei, Liang Qichao, and the Japanese Emperor." In: Joshua A. Fogel (ed.), *The Role of Japan in Liang Qichao's Introduction of Modern Western Civilization to China*, Berkeley: Center for Chinese Studies, Institute of East Asian Studies, University of California, pp. 40-67.

Zeitlin, Judith (1991): "The Petrified Heart: Obsession in Chinese Literature, Art, and Medicine." In: *Late Imperial China* 12/1, pp. 1-26.

Zhang Binglin 章炳麟 (1984): *Qiu shu chongding ben* 訄書重訂本 (Book of Force, Revised Edition). In: *Zhang Taiyan quanji* 章太炎全集 (Collected Works of Zhang Taiyan), vol. 3, punctuated and edited by Zhu Weizheng 朱維錚, Shanghai: Renmin chubanshe.

Zhang Dejun 張德鈞 (1962): "Liang Qichao ji Tan Sitong shishi shibian 梁啟超紀譚嗣同事失實辨 (Corrections of Misgiven Facts in Liang Qichao's Records about Tan Sitong)." In: *Wenshi* 文史 (History of Literature) 1, pp. 81-85.

Zhang Junmai 张君劢 et al. (1997): *Kexue yu renshengguan* 科学与人生观 (Science and the View of Human Life), Jinan: Shandong renmin chubanshe.

Zhang Qiyun 張其昀 (1988): *Zhang Qiyun xiansheng wenji* 張其昀先生文集 (The Works of Zhang Qiyun), 25 vols., Taibei: Zhongguo wenhua daxue chubanshe.

Zhang Rulun 张汝伦 and Lin Hui 林晖 (1996): "Guanyu renwen jingshen 关于人文精神 (On Humanism)." In: Wang Xiaoming 1996, pp. 156-165.

Zhang Zai (1985): *Zhang Zai ji* 張載集 (The Collected Works of Zhang Zai), Beijing: Zhonghua shu ju.

Zhao Xianke 趙縣可 (1982): *Yiguan* 醫貫 (Thoroughgoing Knowledge on Medicine), reprint from 1617, Beijing: Renmin weisheng chubanshe.

Zheng Jinsheng 鄭金生 (1999): *Zhongguo gudai yangsheng* 中國古代養生 (Nourishing Life in Early China), Taibei: Tawain shangwu yinshuguan.

Zheng, Yongnian and Sow Keat Tok (2007): "'Harmonious Society' and 'Harmonious World': China's Policy Discourse under Hu Jintao". In: *Briefing Series Issue* 26 (The University of Nottingham. China Policy Institute, http://www.nottingham.ac.uk/cpi/documents/briefings/briefing-26-harmnious-society-and-harmonious-world.pdf).

Zhou Fucheng 周辅成 (1984): "Tan guanyu rendao zhuyi taolun zhongde wenti 谈关于人道主义讨论中的问题 (On Problems in the Discussion of Humanism)." In: *Shijie lishi* 世界历史 (World History) 2, pp. 8-10.

Zhou Zuoren 周作人(1982): *Zhou Zuoren huiyi lu* 周作人回忆录 (Memoirs of Zhou Zuoren), Changsha: Hunan renmin chubanshe.

—— (2002a): *Yishu yu shenghuo* 艺术与生活 (Art and Life), edited by Zhi An 止庵, Shijiazhuang: Hebei jiaoyu chubanshe.

—— (2002b): "Human Literature 人的文学 (Rende wenxue)", in: Zhou Zuoren 2002a, pp. 8-17.

—— (2002c), "Xinwenxue de yaoqiu 新文学的要求 (The Demand of a New Literature)." In: Zhou Zuoren 2002a, pp. 18-23.

Zhou Yi 周易 (The Book of Changes), Beijing: Zhonghua shuju, 2007.

Zhu Dongrun 朱东润 (ed.) (2007): *Zuozhuan xuan* 左传选 (A Selection of the Commentary of Zuo), Shanghai: Shanghai guji chubanshe.

Zhu Weizheng 朱維錚 / 朱维铮 (1989): "Shiluole de 'wenyi fuxing' 失落了的文藝復興 (The Forfeit Literary Recovery)." In: Lin Yusheng 林毓生 et al., *Wusi: duoyuan de fansi* 五四：多元的反思 (The Fifth-May Movement: Rethinking It's Multiple Origins), Hong Kong: Sanlian, pp. 82-91.

—— (1990), *Coming Out of the Middle Ages. Comparative Reflections on China and the West*, Armonk and London: Sharpe

—— (1996): "Hewei renwen jingshen? 何谓人文精神 (What is Humanism?)." In: Wang Xiaoming 1996, pp. 129-136.

—— (2002): *Zhongguo jingxueshi shi jiang* 中國經學史十講 (Ten Discourses on the History of Chinese Classical Studies), Shanghai: Fudan daxue chubanshe.

Zhu Xi 朱熹 (1986): *Sishu zhangju jizhu* 四書章句集注 (Explanations and Collected Commentaries on *The Four Books*), Beijing: Zhonghua shuju.

Zhu Xi ji 朱熹集 (Zhu Xi's Collected Works), punctuated and edited by Guo Qi 郭齊 and Yin Bo 尹波, 10 vols., Chengdu: Sichuan jiaoyu chubanshe, 1996.

Zhuangzi, translated by Fung You-lan, Beijing: Foreign Language Press, 1989.

Zhuangzi jishi 莊子集釋 ([The Writings of] Master Zhuang, with Collected and Commentary), edited by Guo Qingfan 郭慶藩 (1844–1896), Taipei: Muduo Press, 1983.

Zhuangzi jin zhu jin yi 莊子今注今譯 ([The Writings of] Master Zhuang, with Present-Day Translations and Annotations), edited by Chen Guying 陳鼓應, Beijing: Zhonghua shuju, 1983.

Zhuangzi yizhu 庄子译注 ([The Writings of] Master Zhuang, with Translation and Commentary), edited by Yang Liuqiao 杨柳桥. Shanghai, Shanghai Guji Press, 2007.

Zhuzi yulei 朱子語類 (Classified Sayings by Master Zhu [Zhu Xi 朱熹, 1130–1200]), punctuated and edited by Wang Xingxian 王星賢, 8 vols., Beijing: Zhonghua shuju, 1986.

Ziporyn, Brook (2003): *The Penumbra Unbound. The Neo-Taoist Philosophy of Guo Xiang*, Albany: State University of New York Press.

Table of Chinese Dynasties

Shang dynasty	*1766–1122 BC (* refers to traditional counting)
Zhou dynasty	*1122–256 BC
Western Zhou	1045–771 BC
Eastern Zhou	770–256 BC
Spring and Autumn Period	722–481 BC
Warring States Period	403–221 BC
Qin dynasty	221–207 BC
Han dynasty	206 BC–220 AD
Western Han	206 BC–8 AD
Xin Dynasty (Interregnum)	9–23
Eastern Han	25–220
Three Kingdoms	220–420
Wei	220–265
Shu	221–263
Wu	222–280
Western Jin	265–316
Eastern Jin	317–420
Southern and Northern dynasties	420–589
Southern dynasties	420–589
Northern dynasties	386–581
Sui	581–618
Tang	618–907

Five Dynasties	907–960	
Song dynasty	960–1279	
Northern Song	960–1126	
Southern Song	1127–1279	
Yuan dynasty (Mongols)	1271–1368	
Ming dynasty	1368–1644	
Qing dynasty (Manchus)	1644–1911	
Republic of China	1912–1949	(since 1949 on Taiwan)
People's Republic of China	since 1949	

List of Chinese Characters

ai 愛 (care, love)
ai 薆 (secluded)
ai er bu jian 愛而不見
aili 愛力
ai qi qin 愛其親
ai ren 愛人
ai wu 愛物
aixi 愛惜
anning 安寧

ba 霸
bachu baijia duzun rushu 罷黜百家，獨尊儒術
badao 霸道
baihua 白話
baijia 百家
Baoyan tang Miji guanghan 寶顏堂祕笈廣函
ben bing 本柄
ben xin 本心
bi fa 必法
bili 比例
boshi 博士
bu ren 不仁
bu jin renqing 不近人情
buyi 布衣

cai 才
Cao Shen 曹參

ceyin 惻隱
ch'ien see qian
Chan, Wing-tsit 陳榮捷
Chang'an 長安
Chen Jiru 陳繼儒
Chen Ping 陳平
Chen Sheng 陳勝
Chen Shiduo 陳士鐸
chengren quyi 成仁取義
Cheng Shude 程樹德
Cheng Yi 程頤
chengxiang 丞相
Chunqiu 春秋
Chunqiu fanlu 春秋繁露
Chunqiu jing 春秋經
Chunqiu jueshi bi 春秋決事比
congshu 叢書

da qi 大器
da ren 大人
Datong shu 大同書
Daxue 大學
Daxue wen 大學問
da yitong 大一統
Dazhuan 大傳
Daifang lu 待訪錄
dangyu shier guan pingdeng 當於十二官平等
dao 道

173

Daodejing 道德經
Daojia 道家
daoli 道理
dao xin 道心
daoyin 導引
de 德
deyi 德醫
deng 等
Ding Wenjiang 丁文江
dong 動
Dong Leshan 董樂山
Dong Zhongshu 董仲舒
du ren 度人
dusheng 獨聖
Dushu 讀書
Du Zhou 杜周

Erya 爾雅

Fajia 法家
fangji 方技
Fan Li 范蠡
fangzhong 房中
fei 非
fei renqing 非人情
fenshu kengru 焚書坑儒
fengchang 奉常
fengshan 封禪
Fengshan shu 封禪書
Feng Menglong 馮夢龍
Fu Shan 傅山

gao seng 高僧
Ge Kuanrao 蓋寬饒
gewu zhizhi 格物致知
gong 工
gongfa 公法
gongli 公利
Gongsun Hong 公孫弘
Gongyang chunqiu 公羊春秋
Gongyang Gao 公羊高
Gongyang Shou 公羊壽

Gongyang zhuan 公羊傳
Guliang zhuan 穀梁傳
Gu Yanwu 顧炎武
guwen 古文
guwen xue 古文學
Guo Xiang 郭象
Guandong 關東

hai ti zhi tong 孩提之童
Han Aidi 漢哀帝
Han Fei 韓非
Han Feizi 韓非子
Han Gaozu 漢高祖
Han Huidi 漢惠帝
Hanshu 漢書
Han Wudi 漢武帝
Han Xin 韓信
Han Xuandi 漢宣帝
Han Yu 韓愈
Han Yuandi 漢元帝
he 和
hetong 合同
hexie 和諧
He Xinyin 何心隱
He Yan 何晏
Hu Shi 胡適
Hu Xiansu 胡先驌
Huangdi 黃帝
Huanglao 黃老
Huang Zongxi 黃宗羲
hui 會
Hunnu 匈奴
Huo Guang 霍光
Huozhi liezhuan 貨殖列傳

Ji An 汲黯
ji fa 急法
jixin 機心
jian'ai 兼愛
jian ye 賤業
jianyi 奸醫
jiang 匠

Jiang Guilin 蔣貴麟
Jiaoyou lun 交友論
Jieshuo 界說
jinwen 今文
jinwen xue 今文學
jing 經 (wrap, canonial scripture)
jing 敬 (respectful)
jing 靜 (tranquility)
Jingjie 經解
jingxue 經學
jingxueshi 經學史
jingyan 經筵
jing zuo 靜坐
jun 軍 (military)
jun 均 (equally [distributed])
junren nanmian zhi shu 君人南面之術
jun tian 均田
junzi 君子

Kang Youwei 康有為
ke ji 克己
keju 科舉
kexuan lunzhan 科玄論战
kexue renwen zhuyi 科學人文主義
kexue wanneng lun 科學萬能論
Kongzi 孔子
kou chi 口齒

leishu 類書
li 禮 (etiquette, rites, propriety)
li 理 (principle, order)
Li Bo 李白
Liji 禮記
Liji zhengyi 禮記正義
Li Si 李斯
li wu 利物
Li yun 禮運
Li Zhi 李贄
li zhi 勵志
lian 憐

Liang Qichao 梁啟超
liangzhi 良知
Lin Yutang 林語堂
ling 令
Liu Bang 劉邦
Liu, Lydia 劉禾
Liu Xiang 劉向
Liu Xin 劉歆
liuyi 流醫
Liu Zehua 劉泽華
Lu Aigong 魯哀公
Lu Bi 盧弼
Lu Jia 陸賈
luan 亂
Luntai zuiji zhao 輪台罪己詔
Lunyu 論語
lü 律
Lü Huanghou 呂皇后
Lüshi chunqiu 呂氏春秋

manmo 蠻貊
men 門
Mengzi 孟子
min 民
Minyue 閩越
ming 名 (name; position and function)
ming 命 (command)
ming 明 (acumen)
mingchao 明朝
Mingjia 名家
mingmen 命門
Ming Taizu 明太祖
mingyi 名醫 (famous physicians)
mingyi 明醫 (illustrious physicians)
mingyi 明夷 (Ming loyalist scholars)
Mingyi Daifang lu 明夷待訪錄
Mojia 墨家
Mozi 墨子
Mou Zongsan 牟宗三

175

nei duo yu er wai shi ren yi 內多欲而外施仁義
Ni Kuan 兒寬
nong 農
nüyi 女醫
Ouluoba tongshi 歐羅巴通史
Ouyou xinying lu 歐游心影錄

Peng Guoxiang 彭國翔
pi 癖
Pi Xirui 皮錫瑞
pian 篇
ping 平
pingdeng 平等
pinghang 平行
pingmian 平面
Pingzhun shu 平準書

qi 氣
qi chaoyi 起朝儀
qilin 麒麟
qimeng 啟蒙
qiren 奇人
qi ren zhi yu ruzi er wei yi ti 其仁之與孺子而一體
qi ren zhi yu washi er wei yi ti 其仁之與瓦石而為一體
qian 乾
Qian Mu 錢穆
Qin Ershi 秦二世
qin qin 親親
Qin Shihuang 秦始皇
qing 情
qingchao 清朝
qinghua 情化
qingjiao 情教
Qingshi 情史
Qu Weiguo 曲衛國
quanyi 權宜
quegu 郤穀

ren 人 (man, human being)

ren 仁 (humaneness, benevolence, compassion, etc.)
renben zhuyi 人本主義
rendao 人道
rendao zhuyi 人道主義
Ren de wenxue 人的文學
ren guan 任官
Renlei gongli 人類公理
renlei men 人類門
ren min 仁民
renqing 人情
renquan 人權
Rensheng guan 人生觀
renwen 人文
renwen jingshen 人文精神
renwen zhuyi 人文主義
ren wu 仁物
ren xin 人心
Renxue 仁學
renzhe 仁者
renzheng 仁政
renzhi 人治
riyong leishu 日用類書
ru 儒
Rujia 儒家
Rulin liezhuan 儒林列傳
rushu 儒術
ruyi 儒醫

sanjiao he yi 三教合一
sengyi 僧醫
shanrang 禪讓
shang 商
Shangshu 尚書
Shanghai wenxue 上海文學
shang ren hu 傷人乎
Shang Yang 商鞅
shen 身
Shen Buhai 申不害
Shenbao 申報
sheng 生

sheng 聖
sheng ren 聖人
shengyuan 生員
shi 是 (affirmation)
shi 士 (scholars)
Shiji 史記
Shijing 詩經
shili 實理
Shili gongfa quanshu 實理公法全書
Shisan jing 十三經
shi tianxia wei yijia 視天下為一家
shiyi 時醫 (temporary physicians)
shiyi 世醫 (heredity physicians)
shiyin 市隱
shu 恕 (reciprocity)
shu 術 (thoroughfare, statecraft)
Shujing 書經
Shusun Tong 叔孫通
Shun 舜
si de 四德
si duan 四端
Siku quanshu 四庫全書
Sima Guang 司馬光
Sima Qian 司馬遷
Sima Tan 司馬談
sishi 四時
Sishu 四書
Sishu wujing 四書五經
siwen 斯文
si yi 四夷
songchao 宋朝
Sui Hong 睦弘

taichang 太常
taifu 太傅
Tan Sitong 譚嗣同
Tang Caichang 唐才常
Tang Junyi 唐君毅
Tang Xianzu 湯顯祖
Tang Zhen 唐甄

Tang Zhijun 湯志鈞
ti ren 體仁
tian 天
tiandao 天道
Tian Fen 田蚡
tian li 天理
tianming 天命
Tianren sance 天人三策
tianwen 天文
tianxia 天下
tianxia wu yi yi 天下無異意
tianxia zhi dadao 天下之達道
tong 同 (community, co-existence)
tong 通 (communication)
tongjing zhiyong 通經致用
tugu naxin 吐古吶新
Tu Weiming 杜維明
tui chuan yu lu 推船於陸

wan wu 萬物
wang 王
Wang Anshi 王安石
Wang Bi 王弼
wangdao 王道
Wang Fuzhi 王夫之
Wang Mang 王莽
Wang Taiqing 王太慶
Wang Xiaoming 王曉明
Wang Yangming 王陽明
wei chi see *wei ji*
wei hanjia ruzong 為漢家儒宗
wei ji 未濟
wei ren 為仁
wei rensheng er wenxue 為人生而文學
wei shi ruzong 為世儒宗
wei yishu er yishu 為藝術而藝術
wen yi zai dao 文以載道
wo gu 握固
wu 武 (rigor)
wu 無 (nothingness)

wu chang 五常
wu duidai 無對待
Wujing 五經
wu lun 五倫
Wu Mi 吳宓
wuming 無明
wu shen 吾身
wu suo bu shi 無所不施
wu suo you 無所有
wuwei 無為
wuwei er zhi 無爲而治
wu xing 五行

xili 吸力
Ximing 西銘
xianren 仙人
Xiang Yu 項羽
xiao dao 小道
Xiaojing 孝經
Xiao He 蕭何
xiaoren 小人
xin 心 (heart, mind-heart)
xin 信 (trust)
Xin Erya 新尔雅
xinli 心力
Xin qingnian 新青年
xin shang 信賞
xinshu 心術
Xin rujia 新儒家
Xinwenhua yundong 新文化運動
xinxue 心學 (Learning of the mind-heart)
xinxue 新學 (new learning)
xing 性 (nature)
xing 行 (putting into practice)
xing er shang 形而上
xing er xia 形而下
xing jiaohua 興教化
Xingli jingyi 性理精義
xing ming 刑名
xiu shen 修身

xiu zhengzhi 修政治
Xu Fuguan 徐复觀
xu xin shun li 虛心順理
xuanxue 玄學
xue 大學
xueheng 學衡
Xueheng pai 學衡派
Xueqi xingzhi 血氣形志
xue sui shu bian 學隨術變
Xun Kuang 荀況
Xunzi 荀子

Yamen 衙門
Yan Hui 顏回
Yantie lun 鹽鉄論
Yan Yuan 顏元
yang baixing 養百姓
yangsheng 養生
Yang Shi 楊適
Yang Xiong 揚雄
yangyi 瘍醫
Yao 堯
yeshi 業識
yi 義 (righteousness, duty)
yi 宜 (handling matters in an appropriate way)
Yiguan 醫貫
Yijing 易經
Yili 儀禮
yiren 異人 (extraordinary people)
yiren 逸人 (hidden people)
yi renshu ye 醫仁術也
yishu 醫術
yitai 以太
yi tian di wanwu wei yi ti 以天地萬物為一體
yinren 隱人
yin yang 陰陽
Yinyangjia 陰陽家
yinyi 隱醫 (hidden, reclusive physicians)

178

yinyi 淫醫 (immoral, licentious physicians)
yong yi 庸醫
youhun 游魂
Youlun 友論
you xue qi zhe 有血氣者
yu 欲
yulu 語錄
yushi daifu 御史大夫
Yu Yingshi 余英時
Yuan Hongdao 袁宏道
Yuan Shikai 袁世凱
Yuejing 樂經

Zaiyu 宰予
zhang 章
Zhang Binglin 章炳麟
Zhang Chunnian 張椿年
Zhang Junmai 張君勱
Zhang Liang 張良
Zhang Qiyun 張其昀
Zhang Rulun 張汝論
Zhang Tang 張湯
Zhang Taiyan 章太炎
zhangtong gujin 掌通古今
Zhang Zai 張載
Zhao Gao 趙高
Zhao Qi 趙岐
Zhao Xianke 趙縣可
zheng 政
Zhengmeng 正蒙
zheng qi xin 正其心

zheng xin 正心
Zheng Xuan 鄭玄
zhi 智 or 知
zhizhe 智者

zhongyi 眾醫
Zhongyong 中庸
Zhou Bo 周勃
zhouchao 周朝
Zhou Fucheng 周輔成
Zhouli 周禮
Zhou Yi 周易
Zhou Yutong 周予同
Zhou Zuoren 周作人
Zhufu Yan 主父偃
Zhu Xi 朱熹
zhu xin 誅心
zhuyi 主義
Zhu Zhenheng 朱震亨
Zhuzi 朱子
zhuzi baijia 諸子百家
Zhuang Zhou 莊周
Zhuangzi 莊子
zi ai, ren zhi zhi ye 自愛，仁之至也
Zigong 子貢 or 子贛
Zizhi tongjian 資治通鑒
zhongnong yishang 重農抑商
zun 尊
Zuozhuan 左傳

Indices (of Names and Subjects)

Part 1: Index of Names

Ai of Lu, Duke (r. 495–468 BC) 78
Ankersmit, Franklin (born 1945) 132
Aristotle (384–322 BC) 143

Babbitt, Irving (1865–1933) 131, 135, 142-143
Bergson, Henri (1859–1941) 141
Bullock, Alan (1914–2004) 132, 148
Burckhardt, Jacob (1818–1897) 134

Cao Shen (d. 190 BC) 25
Chan, Wing-tsit (1901–1994) 77, 84-85, 93,
Chen Jiru (1558–1639) 109
Chen Ping (d. 178 BC) 29
Chen Sheng (d. 208 BC) 21
Chen Shiduo (1627–1707) 100
Cheng Shude (1877–1944) 35
Cheng Yi (1033–1107) 104
Chow Tse-tsung (1916–2007) 83, 138
Confucius (ca. 551–479 BC) 10, 12-14, 20, 27, 32, 35, 39, 41-44, 47, 51-55, 58, 61-63, 66, 69-71, 73, 76, 78, 84, 109, 143

Davies, Tony (born 1940) 148-149
De Bary, Wm. Theodore (born 1919) 95, 111, 113
Derrida, Jacques (1930–2004) 132
Ding Wenjiang (1887–1936) 141
Dong Leshan (1924–1999) 132
Dong Zhongshu (179–104 BC) 14, 29-35, 37, 43, 45-46
Du Zhou 33

Elvin, Mark 72
Emperor Hui of Han (210–188 BC) 26, 44
Emperor Wu of Han (156–87 BC) 20, 29-45
Emperor Xuan of Han (91–49 BC) 44, 46
Emperor Yuan of Han (74–33 BC) 31
Empress Lü (241–180 BC) 28-29

Feng Menglong (1574–1646) 93-94
First Emperor of Qin (259–210 BC) 12, 20, 22-23, 27-28, 33, 35, 39-40, 43-44
Fu Shan (1607–1684) 110

Ge Kuanrao (d. 60 BC) 46-47
Gongsun Hong (200–121 BC) 29, 35-39
Gongyang Gao 32
Gongyang Shou 32
Graham, A.C. (1919–1991) 50-51, 53, 56-61, 63-66
Great Founder of Han (256/247–195 BC) 21-29, 41, 45
Gu Yanwu (1613–1682) 97
Guo Xiang (252–312) 15, 53-54, 65

Han Fei (ca. 281–233 BC) 12, 28, 31
Han Feizi see Han Fei
Han Gaozu see Great Founder of Han
Han Huidi see Emperor Hui of Han
Han Wudi see Emperor Wu of Han
Han Xin (d. 196 BC) 24, 28
Han Xuandi see Emperor Xuan of Han
Han Yu (768–824) 85
Han Yuandi see Emperor Yuan of Han
He Xinyin (1517–1579) 109-110
He Yan (195–249) 35
Hobbes, Thomas (1588–1679) 50
Hu Shi (1891–1962) 20, 85, 131, 136, 138-141
Hu Xiansu (1894–1968) 131, 135, 142
Huang, Martin W. 89
Huang Zongxi (1610–1695) 97, 104-105, 110-115, 120, 127, 129-130
Huangdi see Yellow Emperor
Huo Guang (d. 68 BC) 20, 46

Ji An (d. 112 BC) 37
Jiang Guilin 117

Kang Youwei (1858–1927) 16, 104-105, 114, 116-121, 127, 129-130

Kongzi see Confucius

Laozi 12, 25, 30
Li Bo (701–762) 110
Li Si (280–208 BC) 22, 27-28
Li Zhi (1527–1602) 110
Liang Qichao (1873–1929) 121, 141
Lin Yutang (1895–1976) 143
Liu Bang see Great Founder of Han
Liu, Lydia (born 1957) 133
Liu Xiang (77–6 BC) 31
Liu Zehua (born 1935) 148
Lu Aigong see Ai of Lu, Duke
Lu Bi (1876–1967) 38
Lu Jia (ca. 228–140 BC) 26
Lü Huanghou see Empress Lü

Marx, Karl (1818–1883) 134
Mengzi see Mencius
Mencius (372–289) 12-13, 43, 51, 69, 74, 84, 85, 101
Ming Taizu (1328–1398) 96
Mirandola, Pico della (1463–1494) 84
Moeller, Hans-Georg 65
Mozi (ca. 490–381 BC) 12, 58, 74
Mou Zongsan (1909–1995)

Ni Kuan (d. 103 BC) 29, 36
Niethammer, Friedrich Immanuel (1766–1848) 133
Nietzsche, Friedrich (1844–1900) 50, 139

Peng Guoxiang 86
Pi Xirui (1850–1908) 29, 38, 43-44

Qian Mu (1895–1990) 145
Qin Ershi see Second Emperor of Qin
Qin Shihuang see First Emperor of Qin
Qu Weiguo (born 1958) 148

Ricci, Matteo (1552–1610) 109, 134
Roetz, Heiner (born 1950) 9-10, 70, 83, 88
Ruge, Arnold (1802–1880) 134

Second Emperor of Qin (230–207 BC) 23
Shang Yang (395–338 BC) 31
Shen Buhai (420–337 BC) 28
Shusun Tong (ca. 250–180 BC) 23-28, 43
Shun (founder of the Zhou dynasty) see also Yao 22, 27, 47, 52, 54
Sima Guang (1019–1086) 78-79
Sima Qian (145/135–90/85 BC) 25, 27, 30-31, 41-42
Sima Tan (165–110 BC) 27, 30
Sui Hong 46

Tan Sitong (1865–1898) 16, 84, 104-105, 120-130
Tang Caichang (1867–1900) 121
Tang Junyi (1909–1978) 144-145
Tang Xianzu (1550–1616) 93
Tang Zhen (1630–1704) 110
Tang Zhijun (b. 1924) 117, 121
Tian Fen (d. 131 BC) 30
Tu Weiming (born 1940) 146

Voigt, Georg (1827–1891) 133

Wang Anshi (1021–86) 71-72, 76, 78, 80-81
Wang Bi (226–249) 96
Wang Fuzhi (1609–1692) 97
Wang Taiqing (1922–2000) 137
Wang Xiaoming (born 1955) 131, 146-147
Wang Yangming (1472–1529) 16, 84, 89-93, 97, 101, 110
Wood, Henry (1834–1908) 124
Wu Mi (1894–1978) 131, 135-136, 142-143

Xiang Yu (232–202 BC) 22, 24
Xiao He (257–193 BC) 25, 28, 31
Xu Fuguan (1903–1982) 144,-146
Xun Kuang (ca. 312–230 BC) 35, 43, 51, 75, 84
Xunzi see Xun Kuang

Yan Hui (514–483 BC) 72
Yan Yuan (1635–1704) 97
Yang Shi (born 1932) 137
Yang Xiong (53 BC–18 AD) 74-76
Yao (founder of the Zhou dynasty) see also Shun 22, 27, 47, 52, 54, 56, 61, 91
Yellow Emperor 47, 100
Yu Yingshi (born 1930) 17, 144
Yuan Hongdao (1568–1610) 93
Yuan Shikai (1859–1916) 120

Zaiyu (522–458 BC) 42
Zhang Binglin (1869–1936) 23, 34
Zhang Chunnian (1889–1927) 137
Zhang Junmai (1887–1968) 141, 144-145
Zhang Liang (d. 186 BC) 24
Zhang Qiyun (1900–1985) 142-143
Zhang Rulun (born 1957) 147-148
Zhang Tang (d. 115 BC) 32
Zhang Taiyan see Zhang Binglin
Zhang Zai (1020–1077) 90, 107
Zhao Gao (d. 207 BC) 28
Zhao Qi (108–201) 35
Zhao Xianke (ca. 1567–1644) 100
Zheng Xuan (127–200) 45
Zhou Bo (d. 169 BC) 29
Zhou Fucheng (1911–2009) 137
Zhou Yutong (1898–1981) 43
Zhou Zuoren (1885–1967) 135, 138-140
Zhu Xi (1130–1200) 69, 72-75, 77-78, 80, 84-85, 88-89, 93, 95, 104, 108

Zhu Zhenheng (1281–1358) 99-100
Zhufu Yan (d. 126 BC) 37
Zhuzi see Zhu Xi
Zhuangzi see Zhuang Zhou

Zhuang Zhou (d. 286 BC) 12, 15, 49-50, 65-66
Zigong (520–456 BC) 21, 41-42

Part 2: Index of Subjects

abdicate the throne 46-47
abstention from grains 97
Academy of Actual Affairs 120-121
act according to expediency 75
activity/movement 71, 89, 93
acumen 78-79
affirmation, affirm 56-57, 126
ai 愛 see care, love
ai 薆 see secluded
aili see attraction
all beings of blood and *qi* 91
allowing plenty of desires inwardly, yet outwardly exhibiting benevolence and righteousness 34
all under heaven 13, 28, 47, 78, 92, 109-114
    all under heaven as one family 110
    no dissent under heaven 13, 15, 28, 33, 43
altruistic 114, 122
American New Thought 124
Analects [of Confucius] 13, 20, 35, 42, 45, 52-55, 69-73, 84, 109
ancient cultures 52
anning see peace, internal peace and stability
anti-intellectualism 23, 26
aphasia 147
appropriate action 53
art exists for its own sake 138
art of one's heart 80-81
artisan 99
assessment 50-51, 57-66

attraction 122
authoritarian 10, 105
authority 27, 36, 73-74, 52, 63, 66, 96, 98, 104-114, 119, 129, 140, 148
    clan authority 107, 114
    political authority 107, 08, 114
    radical denying of any authority 129
    social authority 107, 112, 115
    symbolic authority 114
autocratic monarchy 13, 29
avidyā (Skr.) see ignorance

ba see overlord
bachu baijia duzun rushu see Hundred Schools of Thought; see also Confucianism, Confucian statecraft
badao see overlord, way of the overlord
bai jia see Hundred Schools of Thought
baihua see Vernacular Chinese
Baoyan tang Miji guanghan see *Confidential and Public Writings of the 'Hall of Esteemed Persons'*
ben bing see root and trunk
ben xin see original mind
benevolent government of the people 72
bili see proportion
Biographies of Confucian Scholars 31

INDICES (OF NAMES AND SUBJECTS)

Biographies of the Money-makers 41
Book of Changes 13, 19, 22, 44-45, 71, 79, 96, 106, 122, 127-128, 136
Book of Documents 13, 36, 44-46
Book of Great Unity 117
Book of Mencius 13, 69, 72, 74, 80, 84-85, 92, 112, 122,
Book of Music 13, 45
Book of Odes 13, 44-46, 74, 77
Book of Rites 13, 45, 84, 110, 121
Book of Zhuangzi 49-66, 76
boshi see erudite
brand, branded 56-57, 61, 99
breathing practices 97
bringing something to peace 114
bu ren see numb, being without sensation, to have no feeling
Buddhism, Buddhist 12, 15-16, 89, 95-102, 104, 114-117, 122-124, 127
    Buddhist conception of mind 123
    Buddhist enlightenment 122
    Buddhist monasteries 96
    Buddhist monk 15, 100
    Buddhist Vijñānavada theory 123
bureaucracy 15, 27, 40, 116
burning books and burying scholars 23, 28
butterfly dream 65
buyi see cloth gown

cai see competent and capable
care, love 70-75, 85
caritas 73
Ceremonies and Rites 13
ceyin see commiseration
ch'ien see creation

Chancellor 30, 37
change 9, 22-29, 46, 53, 62, 66, 77, 83, 86, 103-106, 113, 126-129
    changing society 9
    transformation processes 10, 87
    societal transformation 10
    societal changes/shift 13, 15-16
charity 75
chengren quyi see die for a noble cause
chengxiang see chancellor
Chinese Axial Age 70
Christian 75, 109-110, 118, 134-135, 139
    Christian doctrine 118
    Christian mission 109
Chunqiu see *Spring and Autumn Annals*
Chunqiu fanlu see *Rich Dew of the Spring and Autumn Annals*
Chunqiu jing see *Spring and Autumn Annals*
Chunqiu jueshi bi see *Collection of Adjudications Based on the Spring and Autumn Annals*
civil government 26
civilization 145
Classic of Virtue and the Way 49
Classical Chinese 138
Classical Learning 21, 36, 38, 43-44
history of Classical Learning 21, 27, 31
clenching the fists 97
cloth gown 21
cognition 112, 123, 124
    false cognition 123-124
    karmic cognition 123-124
collectanea 96
Collection of Adjudications Based on the Spring and Autumn Annals 35

185

collective 112, 123-125, 128
  collective identity 125
  collective mental activity 123
  collective mentality 123
  collective mind 125
command 107
Commentary of Gongyang 13
Commentary of Guiliang 44
Commentary of Zuo 13, 136
commercial companies 87
commiseration 72
common 9, 21, 22, 29, 33, 43-44, 51, 53, 73-77, 97-98, 104-106, 110-126, 129
  common benefit 111-112
  common good 111-116, 120, 129
  common harm 111
  common laws 117, 119
  common physicians 98
commoners 23, 99
communication 113, 118, 122-126
community 110, 112, 115, 125
  co-existence 115
competent and capable 79
Complete Collection of Books in the Four Treasuries 34, 99-100
Comprehensive Mirror for Aid in Government 78-79
Comprehensive Writings on the Common Laws [based on] the Principles of Reality 116-117
conditio humana 12, 69
Confidential and Public Writings of the 'Hall of Esteemed Persons' 109
Confucianism 10, 13, 16-17, 26, 34, 43, 51, 55, 58, 65, 70, 76-78, 86, 95-96, 102, 104, 110, 135, 143-146

Confucian Classical Learning, Confucian classics 14, 43, 86, 136
Confucian ideal of humaneness 15
Confucian Institutes 10
Confucian moral virtues 51
(Confucian) naturalistic view (of society) 104-107, 114, 118-122, 126, 129
Confucian pantheon 42
Confucian scholars 23-24, 30, 36-37, 91, 98
Confucian state ideology 12-17
Confucian statecraft 13-14, 29-37, 42-46
Confucian values 15, 75
imperial state ideology 14, 20-21
Neo-Confucian anthropocentrism 90
Neo-Confucianism, Neo-Confucian(ist) 16, 17, 77, 84-85, 88-93, 96-101, 139
New Confucianism, New Confucian(ist) 13, 142-146
paragon of Confucianism 14, 25, 35, 43
paragon of present-day Confucianism 31, 34
predicament of modern Confucianism 17, 144, 147-148
revival of Confucianism 86
revival of traditional Confucian thought 10
re-affirmation of Confucian values 17, 126
socio-political order of Confucianism 12
state-sponsored theology 14, 35

traditional Confucian social theory 104
victory of Confucianism 20
congregations 116
congshu see collectanea
context shifting 125
control over political ideology 15, 40
converting others 127-128
Correct Meaning of the 'Book of Rites' 110
Correction of Obstruction 90, 107
corruption 73
cosmological re-integration of men 90
Court of Imperial Sacrifices 26
craft 16, 99
craftsmen 41, 99
creation 106-108, 128
criminal 31, 56-58, 64
critique 8, 90, 96, 113, 142
culture 7, 9-17, 20, 85, 95-101, 104, 109, 134-145, 149
   breaking with culture, half way broken with traditional culture 11, 17
   consumptive culture 147
   cultural concepts 83, 101-102
   cultural conservatism 144
   cultural differences 7-8
   cultural heritage 140
   cultural mainstream 101
   cultural relativism 10, 104
   defend traditional Chinese culture 143
   human culture 15
   humanist culture 137, 140
   moral spirit of Chinese culture 145
   reappraising Chinese culture 144
   traditional culture 11, 17, 20, 139-140, 144-145
   Western culture 139, 146

da qi see large utensils
da ren see great man
Datong shu see *Book of Great Unity*
Daxue see *Great Learning*
Daxue wen see *Questions on the 'Great Learning'*
da yitong see great unity
Dazhuan see *Great Treatise*
Daifang lu see *Records while Waiting for Appointment [in a Time of Obscured Light]*
dao see way
Daodejing see *Classic of Virtue and the Way*
Daoism, Daoists 12-16, 27, 30, 33, 49-50, 53, 60, 64, 89, 95-96, 102, 135
   Daoist critique of the Confucian search for humaneness 12-15
   Daoist classics 15
Daojia see Daoism
daoli see principle, order
dao xin see moral, moral mind
daoyin see breathing practices (lit.: guiding and pulling)
dark learning (movement) 53
de see honest and straight
De amicitia 109-110
Debate over Science and Metaphysics 141-144
decapitation 91
Declaration of Independence 104
Definitions (part of the *Renxue*) 128-129
deyi see virtuous physicians
deng see equal, equation
denial, deny 7, 50, 56-61, 65-66, 76, 129, 132, 141; see also assessment
desires 8, 89, 92-94, 111
devious physicians 98

die for a noble cause 128-129
dignity, respect 7, 11, 15, 79, 55-56, 84, 106, 110, 112, 120, 130
Discourses on Salt and Iron 73, 75
disorder 13, 15, 45, 50-51, 59, 62, 64
divine principle 11
divinity 134
do ut des 70
Doctrine of the Mean 13, 69, 78, 84-85, 108
dong see activity/movement
draw up the court rites 24
drifting soul 17, 144
du ren see converting others
dusheng see sage, lone sage
Dushu see *Review*

East and West 85, 121
economic reform 146
education 14, 40, 78, 108, 113-114
emancipation, emancipate 140
embodying *ren* 72, 79; see also *ren* 仁
emoluments and benefits 38, 43-44
emotion, love, passion 93-95
empathy 92-93, 101, 126
emperor 15, 21-46, 96, 99, 110-116, 120
encounter of the two traditions 17, 109
encouraging agriculture and disfavoring commerce 41
encyclopedias for every day usage 88, 96
enlightenment 91, 147
entrance 118
entrance of mankind 118
epistemological revolution 89
equal 10, 16, 42, 103-120, 124-130
    economic equality 103
    equal dignity 104, 119
    equal distribution of land 115
    equal status of women 116

equally [distributed] 115
equality 16, 100, 114-115, 120, 124-126, 128-129
equation 103, 107-108, 112-117, 125-129, 133
    human equality 16, 104-105, 109-112, 115, 120
    inequality 16, 104-106, 116, 129
    unequal 10, 105-108, 114, 124, 129
    "unequal" hierarchical principles 106
erudite 23-26, 31, 36-37, 39, 43-44
    Erudite of the *Five Classics* 37, 39, 43-44
Erya see *Luxuriant and Refined Words*
eschatological goal 116
The Essence of Human Nature and Principle 77
ethics 14, 50, 56-60, 64, 70, 80, 86, 98
    Confucian political ethics 78
    ethic of intention 80
    ethical and political concerns 11, 13
    ethical conduct 11
    ethical guidelines 10
    ethical norms 40, 109
    ethical refinement 97
    ethical view 57
    lack of concern for ethics 51
    "post-conventional" ethics 70
    traditional Confucian ethics 105, 121
    Zhou ethics and rituals 76
etiquette, rites, propriety 24-27, 59, 70, 77, 80, 88
Europe, European 20, 84, 103, 106, 109, 131, 134, 139-141, 146
European History 131, 134

even 114-116
exegesis 13, 43, 74, 77
exercising the law 33
exhausting one's life potential 95
exile 116-117
existential transformation 17, 122-123
extraordinary people 93

Fajia see Legalism, Legalists
famous physicians 98
fangji see craft
fangzheng see sexual practices
farmers 41, 99, 110
fei see denial
female physicians 98
fenshu kengru see burning books and burying scholars
feng and *shan* sacrifices 38
fengchang see Court of Imperial Sacrifices
fengshan see *feng* and *shan* sacrifices
Fengshan shu see Treatise on the *Feng* and *Shan* Sacrifices
feudal state 22, 41
filial piety 98, 99
   Classic of Filial Piety 13, 45
   filial child 113
   unfilial child 113
five bonds 105-106, 109, 112, 123, 125
Five Classics 13, 36-37, 39, 43-44, 84
five phases, five elements 28, 35, 45, 77, 90
footprints 53-54, 61-62, 67
foreign rule 13-14
forming one body with (heaven, earth, and) all things 92
fortitude 78-79
four beginnings 77, 80
Four Books 13, 69-70
four classes 41, 99

four seasons 46, 77
French Revolution 104, 116
friendship 69, 109-110, 115

gao seng see Buddhism, Buddhist monk
gentleman, noble, superior man, son of an official 16, 52, 55, 72-73, 76, 79, 99, 129
gentry 87, 96
Gesinnung see one's habit of virtuous mind
Gesinnungsethik see ethics, ethic of intention
gewu zhizhi see investigating things to extend knowledge
global society 121
globalized world, Globalization 7, 145
go with the flow 62
Golden Rule 70
gong see artisan
gongfa see common, common laws
gong li see common, common benefit
Gongyang chunqiu see *Gongyang Commentary on the Spring and Autumn Annals*
Gongyang Commentary (on the Spring and Autumn Annals) 13, 32, 34, 36, 44
Gongyang School 31-32, 104
Gongyang zhuan see *Gongyang Commentary*
government 10, 14, 16, 22, 26-29, 37-40, 46, 51, 71, 78-79, 121-122
Grand Master of Ceremonies 26
Grand Mentor 26
Great Learning 13, 69, 84, 110
great man 83
Great Treatise 106, 122

great unity 22
guest emperor 114
guilt by intention 34
Guliang Commentary 13, 44
Guliang zhuan see *Guliang Commentary*
guwen see old script
guwen xue see Old Text School

Han dynasty, Han empire 13, 20-26, 29, 31, 39-43, 59
handling matters in an appropriate way 75
Hanshu see *History of the Former Han Dynasty*
harm, harmful 10, 15, 28, 45, 56-64, 108-116, 127, 138, 146
harmony 10, 28, 108, 116, 138, 146
have no opposite 128
he see harmony
heart, mind-heart, heart-mind 11, 15, 37, 41, 49, 70, 80, 89-96, 100-101
heaven, 19, 32, 34-35, 45, 60, 89, 93, 106-112, 118-122, 136
   consummate way of all-under-heaven 78
   heaven and earth 60, 107-108, 118-120, 122
   heaven and man 34-35
   heavenly command 108
   Heavenly Kingdom of Great Peace 116
   heavenly principle 88, 95
   concrete place of heaven within the human body 101
   integration of heaven and man 11
   mandate of heaven 22, 46, 108
   son of heaven 27-28, 37, 107
   unity of heaven and man 12

way of heaven 11, 35, 45, 104, 106, 108, 122, 136
way of man 10-11, 19, 84, 104, 106, 132-140
hereditary physicians 98
hetong see peaceful coexistence
hidden people 93
hidden, reclusive physicians 98
historical criticism 140
historically constructed 124
History of Love/Emotions 93
History of the Former Han Dynasty 27, 31
honest and straight 75, 79
Huang-Lao School 29-31, 34
Huanglao see Daoism
hui see congregation
human
   human being 9, 15-16, 69, 88-92, 96, 100-112, 118-122, 135, 138-141, 148
   human being as a part of society 9, 14-15
   human dignity 108, 120
   human life 7-8, 106, 111, 135, 139, 141, 143
   human literature 135, 138-139
   human mind 89, 92, 141
   human natural right 103
   human nature 89, 101-108, 118, 129, 138, 146, 148
   human rights 10-11, 16, 84, 104
   human sentiments; common sense 70, 75-77
   human society 16, 104-107, 112, 141
Human Literature 135, 139
humanism 7, 9-18, 19, 84-86, 131-137, 140-149
   Chinese humanism 7, 11-12, 17, 69-70, 133, 135, 138, 141, 143, 146, 149

Chinese Renaissance 20, 136, 139-140
Confucian humanism 15, 133, 146-147
functional human beings 15
human-centered 11, 69, 145
humane 10, 14, 122
humaneness 9-18, 51, 54, 66, 70-74, 83, 88, 92-95, 98-101, 122, 142, 145
Humanismus 131, 133, 137
humanist education 137
humanist movement 85, 131, 140
humanistic concept 11
humanistic spirit 131, 146-147
humanistic tradition 11, 16, 86
iconoclastic humanism 147
intercultural humanism 8, 18
invention of humanism 133, 148
Italian Renaissance (humanism) 85, 134
modern Chinese humanism 17, 138, 141, 149
scientific humanism 142
Western humanism 11
Humanist Tradition in the West 132
Humanistic Education in China and in the West 135
humanitarianism 19, 84, 132-140
humanities 7, 142, 146-147
humanity 7, 10, 11, 15-16, 19-20, 55, 84-85, 88, 104-107, 121-122, 126, 131-149
Hundred Day Reform Movement 121
Hundred Schools of Thought 12, 20, 29-30, 42
Hunnu see Huns
Huns 39

Huozhi liezhuan see Biographies of the Money-makers

identity 95, 99, 113, 124-126, 129
ignorance 112, 123, 132
illustrous physicians 98
immoral, licentious physicians 98
immortals 11
Imperial Censor 37
imperial examination (system) 14, 17, 88
   civil service examination 38, 89, 144
   official examination 87
   traditional examination routine 86
   surplus of licentiates 86
Imperial Seminar 80
imperial tribute system 116
Impressions of a Voyage to Europe 141
incompetent physicians 98
incompleteness 128
individual, individuality 9-10, 36, 53, 83, 104-106, 111-112, 116-129, 138-140, 145, 148
   individual identity 125
   individual mental activity 123-124
industrialization 143
innocence 34
integration of knowledge and practice 11
intercultural discourse 7, 9, 11
international law 115-116
Interpretation of the Classics 45
intuitive, innate knowing 74, 91-92, 129
investigating things to extend knowledge 97, 99-100
itinerants 98

Jesuit 73, 109-110, 115, 134
ji fa see exercising the law
jian'ai see ubiquitous and indiscriminate care
jiang see craftsmen
jianyi see devious physicians
Jiaoyou lun see On Friendship
Jieshuo see Definitions
jinwen see new, new script
jinwen xue see new, New Text School
jing 靜 see tranquility; see also quiescent
jing 敬 see respectful
jing 經 see warp, canonical scripture
Jingjie see Interpretation of the Classics
jingxue see Classical Learning
jingxueshi see Classical Learning, history of Classical Learning
jingyan see Imperial Seminar
jing zuo see meditation (lit. silent sitting)
Jiuchao lü kao see *A Study of the Laws of the Nine Dynasties*
jixin see machine mind
judgment 50-58, 62-65
jun 軍 see military
jun 均 see equal, equally [distributed]
junren nanmian zhi shu see method of the ruler facing south
jun tian see equal, equal distribution of land
junzi see gentleman, noble, superior man, son of an official
justice 34, 55, 103, 119

karmic knowledge 123-124
ke ji see self, selfish desires
kexuan Debate see Debate over Science and Metaphysics

kexuan lunzhan see Debate over Science and Metaphysics
kexue renwen zhuyi see humanism, scientific humanism
kexue wanneng lun see science, scientism
kou chi see lapping the teeth

labor 44, 78, 112
language 11, 18, 42, 60, 90, 127, 129, 132-133, 138-139
   guest language 133
   host language 133
   language of literature 138
   source language 133
   target language 133
lapping the teeth 97
large utensils 76
law 28, 31-40, 44, 46, 54, 117-122, 127
Learning of Humanity 120-125, 129
Learning of the *dao* 90
Learning of the mind-heart 90
Legalism, Legalists 14, 27, 30-35
li 理 see principle, order
li 禮 see etiquette, rites, propriety
Liji see *Book of Rites*
Liji zhengyi see *Correct Meaning of the 'Book of Rites'*
li wu see putting the things of nature to use for the benefit of man; see also usefulness
Li yun see Transformation of the Rites
li zhi see exhausting one's life potential
liberation 148
life gate 100
lian see tender affection
liangzhi see intuitive, innate knowing
ling see ordinances

literature 20, 55, 73, 109-111, 117, 130, 135-147
  literary revolution 138
  literature as the vehicle for the ultimate doctrines 138
  literature for the sake of human life 138
liuyi see itinerants
local elite 87
Logics, Logicians see School of Names
loss of control 87
love among siblings 72
low-born generals and ministers 22-23, 28
luan see disorder
Lun liujia yaozhi see Treatise on the Essential Teachings of the Six Schools
Luntai zuiji zhao see Majestic Terrace Edict of Self-Accusation
Lunyu see *Analects* [of Confucius]
Luxuriant and Refined Words 13
lü see law
Lüshi Chunqiu see *Spring and Autumn Annals (of Lü Buwei)*

machine mind 124
Majestic Terrace Edict of Self-Accusation 39
man of conscientiousness, conscientious man 71
man of wisdom, wise man 71
Manchu, Manchu empire 86-87, 98, 110, 114; see also Qing dynasty
manmo see non-Chinese
market economy 10, 146-147
martyrdom 121, 128-129
Marxist paradigm 147
May Fourth Movement 17, 20, 138-140, 148

medicine 16, 26, 32, 88, 96-101
  medical field 16, 88, 95, 99, 101
  medical professionals 95
  medical skill 16, 99, 101
  medical works 96
  medicine as an alternative career 98
  medicine is humaneness 99
meditation 97, 101, 115
Meiji Japan 116, 136
men see entrance
Mencius see *Book of Mencius*
Mengzi see *Book of Mencius*
mental force, mind force 122, 124
mentality 123-124
merchants 41, 78, 99
  status of traders 87
metaphysical sphere 89, 93
method of the ruler facing south 27, 29
meting out punishments on account of intent 32
military 25-26, 38-39, 59, 63, 75, 91, 99, 120
  military campaign 91
min see commoners
ming 名 see name
ming 命 see command
ming 明 see acumen
mingchao see Ming dynasty
Ming dynasty, Ming empire 13, 87, 96, 108, 111, 120, 129, 130
Mingjia see School of Names
Ming loyalist scholars 87
mingmen see life gate
minister 25, 29, 78, 113
  ministership 113, 114
mingyi 名醫 see famous physicians
mingyi 明醫 see illustrious physicians
mingyi 明夷 see Ming loyalist scholars

193

Mingyi Daifang lu see *Records while Waiting for Appointment [in a Time of Obscured Light]*
modern China 12, 85, 104, 107, 115-116, 131-135, 142, 148
modernity 17, 20, 84, 145
  beginning of modern times 147
Mohism, Mohists 12, 27, 33, 57-60, 104, 107
Mojia see Mohism, Mohists
monetary reward 25
monistic philosophy 95
monk physicians 98
moral 15-17, 31, 51-57, 64-65, 75-79, 80-81, 83-84, 89-92, 108-110, 114, 118, 121-122, 126, 129, 136-138, 142-146
  deterioration of the moral and ritual order 73
  moral brand 57
  moral conduct 92
  moral education 15, 17
  moral excellence 108, 110, 114, 118, 121-122, 129
  moral individual 145
  moral mind 89
  moral perfection 108
  moral philosophy 65, 81
  moral principle 80, 136
  moral realist 143
  moral self-cultivation 16, 83
  moral values 16
  moral virtue 52, 79, 89
moralistic and the pragmatic concerns 16
morality 50-52, 57-64, 94, 134, 138, 143

name 30-31, 42, 57, 125, 148
narrative framework 148
Narrative Logic 132
narrative substance 132

nature 7, 11, 15, 21, 28, 35-36, 40, 44-45, 49-51, 56, 58, 60-67, 69, 71-73, 78, 89, 92-93, 104-122, 126-130, 142
  natural predisposition 104, 108, 114
nei duo yu er wai shi ren yi see allowing plenty of desires inwardly, yet outwardly exhibiting benevolence and righteousness
new
  The New Approaching Correctness 135
  New Culture (Movement) 20, 135, 140-145
  new human being 17
  new learning 121, 125, 128
  new literature 135, 138-140
  new script 43-44
  new spiritual culture 142
  New Text School 43
  New Youth 135
non-Chinese 91
  bandits 86, 91
  "civilize" non-Chinese people 91
  four barbarians 40
non-interference 15, 25, 27, 34
  bringing about order without exertion 27
nong see farmers
normal person 52, 55
not to be born 128
not to die 128
nothingness 126
nourish life 16, 88, 97, 102
numb, being without sensation, to have no feeling 90
nüyi see female physicians 98

obsession 94
official-literati 87; see also four classes

old script 43-44
Old Text School 43
On Friendship 109, 134
one's habit of virtuous mind 80
oppression of women 116
ordinances 33-34, 46
original mind 88
Ouluoba tongshi see *European History*
Ouyou xinying lu see Impressions of a Voyage to Europe
overlord 22, 80
    way of the overlord 80

parallel line 115
Paris Peace Conference 141
patriarchal system 112
peace 13, 22, 28, 33, 39-40, 106, 115-116, 122
    internal peace and stability (for the empire) 13, 22, 28, 33, 40
peaceful coexistence 115
Rich Dew of the Spring and Autumn Annals 31, 34
penal cases 31, 44
penal system 31
philanthropy 135
physical/experiential sphere 89, 93
pi see obsession
ping see even
pingdeng see equal, equality; see also bringing something to peace
pinghang see parallel line
pingmian see plain surface
Pingzhun shu see Treatise on the Balanced Standard
plain surface 115
political 9-17, 21-29, 33-34, 38, 43-45, 52, 59, 78-81, 83, 86, 102-116, 120-129, 139
    human policy 104

humane policy 10
political activism 127-129
political advisor 27
political applicability 13
political misery 124
political reform 116
political theory 103-105
progressive political thinkers 104
popularized fields of knowledge 96
possess *ren* "by nature" 71; see also *ren* 仁
Post-Mao era 147
practice benevolence 88; see also *ren* 仁, benevolence
pragmatic action 76
primal source 126
principle, order 73, 89, 93-94, 108
principles of reality 117-119
progressive 16, 104-105, 110, 117, 123
proper way to conduct 55
proportion 112, 117, 119
punishment 30, 58
    punishments and names 30, 31
put into practice 23
putting the things of nature to use for the benefit of man 71

qi (breath; primordial stuff) 24, 74, 89-90, 92-93, 95-97, 101, 107, 113, 118
    orderly *qi*-flow 97
qi chaoyi see draw up the court rites
qilin see unicorn
qimeng see enlightenment
qiren see extraordinary people
qian see creation
Qin dynasty, Qin empire 12-13, 21, 23, 26-31, 39, 44
qin qin see love among siblings
qinchao see Qin dynasty

qing see emotion, love, passion
Qing dynasty, Qing empire 14, 23, 29, 34, 38, 91, 104, 114, 117, 129
qingchao see Qing dynasty
qingjiao see teaching of emotions, cult of emotions
Qingshi see *History of Love/Emotions*
qu ark 9
quanyi see act according to expediency
quegu see abstention from grains
Questions on the 'Great Learning' 110
quiescent 71

radicalism, radicalization 17, 129
rebuilding new institutions 116
reciprocity 70
recorded actions 53
recorded sayings 72-73, 80
Records of the Grand Historian 21-33, 36-37, 40-42, 46
Records while Waiting for Appointment [in a Time of Obscured Light] 111
recruitment system 15
rectify their hearts, rectification of the heart 91, 95
redistribution of power and wealth 105
reform movement 116, 120
regicide 32, 35
relation 87-90, 93, 99, 103, 109-110, 113-114, 125-126, 132, 145
    disintegration of conventional hierarchies 88
    hierarchy to relationships, hierarchical relationship 55, 73-74
    moral social relations 55
    natural relationship 112-113

    "non clan-bound" relation 109
    social relationship 12, 55
religion, religious 11, 26, 84, 100, 103, 121, 125-126, 129, 139, 143-144, 146
religion of commonsense 143
ren 人 see humanism; see also human, human being
ren 仁 9, 15-17, 51, 54-59, 64, 66, 69-81, 84-85, 88, 92-95, 98-101, 121-122, 125-128
    In this volume are found the following translations of *ren*:
    act in a selfless way, selfless act(ion) 121-128
    altruism 85
    benevolence 27, 36, 52, 63, 66, 73-74, 96, 98, 104-114, 119, 129, 140, 148
    benevolent government 16, 71-72
    caring for someone, taking care for others 70, 72
    care for oneself 74
    conscious and responsible usage of one's medical instruments 100
    conscientiousness 71
    commit suicide 17, 26, 128
    compassion 83, 90, 99, 126-127
    ether 85, 123
    feel or sense 16
    goodness 85, 88
    goodwill 57
    humanity 55, 85, 88, 100, 121-122, 126
    humaneness 9-18, 51, 54, 66, 70-74, 83, 88, 92-95, 98-101, 122, 142, 145
    human-heartedness 55, 70, 72, 85
    human sentiments 70, 75, 77

in accordance with common sense 70
(keen sense of) responsibility in (one's) action 16, 71
love 54-55, 59, 70-75, 85, 94
man's mind 85
men living together 85
perfect virtue 85, 88
selfless humane action 125
sensitive concern for others 72
ubiquitous and indiscriminate care 74
universal love 85
virtue 51, 54-59, 70, 73, 77-78, 85, 88-89, 95, 99
renben zhuyi see humanism
rendao see humanity; see also political, human policy; see also moral, moral principle
rendao zhuyi see humanitarianism
Ren de wenxue see Human Literature
Renlei gongli see universal, *Universal Principles of Humankind*
renlei men see entrance of mankind
ren min see benevolent government of the people
renqing see human, human sentiments; common sense
renquan see human, human rights
Rensheng guan see View of Human Life
renwen see humanity
renwen jingshen see humanism, humanistic spirit
renwen zhuyi see humanism
ren xin see human, human mind
Renxue see *Learning of Humanity*
renzhe see man of conscientiousness
renzheng see political, humane policy

renzhi see rule, rule of man
reproduction 85, 106, 108
respectful (attitude) 97
respecting life
responsible use of the bountiful resources of nature 72
return to nature 50
returning home 50
revaluation 138-140, 148
Review 10, 146
revival of syncretistic movements 96
revolt 21-24, 31, 116, 120
righteousness, duty, sense of justice, moral obligation 54-56, 75-80, 112, 141
rigor 78-79
Rites of Zhou 13
ritual 24, 27, 94, 106
ritualized life-reality 88
riyong leishu see encyclopedias for every day usage
Roman empire 39
root and trunk 73
ru see scholars
Rujia see Confucianism
rule 14, 22, 25-27, 36, 40, 43, 46, 76, 107, 110, 114, 124, 141
rule of law 40
rule of man 36
rule of *ren* 76
ruler 12, 23, 27-28, 32, 39, 44, 74, 78-80, 95, 100-101, 110-113, 116
rulership 12-13, 79-80
Rulin liezhuan see Biographies of Confucian Scholars
rushu see Confucianism, Confucian statecraft
ruyi see scholar physicians

sage 11, 25, 28, 32-35, 46-47, 52-53, 59-60, 63, 65, 72, 80, 83, 88, 92, 96, 110
   actions of past sages 53
   democratization of sagehood 91
   following the sages 52, 54
   imitating a sage 53-54
   lone sage 42
   sage-emperor 28
   sagehood 16, 90-91
   tracing the sages 55
samatā see sameness
sameness 115
sanjiao he yi see unity of the three teachings
scholar physicians 98-100
scholars 13, 16, 18, 21-25, 29-37, 38, 41-44, 80, 86-90, 95-101, 104, 108, 114, 117, 120, 132-137, 140-148
scholarship 21, 36, 41-45, 86, 198
   scholarship follows changes in the ways of governing 42, 44
School of Names
science 141-144
science and democracy 144
science and technology 141, 143
scientism 141-144
scripture, refinement, culture 19-21, 94, 100, 118, 136-138
secluded 74
secular 11
self 10, 14, 38, 57, 65, 83, 88-101, 108, 111, 122-126, 134, 138-140, 143-147
   self, body, person 58, 83, 85, 90-97, 100-102, 106, 113, 118
   self-accomplishment 92
   self-cultivation 16, 83, 88-92, 96-101
   self-cultivation for nourishing life 16, 89, 96-97, 102

self-development 134, 139, 140, 143, 145
selfish desires 88
self-less, selfless 16, 108, 114, 121-128
self-perception 10, 14, 122-124
sengyi see monk physicians
seniority 106, 113
sentiment and reason 143
sexual practices 97
shanrang see abdicate the throne
shang see merchants
Shanghai Literature 146
Shanghai News 115-116
Shanghai wenxue see *Shanghai Literature*
Shangshu see *Book of Documents*
shen see self, self, body, person
Shenbao see *Shanghai News*
sheng (ren) see sage
shengyuan see imperial examination system, surplus of licentiates
shi 士 see scholars
shi 是 see affirmation; see also assessment
Shiji see *Records of the Grand Historian*
Shijing see *Book of Odes*
shili see principles of reality
Shili gongfa quanshu see *Comprehensive Writings on the Common Laws [based on] the Principles of Reality*
shi tianxia wei yijia see all under heaven, all under heaven as one family; see also heaven, heavenly unity
Shiwu xuetang see Academy of Actual Affairs
shi yi see temporary physicians
shiyi see hereditary physicians
shiyin see town-hermits

shu 恕 see reciprocity; see also Golden Rule
shu 術 see statecraft; see also skill
Shujing see *Book of Documents*
si de see virtues, four virtues
si duan see four beginnings
Siku quanshu see *Complete Collection of Books in the Four Treasuries*
sishi see four seasons
Sishu see *Four Books*
siwen see this tradition of *wen*
si yi see non-Chinese, four barbarians
signification, signified 132-133, 136, 138
sino-centrism 11
Sinic cultural sphere 10
Six Classics 13, 21, 30, 38, 43, 45
skill 66, 99
social 10-12, 16, 24, 55, 83, 87-88, 94, 96, 103-129, 141, 144-147
   commercial society 147
   hierarchy of fixed positions 105
   humane society 122
   ideal social order 112
   nature and society 11, 108, 111-112, 114, 117, 120, 122, 126, 129
   open society 109
   social action 111-112, 120
   social and cultural crisis 141
   social autonomy 119-120
   social class 106
   social communitarian ideals 105
   social hierarchy, social hierarchical positions 106-108, 112, 125
   social identity 12, 109
   social life 83, 112
   social mentality 124
   social policies 105
   social positions and functions 107
   social power 87
   social pressure 116
   social reality 88, 105
   social roles 88, 96
   (social) stratification 12, 16, 104-105, 108
   social structure 107, 118, 144
   social theory 103, 107, 120
   (social) welfare 11, 80, 104, 106, 116, 120, 141
songchao see Song dynasty
Song dynasty, Song empire 12, 15, 31, 71, 77, 91, 98, 104, 107
soteriology 126
   Buddhist soteriology 127
   soteriological beliefs 105
   soteriological context 126
spiritual 11-12, 15, 27, 35, 96, 118, 125-127, 143-144
   spiritual realm 126, 144
Spring and Autumn Annals (of Lü Buwei) 13, 27, 31-36, 44-46
St. Martin 75
state orthodoxy 43, 78
statecraft 12, 16, 20-21, 30-33, 36, 38, 41-44, 99, 116
   statecraft learning 21
   thoroughfare 33
A Study of the Laws of the Nine Dynasties 35
studying thoroughly the canonical texts to employ them for political application 33
suffering 25, 94, 105
suppression 140, 148

taichang see Grand Master of Ceremonies
taifu see Grand Mentor

Taiping tianguo see heaven, Heavenly Kingdom of Great Peace
teaching of emotions, cult of emotions 93
temporary physicians 98
ten thousand things 108
tender affection 74
Thirteen Classics 13
this tradition of *wen* 20
thorough knowledge of the past and the present 27
Thoroughgoing Knowledge on Medicine 100
Three Treatises on the Relationship between Heaven and Man 30
ti ren see embodying *ren*
tianming see heaven, mandate of heaven
tian see heaven
tiandao see heaven, way of heaven
tian li see heaven, heavenly principle
Tianren sance see Three Treatises on the Relationship between Heaven and Man
tianxia see all under heaven
tianxia wu yi yi see all under heaven, no dissent under heaven
tianxia zhi dadao see heaven, consummate way of all-under-heaven
tianzi see heaven, son of heaven
tong 同 see community, co-existence
tong 通 see communication
tongjing zhiyong see studying thoroughly the canonical texts to employ them for political application
town-hermits 93
traces 12, 17-18, 27, 53-54, 62, 67, 83, 94
  traces of humanism 12, 17-18

tranquility 71, 89, 93
Transformation of the Rites (chapter of the *Book of Rites*) 110, 121
Treatise on the Balanced Standard 41
Treatise on the Essential Teachings of the Six Schools 27
Treatise on the *Feng* and *Shan* Sacrifices 41
true king 80
  kingly way 80
trust 37, 77-80
truth 12, 35, 52, 65
tugu naxin see breathing practices (lit.: expelling the old and taking in the new)

ubiquitous and indiscriminate care 74
undivided whole 15, 61
unicorn 80
unification of thought 43
unity of the three teachings 95-96, 102
universal 7, 12, 33, 85, 104, 107-108, 111, 117, 123, 126, 147
  universal function of *ren* 126; see also *ren* 仁
  universal patterns 126
  Universal Principles of Humankind 117
  universal results 126
  universally valid concept 131
uprising 22
usefulness 71

values 7, 12, 15, 33, 36, 40-41, 50-52, 70, 94, 108-109, 115, 119, 120-123, 138-139, 147
  ephemeral value 127
  human value 10, 15, 17, 84, 140
  lost values 88
  oppressing the value of the individual 145
  reconstruction of values 147
  renewal of values 88

revaluating all values 139
traditional Chinese values 10
value judgment 51
Vernacular Chinese 138
View of Human Life 141
virtue 15, 28, 46, 50-64, 70-73, 77-78, 85, 88-89, 94-95, 98-99, 143
   civil virtues 116
   five virtues 77
   four virtues 72
   re-evaluation of human virtues 88
virtuous physicians 98
vita activa 71
vita contemplativa 71

wan wu see ten thousand things
wang see true king
wangdao see true king, kingly way
warp, canonical scripture 33
way (*dao*) 64, 75, 77, 89-90, 99, 136
way of governing 21, 36, 42, 45
wei chi see incompleteness
wei hanjia ruzong see paragon of Confucianism
wei ji see incompleteness
wei ren see practice benevolence
wei rensheng er wenxue see literature, literature for the sake of human life
wei shi ruzong see paragon of present-day Confucianism
wei yishu er yishu see art exists for its own sake
wen see scripture, refinement, culture
wen yi zai dao see literature, literature as the vehicle for the ultimate doctrines
West, Western 9-11, 16-18, 22, 29, 38-39, 46, 52, 56, 64-65, 70, 73, 84, 86, 89, 104, 107, 133-140, 146, 148

Western Inscription 107
wisdom 53, 71-72, 77-79, 96
wo gu see clenching the fists
wounds and skin infection physicians 98
wu 武 see rigor
wu 無 see nothingness
wu chang see virtue, five virtues
wu duidai see have no opposite
Wujing see *Five Classics*
wu lun see five bonds
wuming see ignorance
wu shen see self
wuwei see non-interference
wuwei er zhi see non-interference, bringing about order without exertion
wu xing see five phases, five elements

xili see attraction
Ximing see Western Inscription
Xiaojing see filial piety, *Classic of Filial Piety*
xiaoren see normal person
xin 信 see trust
xin 心 see heart, mind-heart
Xin Erya see *The New Approaching Correctness*
xinli see mental force, mind force
Xin qingnian see *New Youth*
Xin rujia see new, New Confucianism
xinshu see art of one's heart; see also one's habit of virtuous mind
Xinwenhua yundong see New Culture (Movement)
xinxue 心學 see Learning of the mind-heart
xinxue 新學 see new learning
xing 行 see put into practice
xing 性 see nature

xing er shang see metaphysical sphere
xing er xia see physical/experiential sphere
Xingli jingyi see *The Essence of Human Nature and Principle*
xing ming see punishment, punishments and names
xiu shen see self, self-cultivation
xuanxue see dark learning (movement)
xue see scholarship
Xueheng 142
Xueheng School 140-145
xueshi see scholars
xue sui shu bian see scholarship, scholarship to follow changes in the ways of governing

Yantie lun see *Discourses on Salt and Iron*
yangsheng see self, self-cultivation for nourishing life; see also nourish life
yangyi see wounds and skin infection physicians
yeshi see cognition, karmic cognition
yi 義 see righteousness, duty, sense of justice, moral obligation
yi 宜 see handling matters in an appropriate way
Yiguan see *Thoroughgoing Knowledge on Medicine*
Yijing see *Book of Changes*
Yili see *Ceremonies and Rites*
yiren 異人 see extraordinary people
yiren 逸人 see hidden people
yi renshu ye see medicine, medicine is humaneness; see also *ren* 仁, humaneness
yishu see medical skills
yitai see *ren* 仁, ether

yi tian di wanwu wei yi ti see forming one body with (heaven, earth, and) all things
yinren see hidden people
yin yang 27, 34, 45
    Yin-Yang School 27, 45
Yinyangjia see *yin yang*, Yin-Yang School
yinyi 淫醫 see immoral, licentious physicians
yinyi 隱醫 see hidden, reclusive physicians
yong see fortitude
yong yi see incompetent physicians
youhun see drifting soul
Youlun see *On Friendship*
you xue qi zhe see all beings of blood and *qi*; see also *qi* (breath; primordial stuff)
yu see desires
yulu see recorded sayings
yushi daifu see imperial censor
yuan see primal source
Yuejing see *Book of Music*

zhangtong gujin see thorough knowledge of the past and the present
zheng see government
Zhengmeng see *Correction of Obstruction*
zheng (qi) xin see rectify their hearts
zhi see wisdom
zhizhe see man of wisdom, wise man
zhongnong yishang see encouraging agriculture and disfavoring commerce
zhongyi see common physicians
Zhongyong see *Doctrine of the Mean*
Zhou dynasty, Zhou empire 22, 46, 52, 62

zhouchao see Zhou dynasty
Zhouli see *Rites of Zhou*
Zhou Yi see *Book of Changes*
zhu xin see meting out punishments on account of intent; see also guilt by intention
zhuzi baijia see Hundred Schools of Thought
Zhuangzi see *Book of Zhuangzi*
Zizhi tongjian see *Comprehensive Mirror for Aid in Government*
zun see dignity, respect
Zuozhuan see *Commentary of Zuo*

Authors

D'Ambrosio, Paul is currently holding a MA in Chinese Philosophy from Brock University in Canada and is about to start research on a PhD in Philosophy at Cork University in Ireland. His field of interest covers Chinese Philosophy, particularly Daoist thought (e.g. *Zhuangzi*) and Chinese literature. He has completed a two year independent research stay in under the guidance of different professors both in China and abroad. Among his recent publications are: "From Foolish Laughter to Foolish Laughter. Zhuangzi's Perspectivism Leads to Laughter." Paper held at the conference of the Académie du Midi on "Laughter — East and West" 2008, to be published by Parerga Verlag (Berlin); Book Review *Virtue, Nature, and Moral Agency in the Xunzi*, ed. by T.C. Kline III and Philip J. Ivanhoe. Monumenta Serica: Journal of Oriental Studies 56, 2008.

Meinert, Carmen, Sinologist and Tibetologist, obtained her PhD from the University of Bonn in 2001 with a comparative study on Chinese Chan Buddhism and Tibetan rDzogs chen. Currently she works as a research fellow at the Institute for Advanced Studies in the Humanities (KWI) in Essen and at Bonn University (Germany). She has been the coordinator of the project "Humanism in the Era of Globalization" at the KWI. She is an associated member of the Center for Buddhist Studies and the Center for Tantric Studies at Hamburg University. Her fields of research are Chinese and Tibetan intellectual and religious history, Buddhist interchange between China and Tibet, early tantric/esoteric traditions, Dunhuang manuscripts and more recently topics related to engaged Buddhism. One of her current research projects focuses on aspects of violence in Chinese and Tibetan esoteric Buddhism. Among her recent publications are: with Hans-Bernd Zöllner (eds.), *Buddhist Approaches to Human Rights — Dissonances and Resonances* (2010); "'Glatte Worte und schmeichelnde Mienen...'. Humanistischer Anspruch und (in)humane Wirklichkeit in China". In: *Von der*

Kultur der Verantwortung zwischen Anspruch und Wirklichkeit, ed. by Christopf auf der Horst (2010).

Messner, Angelika C., was born and educated in Italy. She studied Medicine, Chinese Studies, Anthropology/Ethnology and History of Medicine in Austria (Innsbruck and Vienna), PR China (Beijing) and Germany (Freiburg i. Br.). She is currently an Associate Professor of Chinese Studies at the University of Kiel, Germany. Her doctoral dissertation is on madness in Late Imperial and Republican China and her second book (Habilitationsschrift) is on the reconstruction of knowledge of emotion in China. She has written on a wide range of topics related to the broad field of emotions (including investigations on literary, medical and scientific views and paradigms) within the Chinese historical context. Her current research interests include material culture; scientific personae, their self-perceptions and their histories; meanings and contexts of science in China in its historical and present context. Among her publications are *Medizinische Diskurse zu Irresein in China (1600-1930)* (2000); with Konrad Hirschler (eds.), *Heilige Orte in Asien und Afrika. Räume göttlicher Macht und menschlicher Verehrung* (2006); with Martina Siebert, "Science and technology from the fall of the Han Dynasty to the decline of the Qing Dynasty". In: *Grandi Opere Einaudi: The Chinese Civilization: From Its Origins to Contemporary Times* (2010).

Mittag, Achim has been trained in Munich, Taipei and Shanghai. He obtained his PhD from Munich University in 1989 for a thesis on Song *Shijing* exegesis. In 2005, he was appointed professor for Sinology at the Institute of Chinese and Korean Studies, University of Tübingen. His special field of interest lies in Chinese historiography and the intellectual history of early modern China, including China's encounter with the West. He has been working on various projects of comparative historiography. His latest publications include: with J. Rüsen and H. Schmidt-Glintzer (eds.), *Historical Truth, Historical Criticism, and Ideology* (2005); with Th. Göller, *Geschichtsdenken in Europa und China* (2008); with F.-H. Mutschler (eds.), *Conceiving the "Empire". China and Rome Compared* (2008).

Schilling, Dennis has studied Sinology, Japanology and Philosophy at the Universities of Würzburg and Munich and Chinese Philosophy at the University of Wuhan. He received his Ph.D. with a thesis about the *Taixuan jing* (*Canon of Supreme Mystery*) and *Yilin* (*Grove of Changes*) and other oracle books imitating the *Yijing* (*Book of Changes*) and attained his Habilitation with a study about the use of Buddhist psychology in modern Chinese political thought. A new German translation of the *Yijing* prepared by him was published in December 2009. His research interests are in the Chinese intellectual history, methods and theories of the history of ideas, the Buddhist theory of mind, ancient Chinese philosophy, comparative ethics, and on the relationship between language and culture. Dennis Schilling taught as assistant and associate professor at the University of Munich. At present, he teaches as a guest professor in Taiwan.

Zhang, Ke is a postdoctoral research fellow at the Philosophy Department of Fudan University, Shanghai. He received his PhD degree from the History Department at Fudan University in 2009. His fields of research include the intellectual history of modern China and the exchange of knowledge between China and the West. His doctoral dissertation is entitled "The Origin of Humanism in Modern China".

Zhu, Weizheng studied history between 1955 and 1960 and has been teaching at Fudan University in Shanghai since 1960. He was a visiting professor in the US, Canada, Taiwan and Germany (Munich, Göttingen, and Heidelberg). His field of research covers Chinese canonical scholarship (*jingxue shi*) and historiography, the history of ideas in the late Qing and early Republican Era, as well as China's encounter with the West. Prof. Zhu has been editing numerous books. Among his most well-known works is a systematic collection of essays on the history of Late Imperial China entitled *Coming Out of the Middle Ages* (*Zouchu zhong shiji*) (1990). Beyond his academic achievements, Prof. Zhu is well known as a critical spirit of the time who contributes to contemporary intellectual discourses and courageously gives his view on attempts at political control of teaching and research in the PR of China. In July 2006 he was granted an honorary doctorate at Hamburg University as the first Chinese sinologist and historian.

Der Mensch im Netz der Kulturen –
Humanismus in der Epoche der Globalisierung/
Being Human: Caught in the Web of Cultures –
Humanism in the Age of Globalization

HUBERT CANCIK
Europa – Antike – Humanismus
Humanistische Versuche
und Vorarbeiten
(hg. von Hildegard Cancik-Lindemaier)

Juli 2010, ca. 350 Seiten, kart., ca. 34,80 €,
ISBN 978-3-8376-1389-6

HELMUT JOHACH
**Von Freud zur Humanistischen
Psychologie**
Therapeutisch-biographische Profile

2009, 340 Seiten, kart., 29,80 €,
ISBN 978-3-8376-1294-3

OLIVER KOZLAREK (ED.)
Octavio Paz
Humanism and Critique

2009, 266 Seiten, kart., 32,80 €,
ISBN 978-3-8376-1304-9

Leseproben, weitere Informationen und Bestellmöglichkeiten
finden Sie unter www.transcript-verlag.de

Der Mensch im Netz der Kulturen –
Humanismus in der Epoche der Globalisierung/
Being Human: Caught in the Web of Cultures –
Humanism in the Age of Globalization

CARMEN MEINERT,
HANS-BERND ZÖLLNER (EDS.)
Buddhist Approaches to Human Rights
Dissonances and Resonances

Januar 2010, 248 Seiten, kart., 29,80 €,
ISBN 978-3-8376-1263-9

JÖRN RÜSEN (HG.)
Perspektiven der Humanität
Menschsein im Diskurs der Disziplinen

Juli 2010, ca. 380 Seiten, kart., ca. 32,80 €,
ISBN 978-3-8376-1414-5

JÖRN RÜSEN, HENNER LAASS (EDS.)
Humanism in Intercultural Perspective
Experiences and Expectations

2009, 280 Seiten, kart., 34,80 €,
ISBN 978-3-8376-1344-5

**Leseproben, weitere Informationen und Bestellmöglichkeiten
finden Sie unter www.transcript-verlag.de**

Der Mensch im Netz der Kulturen – Humanismus in der Epoche der Globalisierung/ Being Human: Caught in the Web of Cultures – Humanism in the Age of Globalization

Gala Rebane, Katja Bendels,
Nina Riedler (Hg.)
Humanismus polyphon
Menschlichkeit im Zeitalter
der Globalisierung

2009, 288 Seiten, kart., 29,80 €,
ISBN 978-3-8376-1172-4

Leseproben, weitere Informationen und Bestellmöglichkeiten
finden Sie unter www.transcript-verlag.de